The
Theatre of
Veenapani
Chawla

The
Theatre of
Veenapani
Chawla

THEORY,
PRACTICE, AND
PERFORMANCE

EDITED BY
SHANTA GOKHALE

OXFORD
UNIVERSITY PRESS

Oxford University Press is a department of the University of Oxford.
It furthers the University's objective of excellence in research, scholarship,
and education by publishing worldwide. Oxford is a registered trademark of
Oxford University Press in the UK and in certain other countries

Published in India by
Oxford University Press
YMCA Library Building, 1 Jai Singh Road, New Delhi 110 001, India

ISBN-13: 978-0-19-809703-7
ISBN-10: 0-19-809703-4

Typeset in 11/13.2 Goudy Oldstyle Std
by Excellent Laser Typesetters, Pitampura, Delhi 110 034
Printed and bound in India by Repro India Ltd

To
The India Foundation for the Arts

Contents

Photographs

Foreword

Veenapani Chawla's theatre is interesting and intriguing not because it is avant garde but because, instead of either deliberately eschewing tradition or exploiting it from ulterior motives, as is the case in most such theatres where tradition plays a pivotal role, either by its deliberate absence or by its too facile 'interpretation', it glories in tradition, peeling away its superfluities and laying bare its strengths. It requires a modern perspective of life and theatre along with a deep respect for the old to be able to create a true fusion between the modern and the traditional. A genuinely creative vision unfailingly imbibes the vitality of a tradition and marries it to modernity to give the resulting work its spine.

Although I have not been able to see all of Chawla's productions, I have seen some of her major ones and realized that her work in theatre has been a continuous journey from one point to the next. She has travelled a great distance from *Oedipus* to her latest play, the journey being at once a search for the deepest meaning of theatre and an almost religious probe into the mystique of it. That makes every new work of hers a work in progress that points to the unfolding of yet another vista in the next work. It is a journey that never ends. It could go on for ever. There will never be anything like the ultimate truth, nothing like the final arrival at a destination.

An artist who embarks on such a quest has no alternative but to continue trudging on. For how long s/he can do it depends on how much steam and how much patience s/he has, and also on how deep her/his desire to know is. This is one of the reasons why nobody, least of all I, should attempt to talk about any single work of hers independently of the others. It would be unfair to single out a production for analysis when every play is just another step, leading her and us to something still unexplored from the indefinable territory of human experience. When you talk about Veenapani Chawla, you have to talk about her oeuvre.

Veenapani Chawla's theatre is perhaps the most traditional theatre in India if the meaning of tradition is understood correctly. She manages to cut off all the dead wood accumulated over centuries and tries to reach the never-changing dynamic vital core of it, internalizing and expressing it in a newly forged idiom which is uniquely her own. Tradition is different from custom or convention or norms. Over a period, conventions become redundant, customs obsolete, norms die. Tradition must not be confused with them. Tradition springs from and is deeply embedded in the spiritual life of a people. It influences a whole way of living and thinking of a particular community for infinity. The very fabric of a community's life is shot through with it. It is invisible yet pulsates ceaselessly, giving it a unique riverness. It may change its face over time, accumulating much that is undesirable. The next generation has to learn to discard this and rediscover its core, that which has remained intact through the centuries, and draw sustenance from it.

What Chawla is doing and what she is discovering in the process is not exactly new. The supremacy of the actor in theatre and the hard regimen required of him is something Grotowski has talked about and practised much before her. He has also made eclectic use of many Oriental traditions in training his actors. Shanta tells us that Chawla's response to Grotowski was luke-warm. What makes her different is, according to Shanta, her deep knowledge and practice of Sri Aurobindo's philosophy. Not being a student of this philosophy, I am not in a position to assess the validity of this observation. Shanta, who is usually impatient with and suspicious of anything even remotely 'mystical or spiritual', seems to have surrendered herself to Chawla's position as stated clearly in her interview with Leela Gandhi and her paper 'Space and the Actor'. But if we get any illuminating moment in her theatre, and we certainly do, it is definitely not because of her 'spiritual' approach. We get it because of the innate theatrical-ity of her work. A work of art acquires a spiritual luminosity not because of its stated 'spiritual' content or the spiritual approach of the creator, but because of an unrelenting search, boundless suffering, profoundest compassion, all inherent within it.

Chawla also speaks of Grotowski's 'self-crucifying asceticism' and 'cruelty to body' as being different from Sri Aurobindo's position. Ascetic he was, but there was no self-crucifixion of any kind in his theatre, nor cruelty to the body if I have understood my Grotowski well. That kind of cruelty belongs to Artaud. Grotowski may not have used the word 'sadhak' in relation to his actor, but that is exactly what he trained his actor to be, to fine-tune his body to arrive at a spiritual experience. Negating everything redundant, materially or artistically, is not neces-sarily cruelty to the body; it is the very meaning of Grotowski's asceticism.

His idea of sacrifice is misinterpreted by Shanta. His actor's sacrifice consists in stripping of his self and laying bare his inner-most core to the audience. This involves annihilation of ahankaar, the ego. This sounds familiar, doesn't it? Where is the difference? That is exactly what Indian spiritual traditions advocate if you are on that path. And although I shall accept the fact that Chawla has not borrowed from Grotowski, I must maintain that borrow-ing is always better than being influenced. Robbing is best. It is a conscious choice. You take what is necessary for your growth, spiritual as well as artistic, from anybody, anywhere. Everybody

does it. What I find fascinating in Chawla is that she has toiled and failed and worked undaunted and arrived at certain deliberations (which may change with the passage of time) on her own, and if there are similarities to be found between Grotowski's ideas and hers, they must be superficial and accidental (if we decide to go by Shanta's observations) because there are many dissimilarities as well. This might serve as a good topic for a PhD thesis.

I have already said that to assess Chawla's work one cannot treat any one of her plays in isolation. They are all interlinked. Her entire work is thus one whole unit, a record of an artist's probe and growth. It is against this background that Shanta Gokhale's book on Veenapani Chawla's theatre is most welcome because that is exactly what the book tries to do. One does not hear a solo voice here, defining Chawla's theatre conclusively, but many voices, each with their own approach to Chawla's working methodology and her theatre, leaving the reader to draw her/his own conclusions. There are articles, interviews, and press reviews here that throw light on areas which perhaps one person might not have been able to cover.

Shanta, who has been a sympathetic witness to Chawla's long and arduous journey, has not only documented it beautifully, but also managed to throw light on Chawla's creative impulses. This attempt to share an artist's journey into the interior is a rare event in dramatic criticism.

MAHESH ELKUNCHWAR
Playwright

Acknowledgements

This book could never have been compiled without the unstinted cooperation I received from Veenapani Chawla and the core members of Adishakti, Vinay Kumar, Arvind Rane, and Nimmy Raphel. Veenapani worked hard and meticulously on the performance texts, and carefully went through the many papers she had presented at various seminars to update those that we jointly chose as the most relevant to her work. Since I was doing this project under my own steam without any funding, Veenapani also found ways to invite me to Adishakti to watch the group train, rehearse, and perform. This provided me valuable background in selecting material for the book.

I am also grateful to Veenapani and her office staff for throwing open to me all the files that contained carefully cut and preserved articles on her work that had appeared in the press from her Mumbai years onwards till today. I am also grateful to her and Vinay Kumar for helping me choose appropriate photographs from her collection to support the text.

I am immensely grateful to Leela Gandhi for the time she spent interviewing Veenapani at great length and depth, to delve into the rich philosophical and aesthetic sources of her work; and to Anmol Vellani who made a visit to Adishakti at my request to interview Veenapani on her most complex play to date, *The Hare and the Tortoise*.

I am grateful to Alaknanda Samarth for giving me the photograph of herself, Chandralekha, and Veenapani, taken by Ketaki Sheth during a break in the rehearsals of the two monologues which Alaknanda did under Kumar Shahani's direction with Veenapani as producer. And I am grateful to Ketaki Sheth for granting permission to use the photograph; and once again to Alaknanda and Veenapani for letting me use the letters they recently exchanged about that experience of working together.

I am also grateful to Sara Joseph for having interviewed Koodiyattam actor Usha Nangyar and Koodiyattam *mizhavu* maestro V.K.K. Hariharan, about their work with Veenapani. I am equally grateful to Joy Brooke Fairfield for her essay on Veenapani's training methods written from a theatre scholar's point and the permission playwright-director-actor Ram Ganesh Kamatham gave me to use his essay on his experience as a participant in an Adishakti workshop. I am also grateful to Devina Dutt for agreeing to write the essay on the Ramayana Festival organized at Adishakti.

The most notable thing about all these contributions is that they were done without expectation or promise of remuneration, even of a token kind.

I am grateful to Geeta Doctor and Himanshu Burte for graciously permitting me to include their articles on Adishakti's theatre building in the book, and to Leela Venkataraman, M.D. Muthukumaraswamy, Keval Arora, and Smriti Nevatia for their generous permission for reproducing their reviews of Veenapani's plays.

A Note on the Book

When I first decided that it was time to write about Veenapani Chawla's path-breaking work in theatre so that at least some part of this notoriously transient art would be preserved in words and pictures, I had envisaged a monograph that would be both a description and a critical analysis of it. However, when I began to think about her work, I realized it was multidimensional and equally important in all its dimensions. Chawla's growth in theatre as she moved from doing plays in Mumbai to living the life of theatre in Puducherry, her fortunate acquisition of a plot of land to set up her vision of a centre for theatre research, the revival of old and almost forgotten local technologies to build the theatre and residential structures on the plot, the workshops through which she shared her theatre techniques with actors from all over the country, the world of ideas that she brought into this remote centre through carefully conceived seminars and conferences, all these and more were aspects of her life and work that demanded attention in order to understand it fully.

If this book was to fulfil its purpose of communicating to the reader the diverse ways in which Chawla had widened the world of theatre for herself and for her core group of actors, it would have to include the papers she had read at various seminars and institutions. Further, considering the difficulty of understanding, through mere description, what her plays looked and sounded like, led to the idea that the book should contain full performance texts of the plays. Finally, given that she believed in plurality, a belief that was reflected in the hybridity that she deliberately employed in her work, breaking down old hierarchies and assumptions about what theatre should be and demonstrating what theatre could be, it dawned on me that the most appropriate form for the book had to be multivocal.

This decision taken, I looked for voices that would throw light on the different aspects of her work. I found newspaper articles and reviews in Chawla's archives that covered some aspects of her work and her centre. But there were other aspects that needed to be looked at. To fill this lacuna, I requested scholars, writers, and theatre practitioners who knew her work to contribute exclusively for this book extended interviews with her and reports on their experiences of participating in her workshops and seminars.

Since some of the material I have chosen for the book is prepublished, no changes have been introduced in the text. It stands exactly as it was in its original published form. However, the visuals that go with it have been added for the sole benefit of the readers of this book.

One
Beginnings

The Mumbai Years

SHANTA GOKHALE

Veenapani Chawla is arguably the only practitioner of theatre in India who has fully articulated a theory of the theatre she practices. By what stages she arrived at it from her early days in Mumbai, when she was still exploring her relationship with theatre, to the time she shifted to Puducherry and evolved her unique form of theatre, is the trajectory I hope to trace in this introduction. I will pay particular attention to her Mumbai plays, the springboard for her later work, which forms the focus of this book.

Born in Mumbai (then Bombay) in 1947 just a few months before India won its independence, Veenapani Chawla studied at Welham Girls' School, Dehradun where she had her first encounter with theatre. The school principal, an English woman named Miss Linell, encouraged her to go beyond academics, and to read and explore her talents. Here she read the English classics, learnt to sing, and play the piano. She also participated in dramatics.

It was here, too, that she saw professional theatre for the first time. It was a time when the Shakespeareana Company, founded by actor-manager Geoffrey Kendal, toured the country performing plays, mostly by Shakespeare, but also those by Sheridan, Shaw, and Wilde. Geoffrey and his wife Laura, joined later by their daughters, Felicity and Jennifer, performed in villages, small towns, Maharajas' palaces, and, most importantly, in schools. Two generations of schoolchildren made their first acquaintance with the Bard through the Kendals. Stage and film actor Naseeruddin Shah, who was to play Oedipus in a production of the Greek tragedy directed by Chawla, has stated in an interview that the first play he did as a young boy with a group of friends was *The Merchant of Venice*, in which he played Shylock. 'My inspiration was Mr Geoffrey Kendal of Shakespeareana, whom I had seen playing the role innumerable times.' Chawla, overwhelmed by the experience of seeing the Kendals perform, felt the first tug towards theatre.

Miss Linell's example was also to influence Chawla, to some degree, in her choice of profession. After doing her master's in history from University of Delhi and another master's in political philosophy from University of Mumbai, she joined the newly established Arya Vidya Mandir School in Santacruz, Mumbai, to teach history and literature to 9th and 10th standard students and to supervise drama classes. Teaching was something of a family tradition. Her sisters and brothers-in-law were university teachers. She chose to teach at school because she was fired by the idea of doing for her students what Miss Linell had done for her—opening their minds to things beyond academics through literature, music, and dramatics. With her mind made up to teach, she decided to equip herself with the required qualifications. She did her bachelor's in education from Mumbai University.

As a student at Delhi University, she had seen a great deal of theatre, largely Shakespearean plays, including the Kendals again, but also modern classics like Robert Bolt's *A Man for All Seasons*, Ionesco's *Rhinoceros*, and Pinter's *The Birthday Party*. Her first experience of a traditional drama form had come during the Total Theatre Festival in Delhi, when she had seen a performance of Kathakali. However, her direct experience of the stage was, even now, confined to standing in the wings and prompting or playing ladies-in-waiting.

While Chawla was teaching at Arya Vidya Mandir and doing what she refers to as 'kiddie plays', she was watching plays at Chhabildas Boys High School in Dadar. The school manage-ment had generously allowed the experimental theatre group, Awishkar, to use their hall for its work. Awishkar, in turn, had transformed the space into a hub for experimental theatre activity, throwing it open to new groups with ideas but no place to perform. Amongst the directors who were doing plays there during the 1970s, the most highly regarded and consistent was Satyadev Dubey. Amol Palekar, the director in whose Marathi version of *Roshomon* Chawla was to play the role of the medium years later, also staged several plays in this space, including Badal Sircar's classic *Juloos* in Marathi translation.

The Chhabildas plays were called experimental only in the context of mainstream theatre where melodrama and sentiment reigned supreme. The word 'experimental' implied an exploration of new forms and themes; but in the context of the mainstream, it also referred to plays of raw realism with Vijay Tendulkar being the most powerful playwright of the genre. Chawla remembers seeing two of Tendulkar's path-breaking plays, *Shantata! Court Chalu Ahe* (Silence! The Court Is in Session) and *Sakharam Binder*. However, powerful as these plays were, neither they nor any of the others she was watching in Bombay affected her in a positive way. On the contrary, they convinced her that this was not the kind of theatre she wanted to do. Realism, raw or otherwise, neither touched her imagination nor her spirit. If it still had a hold over urban theatre in India, it had to be resisted. Stanislavski had to be declared irrelevant.

Elsewhere in the world, leading theatre practitioners had been questioning Stanislavski's methods through their own work since the first decade of the twentieth century when Meyerhold began his experiments in symbolist theatre. European theatre practitioners were by now far away enough from his influence to be able to see his importance historically. Stanislavski himself had noted that the time for the unreal on the stage had arrived, making it necessary to picture not life itself as it took place in reality but as it was vaguely experienced in dreams, visions, and moments of spiritual uplift.

Jerzy Grotowski, whom Chawla was to meet in Mumbai years later, wrote, 'Stanislavski … was the first great creator of a method of acting in the theatre, and those of us who are involved with theatre problems can do no more than give personal answers to the questions he raised' (*Les Temps Modernes* [Paris, 1967] and *Flourish*, the Royal Shakespeare Theatre Club newspaper [1967]). Chawla's personal answer, when it came, was to move in the direction of the Meyerhold tradition; that is, to evolve a method that would train the actor's body in such a way that expression of emotion would result from the use of technique, rather than from the recall of emotion.

By 1978, Chawla had grown weary of teaching at Arya Vidya Mandir where the pressure of completing portions set by the syllabus was beginning to eat into the time she valued most with her students, when she could open their minds to things other than academic learning. Meanwhile, Prithvi Theatre opened quietly on 5 November 1978 in Juhu, a northern suburb of Mumbai, with a performance of the Hindi translation of G.P. Deshpande's Marathi play *Udhwasta Dharmashala* by Om Puri's theatre group Majmah. Prithvi was an intimate theatre, lovingly built by Jennifer Kapoor, daughter of Geoffrey and Laura Kendal, whose plays had so inspired Chawla in her school days, and her husband, the Hindi film star Shashi Kapoor. With its thrust stage and steeply raked seating, it was the perfect space for experimental work.

Chawla finally quit her job at Arya Vidya Mandir and proceeded to Puducherry for a year or so. Soon after her return to Mumbai, she joined Prithvi as foyer manager. The first adult play she directed, which caught the notice of audiences and critics alike, was staged here. This was Sophocles's *Oedipus*. She followed this up with Tom Stoppard's *Rosencrantz and Guildenstern Are Dead*, which she had done as a 'kiddie play' earlier, and Euripides's *The Trojan Women*. Her last Mumbai play was *A Greater Dawn*, for which she carved a sparse script out of Sri Aurobindo's epic poem *Savitri*. *The Trojan Women* and *A Greater Dawn* represent her earliest attempts to find a physical language for the kind of theatre she wanted to do.

Chawla's theatre thereafter has been an attempt to explore the metaphysical and philosophical ideas that preoccupy her, emerging from her study of Sri Aurobindo's and the Mother's writings and conversations. But their philosophy was reflected even in the plays that preceded *A Greater Dawn*. For example, *Oedipus*, which we shall soon discuss in greater detail, had after all been a statement of this philosophy which held that the path to a spiritual life necessarily lay through the material and experiential aspects of life.

The question before Chawla was if philosophical ideas were to be the themes of her theatre, how was she to find a theatrical language that expressed them? Whose work could she turn to for direction?

Meyerhold had begun his break with realism by moving away from words to mime and from the human face to masks. Later, he attacked the fourth wall of realism by breaking, by as many means as possible, the distance between spectator and actor. Speech when used, costume, and scenography were all stylized. Artaud, Grotowski, Eugenio Barba, and later Peter Brook had turned for inspiration to the dance and drama forms of the east— Noh, Kabuki, Kathakali, Odissi, and Balinese dance. These had influenced them variously.

At the centre of the work of all these theatre thinker-practitioners stood the actor. Rejecting the primacy of the word, the pioneers of the non-realistic theatre had made the actor the sole vehicle for expressing ideas and emotions through her/his body. Training the actor's body to express emotion through movement and gesture became their common pursuit. Grotowski defined theatre as being, in the ultimate analysis, 'what takes place between spectator and actor'. His was an ascetic theatre of 'secular holiness' in which the actor was trained to 'sacrifice' himself totally to reach what lay within him.

Veenapani Chawla saw this asceticism as having its roots in Catholicism. As a follower of Sri Aurobindo and the Mother, she stood at the opposite end from Grotowski's self-crucifying asceticism. In her system of belief, the material—that is the life experience of the individual and its relationship with history—was to be accepted as valid in itself, but beyond itself it was to be seen as a means to transcend the material in order to move to a higher plane of consciousness. The body was thus an important instrument in this journey. The Aurobindian philosophy lays great stress on this instrument being tuned so perfectly that it can then fulfil its function of enabling the *sadhak* (seeker) to achieve her/his spiritual purpose. Chawla saw the actor's work on the body as a *sadhana* (search) that would lead to a spiritual awakening, radically different from Grotowski's idea of sacrifice.

Compared to her lukewarm response to Grotowski, Chawla formed a more positive relationship with the ideas and methods of his student Eugenio Barba. Barba's theatre too was actor-centric and a rejection of the 'natural' for the 'artificial'. But it did not demand cruelty to the body. It asked the actor to dredge up from her/his unique subjectivity, objective signs that would communicate with the audience. How the actor was to arrive at this subjectivity became the main thrust of her/his work on her/himself.

In order to see the uniqueness of Veenapani Chawla's theatre practice, we must pause here to look at the Indian context in which several theatre practitioners were simultaneously exploring a physical language for theatre around the time that she began her theatre work in Mumbai. All of them believed that the truth of art lay in its difference from the truth of life. Attempting to create an illusion of life on stage was counter-art. Their theatre did not speak exclusively in words but made music and movement equal carriers of meaning. In Thiruvananthapuram, Kerala, on the southwestern coast of India, Kavalam Panikkar had founded a theatre group, Sopanam, whose greatest contribution to Indian theatre was his production of plays by the ancient Sanskrit playwright Bhasa, 13 of whose playscripts had been discovered in Kerala in 1909. Panikkar had evolved a system of training for his actors based on Kerala's martial art form, Kalaripayattu. Later, Chawla too made this the basis of her theatre vocabulary. Unlike Kathakali and Koodiyattam, in which hand and facial gestures were closely associated with emotional meaning, Kalaripayattu provided a neutral repertoire of walks, jumps, throws of the body, and frozen postures that could be invested with chosen meanings.

In Manipur in the northeast of the country, diagonally opposite to Kerala, Ratan Thiyam was drawing upon the dance, drumming, musical, martial, and storytelling traditions of his region. Like Panikkar, he too had returned to the classics—Kalidasa, Sophocles, and Bhasa, and, repeatedly, to the Mahabharata— in the productions he directed for his company, the Chorus Repertory, which he founded in 1976.

Whilst both Panikkar and Thiyam had local traditions of dance, music, and storytelling to draw upon, Veenapani Chawla, a Punjabi growing up in Mumbai, had no readily accessible form of physical culture that she could use. She had, therefore, to travel up and down the country in search of what might answer her need. This was an urgent task. Working on *Oedipus* and *Rosencrantz and Guildenstern Are Dead* had given her some inkling that theatre might possibly be her life's work, and she needed to prepare for it.

Oedipus

As a practitioner of Sri Aurobindo's philosophy, Chawla did not see *Oedipus* as a tragedy. In fact, achieving knowledge at the end, she saw him victoriously arriving at a new equilibrium. She was puzzled by his act of blinding himself. For, to the Greeks, mutilation of the body was abhorrent. But Oedipus justified it by saying that it was his demon, Apollo, who had directed him to do so. This gave Chawla the idea that the myth was a metaphor for seeking internal causes for external events. Tiresias, the blind seer, too advised him to look within himself for the causes of the plague which had afflicted his city. And, at the end, he is a Tiresias-like figure, whose gaze has turned inward towards knowledge of the self and therefore the world. With that, he moves towards his 'awe-full' mystical destiny which plays itself out in *Oedipus at Colonus*.

This interpretation of the play caught Naseeruddin Shah's imagination, leading to his ultimately playing Oedipus.

For this interpretation to hold, Chawla modified the end of the play in two ways. She toned down Oedipus's raving and ranting after his discovery of his predestined sin, and also dropped the scene at the end of the play where Creon brings Oedipus's daughters before him after the blinding.

Oedipus succeeded beyond Chawla's and her cast's wildest imagination. They had expected to do five shows but did 25, each one to resounding applause. The Mumbai press, which gave it wide coverage, hailed it as a landmark production. Besides its superb production values, there were brilliant performances by Naseeruddin Shah as Oedipus and Deepa Lagoo as Jocasta. So elated were Chawla's actors by this success that they clamoured to do another play. And so she directed Tom Stoppard's *Rosencrantz and Guildenstern Are Dead*, a play she had already done with her students at Arya Vidya Mandir.

Rosencrantz and Guildenstern Are Dead

Rosencrantz and Guildenstern Are Dead was staged at the Prithvi Theatre, Mumbai, in June 1983. With the exception of Naseeruddin Shah who played Hamlet, the rest of the cast comprised amateurs. The rehearsals gave every sign of a rollicking production in the making. Chawla has referred to the spirit during rehearsals as 'a state of controlled anarchy'. The play kept its promise. It sparkled with wit and excellent performances. (See Smriti Nevatia's review 'A Triumph' in Appendix I.) The set by Veenapani Chawla and Vinesh Gandhi was specially appreciated as were the costumes. Chawla believed this was her best work to date. However, shortage of funds coupled with inter-actor tensions compelled her to close it down even before it established itself.

Although *Rosencrantz and Guildenstern Are Dead* had a sadly short life, *Oedipus* continued to be remembered as a significant production. As an outcome of its success, Chawla began to receive invitations to participate in workshops, conferences, and seminars. Meeting theatre practitioners from all over the country, hearing discussions on different views about culture, and discovering the many forms and traditions of theatre that existed in this country, were huge learning experiences for Chawla. During one such seminar in Kolkata, where the interaction between traditional dance and theatre was being discussed, she met Guru Krishna Chandra Naik, a well-known exponent of the Chhau form of dance, and decided to learn the art from him.

Chhau is practised, with variations, in the region that surrounds the intersecting borders of three states—Bengal, Bihar, and Orissa. In Purulia (Bengal) and Seraikela (Bihar) the dancers wear masks. In Mayurbhanj (Orissa) they do not. Chawla travelled to the interiors of all three states to discover which of the three forms of Chhau might be most useful for her purposes. She rejected the masked forms because an expressive body had to necessarily include the face, and opted for Mayurbhanj Chhau. She spent some time in Baripada at the Mayurbhanj Chhau Nritya Pratishthan but soon realized that she would not be able to adapt to the life there. So she decided to train under Guru Krishna Chandra Naik at Bharatiya Kala Kendra in Delhi instead.

Here, Chawla received special training in the mornings and joined the general class in the afternoons, occasionally staying back for extra practice in the evenings. She was not learning Chhau to become a performer but to acquire a system of movement that she could use to make texts speak through her actors' bodies. Four months of training sufficed to serve this purpose. At the end of this period, her body had absorbed the vocabulary of the dance form enough for her to use its movements to create an energetic language for her next production, Euripides's *The Trojan Women*.

The Trojan Women

After Veenapani Chawla quit Arya Vidya Mandir in 1978, she went to the Aurobindo Ashram in Puducherry to work on her PhD thesis, 'Sri Aurobindo and Education'. She spent almost a year there during which time she read the Greek classics. Amongst them was *The Trojan Women*. As with *Oedipus*, Chawla had her own interpretation of the play. The fact that the characters in the play did not evolve with their experience militated against the very core of her philosophy. When she chose to do this play after *Rosencrantz and Guildenstern Are Dead*, it was with her own interpretation. Her Hecuba, the central figure of the play, accepted the circumstances of history as inevitable and rose above them. Chawla also recast Helen as a wise woman who inspired the worship of beauty, truth, and refinement, rather than as a temptress.

The play had already begun to germinate in her mind as her next production while she was undergoing Chhau training in Delhi. Back in Mumbai, she gathered a group of women, a mix of trained actors and amateurs, and began the process of training their bodies in the movements of Chhau. Their urban bodies were stiff, and had to be de-schooled and broken into the low, crouching gaits of Chhau. They had to learn to stretch, arch their backs, and do *paltas*—half-turns of the body which allowed the torso and arms to flow in one sinuous, unbroken movement. The exercises began in October 1983. The play was staged the following year, after six months of back-breaking rehearsals. The main roles were played by actors who were later to become well-known names in theatre, film, and television. Sushmita Mukherjee played Hecuba, Neena Gupta, Andromache, Aditya Bhattacharya, Menelaus, and Javed Jaffrey, Talthybios.

Arvind Rane, who had been with Chawla from his student days when she was his teacher, played the *nagara* (drum) for the play. The rise and fall of its beats was the only music there. Rane also designed and constructed the set.

The Trojan Women attracted packed houses and was critically acclaimed. (See Smriti Nevatia's review 'Intelligent Adaptation'

The Trojan Women. Photograph courtesy of Vinesh Gandhi.

in Appendix I.) Several of the women who acted as the chorus in the play were to stay on for Chawla's next production, *A Greater Dawn*. But before that, Chawla produced two monologues, *Kunti* and *The Human Voice*, which expanded her understanding of the nuts and bolts of theatre significantly, and led to the most important phase of her life—her exploration of the theatre and martial art forms of Kerala.

Kunti and *The Human Voice*

The year after Chawla staged *The Trojan Women*, that is, in 1984–5, she produced two monologues to be performed back to back by Alaknanda Samarth. The first was G. Sankara Pillai's *Kunti*, written specially for the actor; the second, Jean Cocteau's *The Human Voice*. Besides being a learning experience, producing the plays also gave Chawla valuable time with Samarth and dancer Chandralekha, who was choreographing them. (See the Samarth–Chawla letters in '*Kunti* and *The Human Voice*'.) Being with these artists proved to be a turning point in Chawla's theatre in many ways.

For instance, Chandralekha spoke to her about the benefits of Kerala's martial art form, Kalaripayattu, for improving breath control and voice quality. This led to Chawla obtaining a grant from the Ford Foundation to research into traditional and contemporary knowledge related to breath, voice, and energy, with a view to developing a methodology for voice training of the actor. The question of how she was going to get into one of the four schools in Kerala where Kalaripayattu was taught, and which of them would suit her best, was solved by G. Sankara Pillai. He was one of the most eminent persons in the theatre field in Kerala, having founded the Nataka Kalari in 1967, which led to the creation of the School of Drama and Fine Arts in Kerala. His word carried a lot of weight.

G. Sankara Pillai assigned one of his students of theatre, Naripatta Raju, himself a significant theatre director today, the duty to take Chawla to all four schools to enable her to make a choice. She decided to train in the *kalari* (school) at Chavakkad village near Guruvayur. Chawla's intention was to learn Koodiyattam at the same time as Kalaripayattu. This is when Pillai arranged for her to be enrolled in the kalari as a special student with a timetable that was different from the other students. When she found that the accommodation available in Chavakkad did not suit her, it was Pillai's word again that helped her find a suitable room in Irinjalakuda, where her Koodiyattam guru Ammannur Madhava Chakyar lived.

Learning Kalaripayattu and Koodiyattam together was a gruelling regimen. Chawla would get up at 5 in the morning, take a two-hour bus ride to the kalari, have breakfast, then train for three hours. After a brief nap, she would take the bus back to Irinjalakuda, where she would have lunch and start her lessons with Chakyar.

Kalaripayattu also involved an annual regimen of body massage with special oil. The massage was done over 15 days and was followed by a 15-day rest period. The guru's wife massaged her with her feet while Chawla lay spreadeagled on the floor. There was no nap for her on massage days. The bus conductor had strict instructions not to let her doze off on the way back. The efficacy of the massage depended on adhering to this rule amongst many others. Chawla trained in this fashion for two years. At the end of it, she was permitted to give her *arangetram* (stage debut), although she had mastered only five of the eight weapons that would normally qualify a student to give a stage performance.

During the two-year Ford Foundation grant period, Chawla also worked with Patsy Rodenburg, the voice coach of the Royal Shakespeare Company, London, learned *pranayama* and *hatha* yoga, and studied the *dhrupad* style of music with the Dagar brothers. In 1989, she received a grant from Det Lange Udvalag to study at Eugenio Barba's Odin Teatret in Holstebro. Equipped now with the means to develop a methodology for breath, voice, and body training of the actor, and insights gained from the training methods of the leading theatre guru of the time, Eugenio Barba, Chawla was ready to take on the challenge of editing and adapting Sri Aurobindo's 24,000-line poem *Savitri* for the stage.

A Greater Dawn

Although *A Greater Dawn* was the last of Veenapani Chawla's Mumbai plays, it was in many respects closer to her first Puducherry play, *Impressions of Bhima*, than to *The Trojan Women* that had preceded it. The first trio of plays in Mumbai had followed each other within a span of five years, from 1981 to 1985. *A Greater Dawn* premiered in 1992 although Chawla had been working on the script since 1984. It was an onerous task to carve out 40 lines and a 75-minute performance text from Sri Aurobindo's epic poem. The hiatus of almost eight years between *The Trojan Women* and *A Greater Dawn* had been filled with rigorous training in theatre skills and in gaining a hold on the aesthetics of performance rooted in the traditions of South Asia. *Impressions of Bhima* used the same sources of body language as *A Greater Dawn*, and had its first show just three years after.

The second link that connected *A Greater Dawn* with the Puducherry plays was its direct engagement with the philosophy of Sri Aurobindo. Whereas earlier this philosophy had caused Chawla to reinterpret existing dramatic texts to bring them in line with it, she was now doing the writing herself in order to explore themes that would reflect it directly. There was thus cohesion in her vision of what she wanted to say and the manner in which it needed to be said. The very structure of the plays was the result of this cohesion.

The third vital link between *A Greater Dawn* and *Impressions of Bhima* was the presence of actor Vinay Kumar K.J. in both. Vinay Kumar was not only Chawla's actor but her collaborator as well. It was his fascination with M.T. Vasudevan Nair's novel on Bhima that was to sow the seeds of *Impressions of Bhima* in Chawla's mind. She had met Vinay Kumar in Trichur where she had gone to work with K.C. Manvendranath, who was playing Death to Mita Vasisth's Savitri. Vinay Kumar had joined Manvendranath's theatre group, attracted by the new methodology of training he was developing for actors.

Listening to the discussions between Manvendranath and Chawla about Sri Aurobindo's interpretation of the story of Savitri and her husband Satyavan, Vinay Kumar found himself getting deeply involved with the ideas and meaning of the poem. Chawla found the suggestions he was making for movement and voice highly valuable. She asked Manvendranath if he could be spared to go to Mumbai with her to help with her other actors. Since she was herself to play Savitri in the second run of the play, an assistant director whose ideas about theatre matched hers would be of invaluable help.

Manvendranath granted permission, and Vinay Kumar accompanied Chawla to Mumbai. He watched the actors closely. Homing in on their specific problems, he worked out solutions for each one, evolving exercises for voice training and body energy. His work with actors prompted Chawla to ask him to play Death in the second run of the play. He agreed with alacrity. But the play was in English, a language that he was not at all comfortable with. Chawla relieved him of anxiety on that count by reverting to an idea she had originally had of Death as a silent force.

A Greater Dawn was the first play of Chawla's in which music—which was to gradually grow in importance in her plays to ultimately become the text itself in *Ganapati*—played a more

Vinay Kumar and
Veenapani Chawla in *Savitri*.
Photograph courtesy of S. Anwar.

vital role than it had done before. She wanted the music to enter
and be part of the movement and vice versa. It was a tough call
to find a musician who could understand this concept in the first
place, and then for him to be imaginative and innovative enough
to give the concept a musical form.

After a search that took her all over the country, Chawla found
the person she was looking for in Mumbai itself—the young tabla
player Aneesh Pradhan. Together they set about constructing
a score that mixed the human voice with an eclectic variety of
musical elements, drawn from sources as diverse as Gregorian and
Buddhist chants, chords, strains of raga music, and notes from
Mozart's *Requiem*. They used an equally varied range of instruments for the effects they desired. These included gongs, drums,
and Manipuri rice bowls that produced richly resonant notes
when the rims were stroked with a short baton. There was also
the haunting dirge that Savitri sang as she came to terms with
Satyavan's imminent death.

Like her earlier plays, *A Greater Dawn* too was widely covered by the Mumbai press and won critical praise wherever it was
staged. (See Keval Arora's review of the play in Appendix I.)

Puducherry

In 1993, Veenapani Chawla moved to Puducherry. Living near Sri Aurobindo Ashram, she contemplated how she was to take her theatre forward. By the following year she had her answer. Vinay Kumar had found his work in *A Greater Dawn* as an actor and assistant director immensely rewarding. This was the kind of theatre he wanted to do. So he enrolled at the university in Puducherry to do a doctorate in drama, to give himself a chance to find out whether his future lay in doing theatre with Veenapani Chawla.

In 1994, Chawla set up Adishakti, a laboratory for theatre arts research. Her aim was to evolve a new vocabulary of theatre. She had already taken a major step in this direction with *A Greater Dawn*. But she needed space that would allow her to work in a systematic, concentrated fashion. Meanwhile she had an actor, Vinay Kumar, and a tiny flat near the Ashram, where they could make a beginning.

Totally unknown to her, there were people around who admired her work and wanted to see it grow. Igor, a resident of Auroville, offered her the plot of land on which the Adishakti Laboratory for Theatre Arts Research stands today. She had no money to buy it but another admirer, a Danish gentleman, did. The first thing Chawla and Vinay Kumar did after he bought the land for her was to plant trees. That meant engaging a gardener to look after them and a watchman to guard the property. But where were their salaries to come from? From the vegetables that they began to grow on the land. Next, Chawla's niece, Leela Gandhi, who had acted in her Mumbai plays, gave her money to build the cottage in which she lives. Gandhi had inherited the money from her Tamil grandmother, and felt it should go back into Tamil soil! Contributions and grants from other people and organizations followed, to fund the guest house and the theatre. The guest house soon became a source of income for Adishakti. It has been regularly hired out for arts residencies, conferences, and seminars. British director Tim Supple rehearsed his widely acclaimed *A Midsummer Night's Dream* with a linguistically mixed cast at Adishakti.

Today, the Adishakti laboratory is abuzz with creative activity all year round. Its core group of actors, Vinay Kumar, Nimmy Raphel, and Arvind Rane, live on the campus. Suresh Kaliyath, a professional Ottan Thullal performer, comes and goes. Chawla's actors train every day to keep their bodies, minds, and spirits tuned. Rigorous daily practice is required for the kind of work they are called upon to do.

Four of the six plays that Chawla has directed since she moved to Puducherry form the focus of this study. They have been the most widely watched and trace a clear trajectory of her search. The audience reception of these plays has not been uniform. The first play, *Impressions of Bhima*, is considered to be Chawla's most accessible after the Mumbai quartet. *Brhannala*, which came next, required a certain amount of annotation to help the audience enter it. *Ganapati*, the third, being almost entirely music and very little speech, caused conservatives and critics amongst the audience to question whether it could be called a piece of theatre at all. Many found the fourth, *The Hare and the Tortoise*, the most difficult to understand. Chawla had to prepare a very long, explanatory programme note, and distribute it before performances to help the audience understand what was going on.

Besides the difficulties presented by Chawla's plays, mainly because of an absence of linear narratives, it needs to be said here that some theatre practitioners and commentators have rejected her work on ideological grounds. Some have rejected it as a consequence of their rejection of Sri Aurobindo's philosophy which forms the very source of her ideas and themes. Some, in the firm belief that theatre must speak of people's contemporary problems, have done so because hers is a theatre of archetypes and spiritual journeys. Some believe that plays which require extensive introductions block the free flow of ideas and emotions that should connect the performer to the spectator. Much as the editor would have welcomed these dissenting viewpoints in this study, they were not forthcoming.

Kunti and The Human Voice

ALAKNANDA SAMARTH AND
VEENAPANI CHAWLA

eminiscences exchanged between Alaknanda Samarth
and Veenapani Chawla when the former recently discovered an old photograph that Ketaki Seth had taken
of the two of them and Chandralekha during a break in the
rehearsals of *Kunti* and *The Human Voice*. They were directed
by film-maker Kumar Shahani. Chandralekha did the choreography and eminent artist Akbar Padamsee, the sets. This
exchange of letters gives us some inkling of how important
an experience doing the monologues was for both Samarth
and Chawla.

Actor Alaknanda Samarth, producer Veenapani Chawla, and dancer-choreographer Chandralekha during a break in the rehearsals of G. Sankara Pillai's *Kunti*, directed by Kumar Shahani. Photograph courtesy of Ketaki Sheth.

We Three

Dear Veena,

This photo was taken by Ketu Seth during a rehearsal break, remember? Some 33 years on, the rehearsals of *Kunti* and *The Human Voice* remain the most tumultuous I've known. A few of us got together to unload the baggage we carried individually in our various disciplines, lay ourselves bare and reshape an idiom of live performance.

Two monologues were acted by one person on one stage. *Kunti* was written for me by G. Sankara Pillai in Malayalam and translated into Hindi by Raghuvir Sahay. *The Human Voice* by Jean Cocteau in French was translated by me into English. Four languages were at work. Played back-to-back the show ran two hours in Hindi and English with a 15-minute interval. It was directed by Kumar Shahani.

A high risk venture, then. You it was, who actually stepped forward to take it on as producer. Weeks before rehearsals even began, anxieties were flying. Akbar Padamsee was designer, Chandralekha choreographer, Bhanu Athaiya costume designer. I wasn't living in India and barely knew you. I wrote you not one, not two, but dozens of handwritten aerogramme letters, which you quietly assimilated.

It was only when we all met in that rehearsal room at the House of Soviet Culture in Bombay, that what we were unleashing began to dawn on us. Something primal. And deeply disturbing. We'd entered a cave of the word, shattering our own respective disciplines, shattering the stereotype, the fossilisation of myth. In those intensely private rehearsals, you sat throughout silently, listening profoundly, above all listening actively.

Kumar Shahani was not just any film director, but one who had evolved a highly sophisticated, unique idiom of acting. He'd never directed live theatre before this. He worked on two maps. With Chandra for *Kunti*, he drew on me a physical mapping of the text in space, stripped of every iota of the motivational, mannered, behavioural. Quite separately, he charted the mathematics of the two texts in two languages for my voice. The show had no music, sounds, or percussion at all. Just the voice without amplification.

'Do Karna with your voice, Kunti with your body', was the directive one day. D'you remember that day? Chandra would evolve a slow-burning move—shoulders at 30 degrees to torso, grip the earth, kneel, lie down, twist torso, rise slowly … How could I do this and speak with resonance at a fast tempo at the same time?

'Either this will be a cacophany or it will be a vibration going out like bronze,' she said.

Bhanu's two costumes gave two starkly different histories of the female form in two different perspectives, lit by cinematographer Piyush Shah. At the end of traumatic eight-hour rehearsal days of four hours on *Kunti*, always followed by four hours on *The Human Voice*, the two halves began to split. Emotional trauma set in. A new joinery began to appear before our disbelieving eyes and ears. Without your grit, humanity, blind faith, this transgressive piece of work wouldn't have known life before an audience.

Kunti and *The Human Voice*, 1987, has become something of an iconic landmark in theatre. Some hated it, some walked out in angry disapproval, some in Delhi stayed to whistle catcalls at me. For some it was catalystic. It changed their lives, set some methodologically free. For some, it's still a cultural reference point. In Kiev post Chernobyl, a lady on the street took off her necklace and placed it in my hand without a word, and two months ago in London 2011, I met someone who said, 'My mother took me to see it. I saw it as a child.'

To you, Veena,
lots of love and thanks,
Alak
5 November 2011
London

Dear Alak,

I know this photograph. I mislaid my copy in transit from Mumbai to Pondicherry! And then you nudged my memory when you showed it to me last year. Three goddesses you said!

I recollect having distinctly mundane preoccupations that evening. We were checking the Homi Bhabha auditorium as a venue for *Kunti* and *The Human Voice*. Kumar wanted *Kunti* to open to the setting sun. But what about the aircraft sounds overhead? And what time would the sun set next month for the performance?

I remember feeling oppressed by the management required for an outdoor performance. Seating to be hired and organised, sound system to be perfect, scaffoldings and grids for the lights. And where was the money?

Kumar was querulous that evening. He wanted Chandra to perform in counterpoint to you in *Kunti*. But she did not have the time to commit to performance. Chandra thought that, with my one year experience in Mayurbhanj Chhau, I would be able to do what Kumar wanted her to do! I was very concerned. I stood in *tribhanga* for 20 minutes and had it! Was she cross!

Yes I remember very well when Kumar asked you to use different tempos for the body and for the voice. I had been so used to the duplication of expressions in our traditional forms, that this really gave me a knock on my nose and woke me up. It has stayed with me in my work since then. Exploring tensions between different modes of expressions, making them speak beyond the obviously expressed.

I was a student all over again, and K and HV was a bridge to somewhere else. One of those liminal phases where one looks for new directions and shapes in thought. Akbar Padamsee told me about the *muladhara chakra* and how to locate it! Chandra opened my eyes to scale. We were driving down from Bandra to Altamount Road for the rehearsals, animatedly in talk, when she paused abruptly mid-sentence, entranced by a billboard covered with scaffolding and tiny people painting on it.

I loved those drives with Chandra. Hearing from her about the letters Sri Aurobindo had written to Harindranath Chattopadhyay, her own interactions with the Mother, her visits to the Ashram to perform there, her notions of the body. And she, sitting totally erect, always erect, spine straight, not leaning against the seat of the car through the long drive.

So many from that time continued to be friends and collaborators in later years. You know that Bhanu created costumes for my production of *Savitri* in 1992, and again for some other work I did in 1995 from Pondicherry. And of course you know that it was G Sankara Pillai who guided my Kerala journey. And years later, when he was with Mahatma Gandhi University, I spoke to him about my dream of creating a theatre laboratory; and he said, 'Remember to involve me.' Sadly he passed on that very year.

For *The Human Voice* I remember an almost last-minute decision that Kumar made, playing the soundtrack of a French film—I forget which—through the performance, and beneath your text. Brilliant! Years later it connected in my mind when I explored Koodiyattam music as a text.

One of the delights was to hear your imaginings. And I recall the day when you 'saw' the bird in *Kunti*. I had always imagined it to be large, somewhat like a seagull. Especially because of the sound you voiced for it. But in your mind's eye that morning, you said you vividly saw a small, yellow bird.

And talking about sound, it was inspirational to observe your commitment to *vachika*. You had a tutor for your Hindi text. Each inflexion had to be just right. But it was not about realism. And I recall our conversation when we met last year, regarding your work with Patsy and your recent research into sound. I remember also your reading of Elkunchwar's text at Adishakti's Winter Festival in 2003 and your advice to Vinay for the text of the last scene of *Brhannala*.

Unique and wonderful. How much of an influence did your mother have on this aspect of your work I wonder? Sound, the word, beyond realism.

I reflect on this as I prepare to delve into the world of vachika myself.

I remember one conversation we had with Rustom—remember he was there too, observing the process?—where you said that the performances were pure *satvika* and therefore demanding.

All this was happening just before I left for Kerala. A great preparation before my plunge into Koodiyattam and the actor's craft. I had directed three plays professionally before this. But the actor's craft had eluded and baffled me.

After this, not so much.

But both of us had crosses to bear during *Kunti* and *The Human Voice*. You had that terrible back pain. I had to deal with money.

Love,
Veenapani
Pondicherry
20 November 2011

Two

The Adishakti Campus and Team

THE DEVELOPMENT OF the Adishakti campus has been an ongoing process from the time Veenapani Chawla acquired the plot of land. In her essay, she tells us what principles led her to design the theatre space as she has done. The article by art critic Geeta Doctor gives us an informed outsider's view of the space. The article by Himanshu Burte, an architect with a special interest in theatre spaces, offers a specialist's response to Adishakti's. Shanta Gokhale profiles Adishakti's core team of performers and Sarah Joseph tracks the work done with Adishakti by two illustrious performers from Kerala.

Architecture and Theatre*

VEENAPANI CHAWLA

Architecture for theatre has to spring out of an aesthetics and philosophy of live performance. The interaction between the audience and performer in theatre is not only sensorial, it is also one wherein the performer's heightened consciousness impacts the spectator through contagion.

In the world of art and aesthetics, both contagion and consciousness are fundamental to experience. Indeed, the value of aesthetic performance lies in its ability to create a heightened or elevated state of consciousness. This uplifting power of performance is inherent in its nature; for it is itself the expression of a

---

* Excerpted from a paper read at a seminar on 'Theatre Space' at Prithvi Theatre, Mumbai, in October 2003.

heightened/elevated consciousness. If the creations of the artist/ performer come from her highest states of consciousness, they will impact the spectator and elevate her to a corresponding state of consciousness. Such an aesthetic and philosophy of the theatre implies that it has a sacred function.

Sacred Space

According to the evidence we have of the traditional performing space both in the *Natyashastra* and in the *Koothambalam*, we find there is a similarity between the organisation of the temple space which is sacred, and the traditional performance space, the *Koothambalam*. It seems therefore, that the tradition also envisaged a sacred role for theatre, although the traditional notion of the sacred possibly varied from ours. While theirs was largely religious, ours can be religiously, morally, politically and socially subversive, and yet retain its sacredness, as that sacredness is not dependent on established formulae, but on the truth of a lived experience.

We see then, that certain important features of the temple are replicated in the *Koothambalam*. The temple has an inner sanctuary, the *garbha griha*, in which the deity is kept; it has a pillared hall, the *mandapa*, in front of the sanctuary for the assembly of devotees; and it has a run-around verandah, the *maha-mandapa*, on each side of the assembly hall. In the *Koothambalam*, the performance area replaces the inner sanctuary, thus signifying the sacred nature of this space; the pillared assembly area of the temple is replaced by the space for the spectator, the two spaces being frequently marked out by a small difference in levels, and pillars. The run-around corridor is also accommodated in the structure of the *Koothambalam*.

It is interesting to note that there is much the same conventional system and disposition of parts in the Christian church and the Greek temple as in the Indian temple. The chancel in the Christian church and the *cella* in the Greek temple correspond to the *garba griha*. The nave of the Christian church, and the columned *naos* of the Greek temple correspond to the *mandapa*.

The architectural principles fundamental to the sacred in the traditional performance space, manifest themselves through the subtle division between the performer's space and the spectator's space, and in the awareness that the centre of the entire constructed space of the theatre—the point of highest energy—is where the performer ought to situate herself so as to have the highest impact.

The justification behind the first principle was that the first principle, while allowing for intimacy and sensorial participation, encouraged a psychical distance between the performer and the spectator. Thus, while the performer could portray a *bhava* like lust/*kama* for instance, the spectator was encouraged to be detached from the feeling of lust while experiencing the *rasa* or aesthetic appreciation of its portrayal. Without this, the performance would be merely a sensorial, rather than an elevating experience.

Insofar as the second principle is concerned, very few performance spaces honour it today. In most, the performance space is placed at the extreme end of the structure. The *Koothambalam*, however, divides the entire constructed space into two, one half of which is the performance space and the green room beyond. This places the performance area at the centre of the structure. In performing at the centre of the structure, the performer avails of the high energy that is available in that location.

Intimate Space and Architecture

The sacred intent of theatre, which is grounded on presence in a true space, dictates that the space is such that neither the presence, nor its contagion, is diffused. It begs for a space which is intimate. It begs for a space which encourages an interactive engagement between the performer and the spectator.

Today theatre practitioners define intimate space in terms of its audience capacity. This could vary from 70 to 200 people. Although this is one yardstick for defining an intimate space, there are others such as the arrangement of the space. A proscenium with a seating capacity of 200, need not be intimate, if it allows for too large a distance between performer and audience; and anything which distracts from an exclusive mutual concentration between performer and spectator, prevents the space from being intimate.

One of the best examples of an intimate space in contemporary times is the Prithvi Theatre. Yes, it accommodates about 200 people; but the space is so arranged, with its thrust stage, black box effect and excellent acoustics, that it holds the performer-spectator in an embrace, allowing for the magic of an intimate performer-spectator relationship to happen. In the Indian tradition, there is recognition of the need for this embrace-like effect of the theatre space. The *Natyashastra* describes such a space as a cave, where nothing extraneous intrudes to disturb the communication between spectator and performer.

To conclude, the ideal space for theatre would be one which transmits the power of the live performer's behaviour to the spectator at the optimum. If the inner spaces of the performer are to be reflected on her face, then each twitch on it ought to be visible to each one of the spectators. Thus the human eye dictates the size of the intimate performance space. If the minutest details on the face of the performer are visible from any point in the space, the size of that space is right.

Additionally, when the space carries the sound of the performer, unaided by technology, beyond mere audibility to resonate within the body of the spectator, then it is truly an intimate space.

The Good Earth

GEETA DOCTOR

Adishakti is an experiment in living theatre created by Veenapani Chawla just outside of Puducherry. A winding track leads to it from the East Coast Road that connects Chennai to Puducherry. People from all over the world pass you on their bikes and two-wheelers on this track, including locals in slow-moving bullock carts. The track winds through densely planted groves of trees and cashew farms and along old temple tanks filled with heads of pink lotus flowers. It is always a surprise to find Adishakti. Suddenly, it is there, its wooden gates hung with a small sign that reads, 'Adishakti'. Beyond is an expanse of land, lush with vegetation.

It wasn't always like this. When the land first came to Veenapani, gifted by a Dane who admired her work, the landscape was covered with red earth and a few scrawny bushes that had struggled up through it. Even these were nibbled at by village goats. Next door was Auroville, envisaged by the Mother as the City of the Future.

'What is it that you would like to do?' one of the elders of the Ashram, founded by Sri Aurobindo and the Mother, had asked Veenapani. 'Would you like to stay here and work with us? There is plenty to do for everyone. Or would you like to take the path less travelled?' After mulling for long over the question, she decided to take the path less travelled. She already saw the barren wilderness of her land filled with trees and flowers, aromatic plants and shrubs, a theatre, and a house for artists and performers. This was going to be the realization of her vision—the Adishakti Laboratory for Theatre Arts and Research.

Today, the entire area is covered with fruit trees, shade trees, flowering trees, and shrubs that bloom during different seasons. In the evenings, as you walk to the communal dining room that visitors and performers share, the night-blooming flowers fill the air with fleeting traces of perfume. In the morning, as you walk around, the mild fragrance of dew-covered grass, mint and lemon

The exterior of the theatre at Adishakti, the Sir Ratan Tata Koothu Kovil. Photograph courtesy of Vinay Kumar.

grass, and the heady scent of frangipani blossoms dropping on the red earth follow you.

As for the red earth, it forms the keystone of the architecture of the buildings that have come up at Adishakti. The most dramatic of these is the theatre itself. It is a magnificent space, built of laterite walls, with pierced openings to let in the light and air, a huge performing space inside, with the black polished floor that was traditionally used in the old palaces of Kerala.

The theatre has more than a passing likeness with *Koothambalams*, the traditional temple theatres of Kerala. But what is extraordinary about it is the sense of 'lived experience'; it communicates even when there is no live performance going on. The circular platform at the front of the building is already suggestive of a performance space. One steps up from the garden onto its brick surface and then stands before the small porch with the carved wooden doorway that leads into the auditorium. Stepping from the brightness of the outdoors into the mysterious space within replicates, almost exactly, the sense of stepping into a sanctum. The vastness of the space is such that it seems to hum with a certain resonance. The performance space fills the foreground and stretches right up to the end of the hall in one continuous expanse of polished wood, contained on three sides by massive pillars that rise like a forest to meet in the darkness of the rafters that hold up the roof. This is the platform where both the performers and the audience may meet in a dialogue.

The stage is 30 feet by 40 feet with a height of 30 feet. It is surrounded on three sides by a 6-foot-wide enclosed verandah or corridor. This space is designed to accommodate not only Adishakti's rehearsal work and performances but also the entire gamut of their performer training, which includes highly physical aspects of their work.

What is interesting, once you are inside, is to see how the light filters in through the *jali*-type work that has been incorporated into the placing of the laterite blocks. The light creates its own dynamics of space, changing at different times of the day. It also makes for a very cool interior. Beyond the performance area are the green rooms, storage space for the props that are needed in the theatre, such as the musical instruments, the toilets, and so forth. Decorative arches frame these doors so that they can be used in a dramatic manner should the need arise.

Looking from the stage towards the front door, you see a circular symbol with the floral design of the Mother placed at the centre top of the entrance, like a distinctive *bindu*, or luminous eye. With spotlights along the sides of the walls, the theatre is a dramatic visual statement of light and shadows that sweep over the red tiled floors, the rough earth colours of the laterite walls, the mellow sheen of the wood that is continually polished by hand, and the limitless span of the black roof that frames it like the vault of the dark sky itself.

At a short distance from the theatre is the guest house built of mud in what Veenapani calls a 'hybrid construction'. Her Kerala-based architect, Sreenivasan Vasthukam, had worked earlier with Laurie Baker, the architect of highly innovative buildings, using age-old building materials and techniques, and at Cosford, where such methods were modified to train traditional craftsmen to work to the standards required in the construction of houses for a more contemporary clientele. Veenapani taught herself the rudiments of building by trial and error. She built her own house first using natural materials. The next project was the guest house. This has been built in a regular *mandala*-like form. Its pitched roofs project fan-like tiers to shelter the walls which have been constructed using traditional local techniques, involving compounded mud, plastered to a shiny finish with several kinds of organic materials from parts of north Kerala. The highly polished black pillars, set on dressed stone bases that outline the central courtyard, contrast dramatically with the red tiled and polished floors.

'The inspiration for these buildings came from our own region,' says Veenapani.

> Mud technology has been used all across South Asia, and from Kashmir to Gujarat to Tamil Nadu, with variations to suit local needs. We adapted the old technology using new inputs, entirely Tamil. The artisans who worked on the construction came

from Kerala, and had to learn the technique from an old Tamil mason, the only one left in this region who had the know-how. Sreenivasan, had only a theoretical knowledge of the process at the time. Over time, with the practical experience of making the Adishakti buildings, he has improved on it for contemporary needs. The guest house was his first mud construction. Subsequently, he has constructed a number of mud buildings in Kerala and other places. I might add that the laterite used in the construction of the theatre is fossilized mud. Being hard and rough in texture, it is ideal for acoustics.

All this digging of mud for constructing the theatre, the dining room that still has a thatched roof, the office, the guest house, and some of the Adishakti community members' homes, had left pits in the ground that had been turned into ponds for rainwater harvesting. But there was one enormous pit a little distance away from the theatre that Veenapani had set her mind on for a swimming pool. This is to date the last feature to appear on the Adishakti campus. Its surrounding walls are built in brick, plastered with mud, and bordered by banana plantations, jackfruit, and guava. But the pool itself is state-of-the-art, tiled in brilliant blue.

At Adishakti, the Mother's work is manifest in the flowering of the good earth.

Home for Theatre*

HIMANSHU BURTE

Stated ideas don't always continue loyally into action. The small campus that Veenapani Chawla has built near Pondicherry for her theatre commune, Adishakti, is a striking exception. Chawla and Adishakti, are known for developing a contemporary theatrical expression that attempts to draw inspiration from the many historical and cultural strands that make us what we are today. Hybridity is the key word for Chawla in her work as well as her space, as the Adishakti campus, and especially the powerful theatre space built in the year 2004, demonstrate.

* Excerpted from the article titled 'The Stage Is a World!' that appeared in *The Mint* on 31 May 2007, with permission of the copyright holder, HT Media Ltd.

What the theatre also reveals is that the hybrid can sometimes have the sacred intensity one usually associates with pure states.

The theatre, named Sir Ratan Tata Koothu Kovil, is the centerpiece of the almost three-acre campus which also has a guest-house, an older rehearsal space, residential spaces and lots of trees. The design of the campus was a collaboration between Chawla and Sreenivasan Vasthukam, a civil engineer practising as an architect in Kerala. Serendipity rules over the story of the campus. Chawla came to stay by the Sri Aurobindo Ashram in Pondicherry in 1993, after years of acclaimed work in theatre all over the country. Soon Vinay Kumar, actor and core team member of Adishakti, joined her, and theatre work began once again after a gap. There was no money but she had an actor to work with. Their work soon caught the interest of a Danish gentleman, who suggested that Chawla start a theatre laboratory. Putting his money where his mouth was, he bought and gifted Chawla the plot on which the campus stands today. The guest-house and the theatre were built with the help of a variety of grants and contributions, that recognised that something interesting was in the process of taking shape.

From outside, the theatre could be mistaken for a church with a difference. The church feeling continues inside into its majestic, glowing darkness, but is tinctured by the ghost of the *Koothambalam* inhabiting the core. Lofty, intimate, dark and glowing all at the same time, the hybrid space has a special personality that is uniquely its own. Conceived as mainly a space where Adishakti's performances are created and rehearsed, it works equally well for other very different kinds of performance, including experimental theatre, traditional Indian forms as well as western classical music. 'A visiting German chamber music group performed Mozart here and thought this was the best space they had performed in,' reveals Chawla, whose vision of a theatrical space supportive of Adishakti's work drove the design.

The flexibility as well as the engaging power of the space probably relates to the simplicity of the design, and the use of natural materials, especially laterite. These also help calm the awkward visual resonances that the unintended cross between a church and a *Koothambalam* could have engendered. Some such unease does remain in the external form of the building—the walls are a bit too high for the suggested intimacy of the *Koothambalam*, and the porch columns on pedestals too weak for the majestic mass above. But this understandable awkwardness is compensated for by the confident stance of the interior space, itself an unconventional compound of types.

Unlike the norm, this theatre is one large hall with an expansive central platform 30 feet by 40, raised one step higher than the aisle that wraps around it on three sides. The space over this wooden platform is raised higher than that over the aisle, which is like an enclosed veranda. Usually, the platform is used as a 'stage' with the audience spread out on three sides, but then there are no strict rules about that. What seals the unconventionality of the theatre is the external *jali* wall with a pattern of perforations in the stone. The perforations stand in for windows that Adishakti could not afford for reasons of cost and maintenance. But they also let in breeze during the day along with intriguing light patterns, while opening up unusual lighting possibilities during evening performances.

The interior of the Sir Ratan Tata Koothu Kovil.
Photograph courtesy of S. Anwar.

The perforated external wall also allows everyday life outside to intervene in the performances and the rehearsal work inside. This may be unbearable to many theatre practitioners whose performances work only when completely secluded from life outside the auditorium; but is an important ally in Chawla's view of her work.

> For us, the sacredness is only in our approach to work, not in the perfect inviolability of the performance. I quite like our more relaxed South Asian approach to audience-performer relationships, where people walk in and out of all-night Kathakali performances, or sleep through parts. Children waving at actors, or going to the far end of the stage to see a performance from unusual angles is alright with us.

Chawla often takes her dog to rehearsals.

The flat floor of the theatre space acknowledges the varied nature of her local audience. Village audiences feel at home sitting down on the floor to watch performances, and the more urban or foreign viewers from Auroville and Pondicherry happily adjust. Chawla is grateful that she did not have the money to build a stepped auditorium like Prithvi, which she might have done if it had been possible. 'That might have been a terrible mistake,' she says; 'because the village audience would have been discouraged by the Prithvi kind of auditorium.'

Not surprisingly, Chawla thinks of her practice as that of a bridge bearing cultural traffic to and fro between east and west, city and village. The bridge is not of any one side. Belonging to both banks, it is also uniquely itself. And it finds its sacred (and provisionally) stable centre in so being. Who knows, then, there may well be a sacred centre at the heart of every hybridity?

The Core Team

SHANTA GOKHALE

The Adishakti team speaks to the author about their backgrounds, how they came to be at Adishakti, and what Adishakti has meant for them as performers.

Arvind Rane

I didn't find theatre. Theatre found me. It was pure happenstance. I'd been doing school dramatics from the time I was in the second standard. When I was in the ninth, Veenapani joined the school to teach us history and English, and started doing plays with the students. She didn't come with any training or experience in theatre. She was just interested in it and was finding her feet. I started acting in her plays because they were happening. There

Arvind Rane. Photograph courtesy of Vinay Kumar.

was no question of believing in her, or being driven by ambition, or anything of the kind. Yet, I have continued to do theatre with her till now.

In 1978, Veenapani was doing Snehalata Reddy's *Sita*. The boy she had cast as Ram fell ill. So I stepped in and played Ram. All through college I continued to do plays. I acted in *Jabberwock* at Prithvi, directed by Aditya Bhattacharya. It was a horrible play and Jennifer [Kapoor] was appalled. Aamir was doing the lights. Yes. Aamir Khan [the film star]. I was playing Alice. I was in Yusuf Mehta's plays and college productions—*Evam Indrajit* and all that.

All through my working years in advertising agencies, I did plays with Veenapani. I was in her first professional production, *Oedipus*. I was in the chorus. I was the flautist in the troupe of players in Veenapani's *Rosencrantz and Guildenstern Are Dead*. Veenapani suddenly threw this thing at me. Compose me the overture she said. I bought a flute from a phenomenal flute-maker that somebody had told me about. He would stand outside Haribhau Vishwanath, the music shop at Dadar, and play his flute. I composed the music for *Rozencrantz and Guildenstern* on that flute. I don't know how I did it. The tune I composed became the motif of the play.

I didn't act in *The Trojan Women*. I designed and constructed the set and played the drum. The set looked like five jagged mountains of varied heights and, funnily, they also looked like women. It was made of thick wood and sacking cloth soaked in hot starch. I climbed up and sculpted the sacking into the shapes I wanted. I made a support structure of scaffolding and ladders at the back.

In *A Greater Dawn*, I was in the chorus and the set was mine. You remember the black, egg-shaped oval which seemed to be suspended in mid-air and at critical points, a halo of blue light would come out from all around like in an eclipse?

After Veenapani shifted to Pondy, I continued to be in touch. When they came to Mumbai with *Bhima*, I met this phenomenal *mizhavu* player from her group, Hariharan. I spent all my days jamming with him in the hotel room. When they returned to Pondy, Vinay Kumar said to Veenapani, this fellow's bumming around in Mumbai, which I was—I was in the wilderness of advertising, I had lost my last job—so call this bum over for 10 days every month. So for two years I did that, working on. And for the remaining 20 days I was freelancing in Mumbai.

Then in 2000 my Mum died. We were scheduled to do our first show of *Ganapati* at the Ashram. My ticket was booked. And she died. Two days after we cremated her, I came to Pondy. What was there to do? She was gone. After that I had no reason to go back to Mumbai. I'd go for a visit now and again but not too frequently. So this is where I stayed. As a musician. Not actor. Though in *Ganapati* the musicans also act—there's facial expression, gesture, stance. Then came *The Hare and the Tortoise*. Veenapani got me to do Bomallattam (the local form of shadow puppetry) and play bass guitar. But my real acting role came in Vinay Kumar's *Rhinoceros*. I enjoyed that very much. I loved working with Vinay because he breaks rules. I like that. Do it, see what happens. So now this is my home. Not theatre. But Veenapani and Adishakti is why I'm here.

Vinay Kumar K.J.

I have done theatre now for 25 years. It began for me when I was at school. I was 13. Many theatre groups used to use the school hall for rehearsals. They would take the power connection from our home. So I was allowed to watch rehearsals and even touch their musical instruments. For the premiere show of one play, I was allowed to draw the curtain. I felt like a hero. Then we started doing plays ourselves. I played Hitler in one. Gandhi and he have a discussion and Gandhi converts him.

But my first real experience of theatre was in a play that told the history of the Communist Party right up to the Emergency. It was three-and-a-half hours long. My mother had helped the director to script it. There was a boy's role in it and the person who was playing it was ill. Days went by and he didn't come. The director had to take a decision. He looked at me and said why don't you do it. I said yes, I will. It was a very emotional role. The boy had to deliver a secret letter to a leader. On the way he got bitten by a snake but he delivered the letter before

Vinay Kumar.
Photograph courtesy of
Nimmy Raphel.

dying. At the end he rose with a red flag in his hand and all the others followed behind him. The top Communist leaders were at the premiere show, including E.M.S. Namboodiripad and Jyoti Basu.

I did 300 shows of the play in three years. Wherever there was a Party event, they wanted the play. I was doing shows from Thursday through Sunday. It was a time of great excitement and learning from all those wonderful people. At the end of that experience, I decided theatre would be my life. I had to go to drama school. But to do that, I had to pass my +2 exam. I kept failing because of English. So I was sent to Orissa to stay with an uncle who was teaching there, and study under his supervision. Although I didn't study much, I managed to get through the exam and joined the drama school in Trichur.

During the 1980s, there was a great divide amongst the students. Some were radical. They wore a serious expression and spoke of Marx. I belonged to a group that didn't have such pretensions. That worked to our advantage. While those chaps were spending time in the library and destroying themselves, our group was getting all the roles in the student plays. We had to do one play every three months. That was a lot of plays in four years. There was no teaching as such happening there. That's how it is in government institutions. But we learned from our seniors. We learnt on-the-job, doing lights, looking after production, etc. During this time I funded myself by directing plays for college festivals and competitions. Once you won a prize, you were on. You could charge Rs 2,000 for a fortnight's work and the work was permanent.

We also formed our own theatre group, to do women-oriented plays. But soon I tired of realism. Just mouthing lines made me feel stagnant. When I played the title role in *Woyzek*, directed by award-winning film-maker Suveeran, I physicalized my performance. I did acrobatics, and at one point almost flew in the air. At 20 your body is very flexible. A friend of my mother's said I should learn Kalaripayattu. But coming from a Christian background that was out. Then something happened. The theatre director Manvendranath came to college. He gave me an offer to join his group where there would be a Kalaripayattu teacher and I would also get a salary. I joined him in 1992 and trained hard for a year-and-a-half.

Then Veenapani came to rehearse with Manvendranath for *Savitri*. I found the play extremely fascinating. I also made some suggestions for movements, etc., which she found useful. So she asked me to go to Bombay to help out with the other actors. Then she proposed that I play Death in the second run of the play. This work was very exciting. But one day it ended. Veenapani went to Delhi and then moved to Puducherry. I was left at a loose end. I decided to mark time by doing my master's in theatre. Puducherry was one of the three universities that offered this degree. I'd visited Pondy three or four times and had liked it. So that's where I went.

I discovered that I was quite disconnected from pursuing mere academics. So I quit the course and urged Veenapani to do another play. She didn't have a play in mind at the time, so she started working on the physical language of theatre and other things, using my body and skills. Despite that, we had a lot of free time. So I offered to translate a Malayalam novel on Bhima written by M.T. Vasudevan Nair that had fascinated me. That was the seed for our play *Impressions of Bhima*. It was to be a solo performance. That made it very problematic. For what is solo acting? It's mimicry. You become one person, then another. I was very sceptical. But Veenapani started using my strengths and incorporated them in the work and we were able to push it with music, movement, singing, storytelling. The most difficult thing was to create those mask-like faces for different characters. We had to find the tools to sustain them and keep the energy going.

Then came what was actually conceived for the dancers at Nrityagram in which I was to play a role. But they got sidelined into another project. So Veenapani decided to do it with me alone. From then on, I have been involved in a process of stripping away all superfluities. In *The Hare and the Tortoise*, one line must have the impact of 30. Also, this was not a one-person performance. I wasn't setting the pace. I had to enter it practically halfway and find my place in it and hold it truthfully. That was a major challenge for me. But it has released me completely. Now I feel free as an actor.

Nimmy Raphel

I come from Wayanad district in Kerala, which lies near the Karnataka border. I joined Kalamandalam at the age of 13. My father was very keen I should learn dancing. The daily routine was tough. We were up at 5 every morning and danced till noon. We had school from noon till 1 o'clock. Vinay Kumar's sister Sangeetha taught us English. But I couldn't speak a word of it. We had an hour's lunch break and school again up to 3 o'clock. Then it was back to dance. After 5 in the evening we rehearsed what we had learnt and went to bed.

I was one of the 20 girls selected to be interviewed at Kalamandalam amongst many who had applied. All the other girls were dressed in pyjamas and tunics. I was the only one in a skirt because the only dance I had done till then was at school. The others were practising their *hasta mudras—pataka, tripataka.*

Nimmy Raphel. Photograph courtesy of Vinay Kumar.

I'd never heard these words before. I was called in. I was shitting bricks. This is Arvind's lingo. For me it is standard English idiom.

In the interview, I could not answer a single question related to dance since I had not learnt any traditional dance form. But I had to get in somehow. So when I was asked to dance, I gave it my all, kicking my legs high, unmindful of the revelations that were coming from under my short skirt. I got in.

In Kalamandalam, you are not allowed to move to other dance forms. You have to stick to the ones you have chosen. Mine were Mohiniattam and Kuchipudi. But all the other forms are there around you. I would have loved to spend some time learning Kathakali and Koodiyattam and to play the mizhavu. It is good to choose one dance form to practise as a performer but there's no reason why you can't move away from it for a while. It's like travelling and returning home. When you return, you bring home your experiences.

So I was, in many ways, totally unprepared for the freedom at Adishakti. Nowhere in my growing-up years had I been expected to think for myself, ask myself questions, and arrive at my own answers. I had been scared at the prospect of coming here because, first of all, I was getting married [to Vinay Kumar], and I couldn't speak English, and I'd never gone out of my village except to Kalamandalam. For the whole of my first month at Adishakti, I would say only 'yes' to anything people said to me. At the end of the month VP barred me from using the word 'yes'. I spoke my first complex English sentence right here. [She points to the corner between the shoe rack on Veenapani's verandah and the front door.] My hands were full with two bags of goodies and I said, 'Can someone help me open the door?'

Given my background of living in a place where I had limited freedom to do what I wanted and trying to get along with everybody, adjusting to the people at Adishakti was not a problem. I knew Suresh from before. He and Hari were Malayalees so I had no language problems there. Arvind was easy because he was kind and protective and treated me like a sister. With Vinay it was a little difficult because I was young. It took me five years to shed my diffidence and think and speak confidently. My body was more or less trained for the work we were doing at Adishakti. It just had to be retrained a little. But it was the mind that was lagging behind. VP has been helping me to explore myself. I love the quietness here, and the Ashram is now the centre of my life.

My first entry on the stage was as a singer in *Brhannala*. Later I replaced Hari in *Ganapati*. At the end of the Beckett workshop, I did *Footfalls* solo with VP's voice offstage. Then came *The Hare and the Tortoise* and Ionesco's *Rhinoceros* directed by Vinay. Theatre is one part of what I have learned to do here but with VP's encouragement, I have helped to manage the place too. She has made me do accounts and general management, and I'm setting menus and supervising the kitchen right now. A wide exposure has also come to me through the seminars that VP has organized. And now I have a piece on the Ramayana ready, written and directed by me with help from VP. I will enact it solo, with help on the music from Arvind.

Suresh Kaliyath

I come from a small village in Kerala. From a very young age I was interested in learning dance. I learned Parichamuttukali at the age of 10 and then shifted to Bharatanatyam and Kuchipudi. I learned the introductory items, seven *padams*, five *varnams*, and two *tharamgams* under Guru Chandrasekhar Kot of Shoranur. There was no art in my family. We were farmers, although my father ran a multi-business store selling ayurvedic medicines, clothes, groceries, and rice mills. But my mother's elder brother, Professor Damodaran Kaliyath, was engaged in a lot of literary work, mainly translations, and had been the secretary of the Kerala Sahitya Akademi. He encouraged me.

After school I joined the government technical college to do mechanical engineering. But my interest in dance continued. One day I happened to see a performance of Ottan Thullal by Guru Kalamandalam Mohanakrishnan. I was completely fascinated by it. I asked him if he would teach me. He agreed. He said I shouldn't find it difficult since I had already learnt dancing. He

Suresh Kaliyath. Photograph courtesy of Anoop Davis.

had trained at Kalamandalam and was teaching freelance then. Now he is back in Kalamandalam.

I was still at college. So I started going to his place over weekends. The family didn't mind as long as my dancing didn't interfere with my studies. After my arangetram, I began to perform with my guru. When I graduated, I got a job in ITI as an instructor in mechanical engineering. I would work there during the day and perform in the evenings. In Kerala, performances are always going on in the temples. Sometimes my guru would be invited to perform in two places on the same day. On such days he would send me to one place and he would go to the other. That's how I began performing independently.

In 1997, I applied for a Central Ministry of Culture scholarship for advanced training. I had to go to Delhi for my interview. Veenapani was one of the interviewers. She asked me to wait after the interview. I waited till everybody else had finished. Then she came out and gave me her card and asked me to visit Adishakti to see the work they were doing. I said I would go one day. But after a week she called me and asked me when I was going.

I told her I'd go the following weekend. I saw them working on *Khandavaprastha*, which I found extremely interesting. Veenapani asked me if I'd like to join Adishakti and I said yes.

I moved to Pondy in 1998. Meanwhile I was informed that I had won the scholarship. So I spent 15 days in Kerala training with my guru, Kalamandalam Mohanakrishnan, and also doing a special course in Kalamandalam itself with my guru's guru, Kalamandalam Gopinathaprabha. I spent the remaining 15 days in Pondy.

My first few years with Adishakti were difficult. I couldn't explore, improvise, visualize the way Veenapani was expecting me to. I was very rigid. I could only work with the eight-beat cycle. But she gave me all her support and kept discussing ideas, always listening to ours. I gradually realized that I wasn't required to cut and paste from Thullal, but to use the steps of Thullal in different ways to mean different things. This training process was helping me gain enough confidence to improvise even in my Thullal performances. Today's audience doesn't have the patience to sit through a performance that is done in one metre. So I began suddenly changing the rhythm during performance and my audience responded. Even my guru approved so long as I didn't break the frame of the form.

I'd never touched a percussion instrument before. But with a lot of effort and hard work, I learnt to play the mizhavu. *Ganapati* was the test for all of us because we were only playing music there. After that experience, I can break any rhythm any time. But we have had to be very careful to avoid forever what we did in *Ganapati*. We have become so conscious of this that in *The Hare and the Tortoise* we changed instruments. I played the xylophone, the tabla, the rhythm-box, and the *chhenda*. In this way every new play has added to my skills.

The latest development in my life at Adishakti is scripting and developing a play based on the Ramayana. The seed for my script was sown when I performed in Ottan Thulal style in 2009 during the first Ramayana Festival. I am now working on a performance of my own concept of *Hanuman Ramayana*. I am going to use the strength of the Ottan Thullal form, like rhythmic delivery of the text with a structure of rhythm, but I'm also going to try and switch between *lokdharmi* and *natyadharmi*. Right now my guru, Kalamandalam Mohanakrishnan, is helping me a lot with the traditional text of Thullal. Once I have something to show Veenapani, she will give me her creative inputs which will help me shape the structure of the performance.

Pascal Sieger

I have been with Adishakti since 2001. I arrived in India in 1996 when I got the opportunity to take a year's sabbatical. I came to Auroville with my family to work on my own music. Back in France I had taken lessons in saxophone from Luciano Paliarini. As a young musician, I was playing with a lot of different bands. But that wasn't the music I wanted to play. When we came to India we found a greater openness. You could do different things here. In that first year, although we lived in Auroville, we travelled a lot.

Somehow, in Auroville also I fell into the same trap, playing with everyone. Again I realized this was not what I had come

Pascal Sieger.
Photograph courtesy of
Adishakti archives.

here for. I took control. I began organizing a weekly concert in Auroville. In 1999, I heard that Veenapani Chawla was looking for a saxophone player. I went for one of her performances. It was the first version of *Ganapati*. Looking at the group of musicians on stage, I remembered hearing them some six months earlier when they were presented as musicians from Kerala. I had thought then that I would like to play with such a group. Naturally I decided to join them. We jammed a lot to understand one another. And then the saxophone became part of the musical text of *Ganapati*.

I am now a member of the group. I have even done voice training for *The Hare and the Tortoise* because I have a few lines to say in it as Zeno. The big difference between *Ganapati* and *The Hare and the Tortoise* is that by the time we did the second play, Veenapani knew me well enough to discuss the theme of the music with me and to tell me what she would like me to compose. That is how I came to compose the saxophone score for *The Hare and the Tortoise*.

Arjun Shankar

Arjun Shankar is a self-taught guitar player, who has been influenced by many styles including jazz, the blues, heavy metal, and disco. He, along with a group of young people, founded Harami Theatre in Bangalore in 2003. He performed as an actor and musician in two Bangalore productions, *Alphabetical Order* and *Butter and Mashed Bananas*. Arjun joined Adishakti in 2006 and has performed in *The Hare and the Tortoise* and *Rhinoceros*, directed by Vinay Kumar. Arjun has left Adishakti now, but will continue to return whenever *The Hare and the Tortoise* is performed.

Come, Work with Me

SARAH JOSEPH[*]

I have always been fascinated by the prospect of interactions between tradition and modernity. Was it possible? Could there be a productive dialogue between the two without a clash of egos? I was fortunate to witness one where not only was the dialogue healthy but which resulted in some outstanding work in both contemporary and traditional theatre. I speak of the dialogue and interactions of contemporary theatre director

* Usha Nangyar, the Koodiyattam performer, and V.K.K. Hariharan, the eminent *mizhavu* player, were Veenapani Chawla's collaborators for many years. Sarah Joseph met them to discover how they had responded to the work they did at Adishakti, and the benefits, if any, that they had reaped from the experience.

Kudiyattam performer Usha Nangyar in *Putana Moksha* at Adishakti, accompanied on the mizhavu by V.K.K. Hariharan. Photograph courtesy of Adishakti archives.

Veenapani Chawla, Koodiyattam actor Usha Nangyar, and Koodiyattam mizhavu maestro V.K.K. Hariharan.

Usha Nangyar recalls how she first met Veenapani Chawla. Usha was 13. Veenapani had come to Irinjalakuda to study Koodiyattam under Ammanur Madhava Chakyar, Usha's guru. He was putting Veenapani through a daily routine of vachika, *abhinaya*, mudras, and eye exercises. One day, as he was engaged elsewhere, he asked Usha to supervise Veenapani's eye exercise class. It seems, even at 13, Usha impressed Veenapani. And subsequently, during her stay in Kerala, she followed Usha's growth as a performer very closely.

They met next years later at Usha's performance at the Manakody Nambor Kavu temple. Usha recalls that while she was preparing for the performance, she heard that Veenapani was in the audience. She waited for her to come backstage before the show. But she did not. Through a small gap in the curtain, Usha saw her sitting in the first row, motionless and still. And that is how she sat right through the two hours of the performance. Motionless, still, and with hungry eyes. And then, after it was over, she went to see Usha and asked, 'Will you work with me?' Usha accepted after consulting Ammanur.

Veenapani wanted to learn the breath technique which Ammanur Madhava Chakyar had evolved. He had told her about it and explained it theoretically, but had refused to part with the knowledge because he felt no one, not even his nephew, his natural heir, was a great enough actor to be given this secret. It was too dangerous. When Veenapani saw Usha's performance that day at the Manakody Nambor Kavu temple, she realized that the Chakyar had found a great actor to pass his knowledge on to. Usha did not deny that she had been given this knowledge that day when Veenapani met her after the show. But she did not think it was such a great thing that someone should go mad for it. She had thought of these breath techniques just as exercises and not something to be used in performance.

According to Usha, the decision to leave Kerala and work with Veenapani was a definite turning point in her career. For the first time she would be working outside the comfort zone of her own form and aesthetic. She would have to deal with a different sensibility and performance style. But it was a challenge and she wanted to face it. Another first was travelling by herself outside Kerala. This too contributed to the richness of the experience.

Usha recalls how difficult the initial few weeks were—being away from family, the alien atmosphere, the different language, and, above all, the different work processes. But Veenapani put her at ease. Then, when the work shifted to the second phase where the research centred around breath and emotion, it became easier and more exploratory for Usha. Also it was during this phase that Veenapani started creating the performance *Khandavaprasta Agni Ahooti* with Usha, a piece based on the Koodiyattam language, but stripped of its customary *aharya* and music. In fact, different musical styles were used in it and she found this interesting and challenging. Unfortunately, this play could not be staged beyond its premiere in Auroville because Usha became a mother and was subsequently completely engaged with her daughter.

Recalling some of the earlier exercises that were devised for the exploration by Veenapani, Usha said that they made significant contributions to her own way of understanding breath. Since the eye is the main means for expressing emotions in the

Koodiyattam performance, Veenapani asked Usha to blindfold herself one day and then try to express all the bhavas/emotions. Initially it was difficult. Because there was no outlet for the emotions! Later she learned to experience emotions internally and found that she could clearly see even the transitions between one emotion and another. This led Usha to expand her own repertoire of performance, including the enlargement of *bhavathrayam* (three emotions).

When I asked her to explain this, Usha elaborated the whole process and illustrated it through the story of Lalitha, the demon woman sent by King Kamsa to kill little Krishna, in the garb of a beautiful woman. Lalitha befriends Yashoda, and one day when Yashoda is not at home she puts poison on her breast and tries to feed Krishna. But Krishna bites off Lalitha's breast and kills her. In the bhavathrayam, this sequence is enacted using three primary emotions—love, pain, and anger. But after the blindfold exercise, Usha felt a disconnect between these emotions, and she started to look at the enactment from a different perspective.

If Lalitha felt motherly love towards little Krishna after seeing him, what would be her previous emotion? This question led Usha to include anger as a starting emotion at the beginning of the enactment, since Lalitha comes with a mission to kill Krishna. After she feels motherly love for Krishna, how could Lalitha jump back to anger again? Here Usha felt that even though Lalitha experienced the emotion of love, at some point she would definitely think about the order of King Kamsa and that would put her in fear of her life. Once that fear was experienced by Lalitha, it was natural to get angry and again get ready for the mission. That made the shift to anger easy. In this process, Usha was able to expand the three emotions—bhavathrayam—into a sequence of nine emotions.

So what the exploration achieved was not only a new way to use breath but also to construct an analysis of a whole performing sequence in Koodiyattam. Not a mere theory but a practice of breath which achieved complexity and believability. Here the performer's experiences were not stock emotions but more complexly felt emotions that would touch the audience.

This new-found opening encouraged Usha to reinterpret more and more women characters in the Nangyar Koothu repertoire and broaden her performance practice. Usha went on to create a number of new Nangyar Koothu performances that were widely appreciated, and made her one of the leading Koodiyattam performers of our times. During this exploration with Usha, another milestone in Veenapani's work was happening. She started a significant collaboration with the mizhavu maestro V.K.K. Hariharan, who had come to Puducherry to visit Usha, his wife. He gave a small performance with her for Adishakti, which showed how the intervention of rhythm transformed Usha's emotive performance.

Vinay Kumar, another actor who was part of this exploration, recalls how in the early stages of exploration, whenever Usha did anything, she would constantly say, 'This is not hundred per cent perfect because there is no accompanying rhythm.' Veenapani, who was working on the concept of 'thought is breath–breath is rhythm', a concept she went on to develop further in her work, immediately knew exactly what Usha was missing. This made her look at the Koodiyattam rhythm from a new perspective. She saw that here rhythm was not a mere accompaniment but directly dictated how the emotional landscape of a performer would evolve.

Hariharan started working with Veenapani as the lone musician in her play *Impressions of Bhima*, and then in her next play, *Brhannala*. By this time the exploration into rhythm was taking a different turn. Veenapani made it compulsory for all Adishakti members to learn how to play the mizhavu. Apart from teaching Adishakti members, Hari and Veenapani started a dialogue on rhythm and its application and performance. According to Vinay Kumar, all these conversations started with Hari lamenting about the lesser hierarchical position that a Koodiyattam percussionist is accorded in the Koodiyattam performance repertoire.

One might logically see this as an outcome of the changing economic and social structures of the Koodiyattam community but Veenapani saw it as the anguish of the individual artist needing recognition, and the urge to go beyond limitations imposed by the structures of tradition on his creative possibilities.

Hari recalled how he would not have been able to explore 'so many strange ideas in any other place' as he could at Adishakti. By this time, Veenapani had started working on her play *Ganapati*, dealing with the concept of rhythm as text. Hari recalled how one day in one of the sessions they were exploring the concept of progressions in a rhythmic structure, such as the beats 2, 3, 4, 5, 7, 8, etc. After working on the improvisation patterns, Veenapani was still not satisfied and asked Hari if there was a concept of 1½ beats in the Koodiyattam structure. Since none was in practice, Hari worked on it and was able to create a 1½ beat to lead the progression of 2, 3, 4, etc., that later become an important motif in *Ganapati*.

Hari says, '*Ganapati* was my own journey in the exploration of Koodiyattam music. The play's first act starts with traditional rhythm structures played on the mizhavu and then develops in a way that leads to a 10-minute free-flowing improvisational structure in jazz. It paralleled my own journey and growth as a performer.' Regarding the play itself, Hari said that audiences felt it was a path-breaking work in theatre. Hari recalls,

> Working with Veenapani meant facing a new challenge every day. As a performer, you needed to constantly challenge yourself to be in any way near her ideas and concepts. I had to leave after *Ganapati* because she was going too fast with her ideas and at that moment I could not catch up, and did not have more to give her. Since then of course I have grown.

Finally, according to Hari, the larger impact on his work of that period helped him to explore his own form quite fundamentally. As an example of what he was able to achieve, he mentioned the response to one of his recent Koodiyattam performances. After the performance, some ardent, scholarly *rasikas* came backstage and told him how they could now see that Koodiyattam music was truly a text and the mizhavu player a performer on par with the Koodiyattam actor, sometimes even going beyond the actor to create the emotional landscape of the play.

Three
All About Sources

Conversations with Leela

An Interview

LEELA GANDHI

In the following conversations which Veenapani Chawla had with Leela Gandhi at the Adishakti campus in Puducherry over four days in June 2011, she speaks of Sri Aurobindo and the Mother, the spiritual forces behind her work; of the gurus who taught her music, dance, and martial arts; and of fellow artists who influenced her work, wittingly or unwittingly, in big ways and small. As the conversations unfold, we get a clear picture of Chawla's journey from her early days in Mumbai to her present work at Adishakti. Leela Gandhi is Chawla's niece and a long-time observer of her work, having acted in two of her Mumbai plays.

Day 1

LEELA GANDHI: Through you I've learnt very much to think of work in the theatre as a philosophical discipline, not to mention spiritual exercise. I'm not a practitioner, so in our conversations I'd very much like to touch on the way working in the theatre is a holistic endeavour for you, a perspective both on world and self. Has your journey been systematic or one of creative accidents which led you willy-nilly, as they say, into theatre? You were teaching history and English in Arya Vidya Mandir, Mumbai, and then, as though out of the blue, you started doing theatre pretty seriously with children.

VEENAPANI CHAWLA: Yes that indeed was an accident! My doing theatre. And starting it with children. Till then I had always looked at theatre rather longingly from the margins. I remember being prompter, wardrobe mistress, and even lady-in-waiting in college plays. And so when I was allowed to take centre stage and direct a performance with children, I felt like a queen. It was in 1975 when the school wanted to celebrate 15 August, which is Sri Aurobindo's birthday, that I chose his *Savitri*, a text I wanted to read but had not yet read.

GANDHI: Even at this early stage, you and the children would spend some rehearsal time doing meditation or some other type of internal preparation in addition to the usual activity. Was this mainly because you were dealing with a Sri Aurobindo text?

CHAWLA: No. Although it was knowing Sri Aurobindo's practice a little which was the inspiration. In any work I did, I followed the practice of clearing the space within, throwing away all other preoccupations, being quiet, and concentrating all my energy for the best and happiest results. I find this practice very useful and practical for everything I do. I still do this. At that time it was with a sense of holiness.

GANDHI: (*Laughs*)

CHAWLA: There is also the sense that by doing this I am preparing myself to rise beyond what I am—to be empty and to

Sri Aurobindo. Photograph courtesy of Henri Cartier-Bresson.

open to the unexpected, to the impossible, to that which I am not yet. And then perhaps this emptiness and expectation will tempt something to leak down and inspire and elevate. I believe that in seeking for inspiration and elevation, one is trying to access that which is a potential of oneself but inaccessible temporarily. Once achieved, the unrealized potential which is waiting will act like a magnet to take you further and beyond.

GANDHI: Your interest, then, was primarily in tuning the instrument—the medium as much as the message, the actor as much as the play—such that the latter was maybe only an occasion for the former's inner work?

CHAWLA: Exactly. I was seeking the perfection of the instrument. That was the fundamental goal. And theatre was beginning to be, possibly, the right process or field for the cultivation of such a perfection because it resonated with something other than the banal and the ordinary. And also because it brought up the greatest complexity of my nature. In the context of perfecting the instrument, it is important that all subterranean movements surface to view, rather than lie dormant and concealed from awareness.

GANDHI: Is it at this point that you started looking for something like a 'sacred theatre'?

CHAWLA: No. I had not started looking for new forms at that stage. But I was already beginning to be frustrated with the little I knew and could do. And this would eventually push me to learn more. But in 1975 I was still very much a school teacher, quite happy to be doing kiddie plays. I did not dare to think that there was an alternative life of theatre which I could pursue.

GANDHI: Whilst you were at Arya Vidya Mandir?

CHAWLA: Whilst I was at AVM. The clear direction came when I came to Puducherry to work on the PhD dissertation, 'Sri Aurobindo and Education'. I was here for almost a year, confused because the dissertation was not going anywhere. My heart was not in it. I approached Nolinida [Nolini Kant Gupta] for advice. He was one of Sri Aurobindo's oldest disciples. A great yogi, philosopher, linguist, and poet. He had been with Sri Aurobindo since his days as a revolutionary. You know that he was my guardian and I would write to him every day, telling him about this and that. At one point I remember writing a letter, which I still have, in which I said, 'I want to develop my mind into a fine instrument. I want to make my emotional being refined and cultivated. I like theatre. Is that the way?' He underlined that and wrote in the margin, 'Yes. Continue.' And then he gave me my name Veenapani, as a goal to achieve. It is a name for the goddess Mahasaraswati, and stands for the power of perfection in work and knowledge.

GANDHI: I see.

CHAWLA: I wanted to do something that was poetic in the true sense of the word, which would take me from banality to something else. And he endorsed that. And I said to him, 'But how.' And he said, 'Continue reading, studying, writing,

Veenapani Chawla's mentor
Nolini Kant Gupta.
Photograph courtesy of
Sri Aurobindo Ashram archives.

reflecting. See where it goes.' I came back to Bombay after this, and another accident happened. I met Naseeruddin Shah, the actor. We decided to do *Oedipus*.

GANDHI: *Oedipus*?

CHAWLA: Direct him in *Oedipus*. I had studied the play while I was in Puducherry. I had some ideas about it which seemed to interest Naseer.

GANDHI: Can you talk a bit about what Nolinida said about Greek theatre? Because you kept very serious company with all that for a while. It's important, isn't it, that Sri Aurobindo was a classicist, that he was one of the rare South Asians to read Classics at Cambridge at the end of the nineteenth century, and that Nolinida in his turn wrote extensively on Sophocles and Euripides, among others, in his wonderful essays?

CHAWLA: Remember, Sri Aurobindo was a linguist. And his cosmopolitanism came from this ability to seize the roots of Europe and of Asia. There was no denial or exclusivism in him. That was a wondrous thing for me when I entered his thought. Nolinida was the dean of the Faculty of Languages at the Sri Aurobindo International Centre for Education. And of course he had read Greek drama in classical Greek. I was amused when, in response to my telling him once that I was directing Euripides's *The Trojan Women*, he said that he was 'somewhat familiar with it'!

About the ancient Greek mind he said that it was luminous, that it had a fluid precision and a flexibly enquiring logic, and this determined the character and field of future European thinking. He said that Greek thought was 'the fountainhead of world culture today'. Regarding Greek tragedy he said that the evocation of the feeling of pity and terror works as a purification because such feelings widen the sympathies, pull us out of our small, egoistic, personal, ephemeral pleasures and put us in contact with what is to be shared in wide commonality. Tragedy initiates the spectator into the enjoyment that is born, not of desire and gain, but of detachment and freedom.

When I wrote to him about my interpretation of *Oedipus*, that I did not see it as a tragedy because of the protagonist's growth into a balanced being, both inward and outward looking, one who ultimately saw his outward circumstances as the consequences of his inner states, a Tiresias-like figure, sacred and profound, he wrote back saying, 'What you say is interesting and seems to be correct so far as it goes. But the denouement and the final victory is at Colonus.'

GANDHI: But then you remained interested actually in the spiritual opportunity that's available in the crisis of *Oedipus*. In your other work as well, if we can look ahead to *Bhima* and the sort of work you are doing now. Your focus is always on the entity who is in psychic trouble of one type or other. There's that beautiful thought you give to Hamlet in *The Hare and the Tortoise* about depression being a grace that allows introspection and growth. Maybe this connects to what you were saying earlier about your interest in being unfinished, in possession of possibilities that are never fully intelligible, or, indeed, known

and fixed in advance until we—to use the theatre metaphor—
actually perform them.

CHAWLA: Yes. Therein lies movement, which is what drama is
about. It is interesting, what you say about *Oedipus* and the
theme of the protagonist in crisis. I suppose that became a
preoccupation because in that wonderful, seminal year at
Puducherry in 1978, I too went through a series of crises which
altered my way of seeing things. For every crisis, Nolinida would
say, 'You have to go through.' This advice was not merely about
endurance but about consenting to be not virtuous and pure.
The solution is never in running away, discarding, avoiding,
circumventing, or being ascetic. It lies in coming to grips, confronting fearlessly, looking for the truth in the situation, and
allowing it to be transmuted into a positive. Philosophically,
it is the opposite of the Shankarite and Buddhist views, where
you have to shun the illusory world in order to realize the highest reality. The process I am talking about is more akin to the
Tantric view, where you try to find the Divine in all of life
and through its smallest details. As Saint Teresa of Avila says
metaphorically, if I remember correctly, 'God is in those pots
and pans.'

    I remember a conversation where I complained bitterly to
Nolinida about the pointlessness of Vishwamitra's *tapasya*,
when he gave in to Menaka's seduction. What a fall! And
Nolinida's opinion was, well yes, if Vishwamitra had avoided
the Menaka temptation, he would have gone straight and fast
towards his goal. But his realization would have been narrow.
It would have lacked amplitude and breadth. Through the
experience with Menaka, although the path was longer, the
result was richer and fuller. He wrote to me, 'The straight path
is not always given to us. Many have to go through winding
zig-zags and tortuous by-lanes.'

GANDHI: Is this the thought behind the hare's song at the end of
The Hare and the Tortoise?

CHAWLA: Yes.

GANDHI: How does it go?

CHAWLA:
There was a knowledge seeker
Hedged in by human limits.
He sacrificed the main road
To take a zig zag by-lane.
And though he lost much time,
He grew a wiser man.

GANDHI: I am already beginning to see here a kind of very productive tension between interest in the perfection of the actor and the instrument, on the one hand, and simultaneously an interest in the handicap of the protagonist, on the other. And maybe a growing interest, in terms of craft as well, in how the actor has to perfect herself in order to play out a handicap well. Is this something that evolves later in your work? You have a quick comment before we stop for today?

CHAWLA: In the process of perfecting the instrument the actor unravels the connection between the handicap/crisis and its relationship to movement, or becoming. It is mainly to do with the nature of the transitional. A painful, liminal state.

Day 2

GANDHI: I'd like to tease out your early interest in Stanislavski and the links there with Sri Aurobindo's sadhana. In both cases there's an emphasis on how the outward perfection of craft proceeds from a seemingly obscure work on the self.

CHAWLA: Let's say that I wasn't aware of Stanislavski till I came to Puducherry for my long stay in 1978. I became aware of him through my interaction with Shaupon Bose, a member of the Sri Aurobindo Ashram who works in the Ashram Library and is a friend, and who subsequently guided actors like Khalid Tyabji and Adil Hussain.

GANDHI: Shaupon felt you should read Stanislavski?

CHAWLA: No. He was reading him.

GANDHI: Why?

CHAWLA: Because he had started doing theatre in the Ashram. And also through Pournaprema [the Mother's granddaughter] he was in touch with theatre people from the West, who made much of Stanislavski. I believe that the scope and amplitude of Sri Aurobindo's philosophy is far vaster than that of Stanislavski. Many of Stanislavski's techniques involved in the inner work of the actor, such as stimulating the imagination, concentration of attention, the subconscious and creativity, performing with detachment rather than being totally identified with the character, are by-products of the discipline involved in the yoga of Sri Aurobindo. Although I do believe that Stanislavski was a yogi too, for he was rigorously in pursuit of the truth in theatre.

GANDHI: Your performance theory uses the trope of the iceberg very often. This seems to have its origin in the Stanislavskian method, namely, in the notion that during preparation, the actor builds this whole emotional storyline that is always going on and growing in her head, but of which she only actually performs a mere fraction, the tip of the iceberg, in the lines or gestures given to her by the script or stage directions. Yet, I suspect you would argue that the iceberg motif gets its true philosophical mettle from Sri Aurobindo?

CHAWLA: The tip of the iceberg is the superficial, external aspect of ourselves that we think is the totality of ourselves. According to Sri Aurobindo, there are many parts and personalities of which we are made up; and we have not learned to distinguish each from the other. It is part of the foundation of the practice, to become aware and conscious of the great complexity of our nature, so as to light it with true knowledge. The beginning of self-knowledge comes when some part of one is able to witness the rest of the parts with a certain detachment.

We know our superficial personality which is made up of a body, mind, and emotional/vital being. But behind this, hidden from us, is what he calls the subliminal part, which is much vaster but not known by us. Our external personality constantly receives influences, touches, communications from this part but the external part does not know from where they are coming. Hidden behind the subliminal is the psychic, the evolving best part of us. One of the important objectives of the practice is to bring this part out into the open, to become conscious of it, to let it direct the life. All I will say about the psychic here is that it is the source of the finest creativity, and that is what is relevant to the field of our conversation. Below the external and the subliminal is the subconscious, and below that is the inconscient. Sri Aurobindo says that just as there are ranges of sight and sound above and below those that are accessible to the human senses, likewise there are ranges of consciousness both above and below the mental. And so, above our mind, accessible to our endeavour to reach it, is our potentiality—the superconscient.

Stanislavski's inner work of the actor does not take into account the subliminal, the psychic, or the superconscient. It is restricted to exploring those parts of the external personality which are somewhat veiled from sight in daily behaviour. There is much we do not know even about our external personality. For it is made up of many parts and we only have a mentalized conception of these parts and tend to lump everything together as mind.

Stanislavski also explores the subconscious to some degree for the creative impulse. However, not to the extent that Grotowski explores it. Grotowski uses the method by which fatigue sets aside the mind so that the subconscious creative can take over. In a certain tradition, the subconscious is considered to be the source of what one really is. And I suppose this is what informed Grotowski and Stanislavski.

In Sri Aurobindo's thought, the subconscious lies between the inconscient—a suppressed or involved consciousness in which there is everything but nothing is formulated or expressed—and the conscious mind, life, body. It has no wakingly conscious thought or will or organized reaction but carries obscure impressions, stores up memories, habits, which surface in dreams, and sometimes in waking thought, as a mechanical repetition of old thoughts, old mental, vital, and physical habits. It is the storage place of discarded things. It is definitely not at all the source of what one really is. Sri Aurobindo calls it the darkest, most perilous, and unhealthiest part of the nature and he is critical of the tendency of the psychoanalytical field, which uses its—the subconscient's—partial truth to generalize and explain the whole field of human nature in its narrow terms. In the practice of yoga, he encourages the practitioner to observe it but to concentrate on the more luminous spaces of self so that they can light it up and reveal what lies there. For it is the storehouse of forgotten and lost experience, both personal and universal, which once lit up yields creative wealth.

GANDHI: You have also had a very strong objection to the excessive psychologism of the Stanislavskian method and the realism of text and form to which it lends itself. Is it helpful to make a distinction between a yogic rather than a psychological outlook for the way an actor prepares?

CHAWLA: Yes, it is. In Sri Aurobindo's practice, the seeker attempts to become conscious of the entire iceberg. And this can become an important preparation by the actor on herself. By observing with detachment, every day and at all times, the origins or initiating impulse of each one of her psychological movements, her physical actions, her habits, the actor can gradually enhance the peripheries of her consciousness. This allows her to not only understand the complexity of human nature experientially, and to draw on it in performance but also to see that the realism and psychologism of the external personality is after all the expression of only a very small slice of her entire being. She may begin to see that the entirety of the iceberg puts her in touch with larger universal modes, more abstract, beyond the personal. And this requires another form of expression.

Also, as I said, the nurturing of and concentration on the psychic is crucial for realizing the great creative touches as it is the space for luminous creativity. You must have seen performances by actors/dancers/musicians, which are touched by a light and a quality quite other than the ordinary, which would constitute a good performance. I believe that such performances are influenced by the psychic. They go beyond the perfection of form and craft. It is altogether another quality which distinguishes them. And the performers themselves sometimes do not even know that they have done something extraordinary.

Additionally, the attempt at enhancing the consciousness or of extending its boundaries also involves the 'colonizing' of our potential or possibility through the thrust for inspiration.

When we talk of inspiration, we talk of it as though it is something which comes to us from outside ourselves, from a space which is other than what we are in, in everyday life. In the intense need to find solutions to creative problems, one sometimes makes great leaps of consciousness into spaces of ourselves, which exist beyond those of daily existence. These are vertical leaps into a potential of ourselves, which at that moment seems beyond us. This is what Sri Aurobindo calls the superconscient. The solutions that come to us from there are instances of inspiration. These spaces can become part of our everyday consciousness if we try to access them often enough. And if that were to happen, inspiration would still tantalize us from even higher reaches, inveigling us to go further beyond, enlarging the boundaries of our consciousness even more. This work has an enormous relevance to performance practice. For the struggle to go beyond the everyday in a process of continuous becoming creates a vibrating, energized being.

GANDHI: Then the yogic-performance project, if we can call it that, is not about making one's identity continuous with what one is but does not know. The psychoanalytic thinker Jacques Lacan says something striking somewhere to the effect that 'I think where I am not, therefore I am where I do not think'. Instead, what you are describing is a project of making one's identity continuous with what one neither knows nor in fact is—yet.

If you follow the logic of this proposal, then preparation, in this case for the actor, can never really be completed. In fact the actor is someone quite committed to recognizing and communicating herself as an unfinished work-in-progress. Am I right?

CHAWLA: Yes.

GANDHI: So not at all interested in communicating a command or mastery over themselves and their materials?

CHAWLA: Command in what way? One is never in command. One is only trying to become more and more limpid. And more and more wide and other than what one is at this moment.

GANDHI: What about the spectator of such work?

CHAWLA: The spectator of such work is impacted by the performer through a contagion of her consciousness. Contagion is important. It happens even in everyday life. You enter a room, you enter a disharmonious situation and there is disharmony within you. Or you enter somewhere else with a certain luminosity and that spreads. The relationship between the performer and the audience is around the notion of contagion. What the performer has done with herself, through the process that I have just described, creates a contagion which reaches out to the spectator and touches her through a contagion of consciousness. It's a contagion of what the performer consists of, the consciousness, the light, the work, the tapasya that one has done on oneself, affects the audience through a contagion.

GANDHI: Is there a craft to contagion? A technique?

CHAWLA: It's not a craft. The craft has to do with the physical instrumentality of the actor. This discipline is about the art of living more consciously on a daily basis. Developing the physical instrumentality of the actor helps in making the body more conscious. It adds to the physical consciousness of the performer.

Day 3

GANDHI: From what you've been saying, it seems your real push into theatre started in Puducherry, with Nolinida and your interactions with Shaupon and with Pournaprema. Wasn't it Pournaprema who introduced you to Grotowski, whom you met later, of course?

CHAWLA: Pournaprema was a friend of Grotowski and she arranged for me to meet him. He had stopped in Mumbai, at the actor Rekha Sabnis's house in 1979, and Pourna sent Grotowski and me telegrams suggesting we meet. We met. But more importantly, the meeting was a prelude to my interaction with Eugenio Barba, which was quite seminal.

GANDHI: What did you get from your exchanges with both?

CHAWLA: Grotowski, as you know, like Artaud, was interested in the East and in Asia because he had certain ideas about what Asian theatre could give to the West. The West was exhausted, I think. They needed a fresh stimulus for a new creative thrust. I gathered, especially through my conversations with Barba, that it did not matter if Artaud misunderstood Asia. It was enough that it acted as a catalyst for a new creative impulse. And this idea has stayed with me and been productive for me. Barba told me that ideas are like crystal, with many facets, and you can see whatever you want to in this crystal, take any facet. This was fantastic. The implication was that, when in interaction with something different, if your overwhelming response to it comes out of a misunderstanding of it, it does not really matter because it makes you think further, and it makes you creative. And may I say here that when I first saw Kathakali in an untutored way, what was enigmatic about it is what fired my imagination. When I became more educated, it disappointed me because my imagination was much more exciting than the reality.

GANDHI: If I remember correctly, Grotowski also met the Mother?

CHAWLA: Yes.

GANDHI: Tell me the story about Grotowski and the Mother.

CHAWLA: I got some of it from Pournaprema and some of it I am sure is folklore. It seems Grotowski came to Puducherry a very fat and sick man, always dressed in black and dark glasses. Before his appointment with the Mother, Pourna recommended to him that he not wear black for his appointment because the Mother did not like black, and that he take off his dark glasses because the Mother would like to see his eyes when she met him. But he went to see her in his black and his dark glasses. And he said something to the effect, I know you don't like these things but I am doing it all the same. And of course she laughed. Soon after, he got off a plane in another city and Pourna said, according to the person who was there to meet him, he was not dressed in black, he was without dark glasses, and he'd lost a lot of weight! When I saw him in 1979 he was thin.

The Mother, self-portrait.
Photograph courtesy of
Sri Aurobindo Ashram archives.

GANDHI: How was that meeting?

CHAWLA: It was a meeting of two hours in which he said very little. He took a long time to answer the few questions I put to him. And I am not sure I understood where he was taking me. But I made my own thing out of it. What I got from him was through a contagion! And I believe that is why people go to great teachers, gurus, and masters; because they know that the most valuable thing is what they pick up from the presence of the guru, what they internalize through the unspoken interaction, much more than what is said or discussed.

Because Grotowski provoked my thought, you will see much similarity I suppose in Grotowski's notion of the sacred theatre, the actor's act of self-penetration, her efforts to discard all masks and encourage the spectator to thereby do likewise, with much of what we have been talking about. But there is a difference in process. At Adishakti, the artists' inner practice is not a public practice, it is done in solitude and at their own individual pace, without anyone interfering with them or guiding them. The work that they do publicly is the training in craft and the creating of performance. With Grotowski, there was a technique involved for the plumbing of the inner spaces but a disinclination to use 'tricks' and techniques in performance. While our craft of performance is full of tricks and devices!

Of course the reason why I wanted to have this meeting with Grotowski was because, by now, I was interested in the body as I believed was he. Through my reading of Sri Aurobindo and the Mother, I had become aware that making the body conscious was an extremely crucial part of the practice. In fact, when I once asked Nolinida if he could guide me on how to meditate, he countered by saying, 'Do you do any exercise with your body?' I told him I could begin and he said, 'But you need someone to guide you.' In due course I approached Pournaprema, who was a ballet dancer and who had worked on the body and developed a system for it. She taught me the exercises and also initiated my investigation into the body for Sri Aurobindo's practice.

The body has its own consciousness, just as the mind has its own consciousness. However, the only way we seem to know it is through our perception and experience of it via the intellectual mind, the emotional mind, the sensory mind, and the physical mind. We are rarely, if ever, conscious from the body's consciousness. In Sri Aurobindo's practice, this is something one tries to achieve. The process of becoming conscious in the body is initially to try to silence all these different minds. And this is very difficult. So the practitioner can at least start by trying to challenge the body's automatisms.

It was with Barba, whom I first met in Calcutta in 1984 at a seminar/workshop organized by the theatre group Padatik, more than with Grotowski, that I made the link from Sri Aurobindo and the Mother's practice and the initial process towards consciousness in the body and its application to performance. From the point of view of making the body conscious for performance, one has to free it from reflexive response. One has to initiate processes which undermine its automatisms. One has to break its normal behaviour by using it in a different way; by relearning how to stand, by using a different balance axis, by moving according to rules which deny those of daily behaviour as is done in our traditional performances. And this calls for a constant awareness in the body. Although I began the process of making the body conscious with Pournaprema's exercises, I soon followed up on this by learning traditional forms such as Mayurbhanj Chhau and Kalaripayattu. There was an additional reason by then for this interest in body dynamics—the need to evolve a physical language of performance expression, and to employ this language as a signifier or text.

GANDHI: Can we say that your intellectual transition from Stanislavski to Grotowski has also been from psychologism to physicality in theatre work?

Veenapani Chawla trains in Kalaripayattu. Photograph courtesy of Adishakti archives.

CHAWLA: Absolutely. And this was the beginning of the under-standing that the performer moves from the outside to the inside, from the external to the internal. The reverse of Stanislavski's approach. The work on becoming conscious of the inner landscape remains the private work of the actor on a daily and constant basis. But in performance, on stage, it is the external instruments that take you inward. This view became reinforced through my experience with, and understanding of, traditional performances, when I went to Kerala for my stay of many years. I could see that, when the performer got into specific body postures and structures, she was using them to enable specific emotions to emerge. These structures, stances, postures, were each dominated by a particular *chakra*/centre spoken of in the Tantric tradition. For instance, when the body's posture is determined by concentrating in the middle of the chest, the emotional experience of the practitioner is very different from when it is determined by the point around the navel. This kind of physicality, leading to a change in emotion, is not ephemeral. It is concrete. It is more predictable than trying to recall an emotion from memory night after night. Actors can find that memory becoming stale.

GANDHI: This might be a good place to refer to the physicality also of Sri Aurobindo's yoga—the fact that the Mother, especially, had such a strong commitment to a sadhana of the body and to taking extra care of material existence; calling on disciples to be very responsible towards the objects we live with, and the physical environment around us. I've always found this very striking.

CHAWLA: Yes. She was particularly concentrated on it from the end of the 1950s right up to 1973. I met her first in 1969, and from then onwards I followed keenly what she had to say of her experiences of the body in 'Notes on the Way', a section which appeared in a quarterly journal of the Ashram.

GANDHI: Your focus on physicality and work on the body is a corrective to being too cerebral in performance. This is something that you've refined in your work on voice but especially on breath, a project you've pursued with Patsy Rodenburg and Cecily Berry, amongst others.

CHAWLA: I started working on the voice and the breath in 1978 during my long stay at Puducherry. In fact, a few of the exercises that I evolved then, I still use when training actors. Rupa Nagarajan, an Ashramite, was my first student! She reminded me of this just a few days ago. We worked in the Ashram's Hall of Harmony in the evenings. Also in 1979, I started learning pranayama from Ambu, another Ashramite, who used to guide Chandralekha as well. I discontinued the pranayama on his advice because of the difficult experiences it started giving me. But the interest in breath as a performance tool continued. By the mid-1980s, I knew this energy had an enormous potential as a trigger for emotion. I shared this with Patsy when we met in Delhi briefly. She said that she too was investigating breath through Shakespeare's texts. In 1987, I went to England to work with her. And it was seminal. She led me into Shakespeare and the breath that he almost notates into his writing. Breath triggers emotion. You do not need to employ any other device.

Breath triggers emotion because it is the physical expression of thought. It does not originate cerebrally. I am fighting against the use of cerebral processes in the craft of the actor. Even when I work on text, I fight against the cerebral understanding of the word in the initial stages. I fight against the attempt to get its significance through the mind before it has been emotionally experienced through its sound. I encourage the actor to seek out the physicality of the sound of the word in the mouth, to experience it sensuously, to experience the breath of the vowel and the consonant in the mouth. For it is only when we experience the sound of the word in this manner, that there will be an immediate release of our emotions and imaginings. If the text is dissected cerebrally, it is very difficult to get an immediate emotional response to it. Rather, the danger is that the actor will impose emotions on the words dictated by reason. Sound and significance are closely linked in language and we are emotionally more linked to the sound than to the significance.

When I went to Kerala in 1988 to learn from Ammanur Madhava Chakyar, the great performer of Koodiyattam, he too emphasized the great technique of breath. To my query on emotional recall, he said that he did not use processes like that. He depended rather on the use of particular patterns of breath for generating particular emotions. My guess was that the tradition had, somewhere down the line, developed a codified system out of an observation of breath expression in daily life. How the breath behaves during fear, excitement, anger, disgust, etc., was observed and then codified. But the problem with this is that it is too neat and pat. It doesn't necessarily apply exhaustively to our lives now, which are much more complex.

GANDHI: You've spoken on other occasions about how your excitement at discovering the codification of breath in traditional performance was coupled with disappointment and alarm at how these practices were almost too codified. Am I right?

CHAWLA: Yes absolutely. So then, although I use this, I do so only as a reference. One has to extend the principle and expand the scope.

GANDHI: By extend you mean?

CHAWLA: Not to think of breath as resulting only in the given eight emotional states but also its tactile effect in the mouth in the saying of the word, its impact through application to qualities of body expression, its length through a thought in text, and the emotional consequences and effects thereof. One has to keep on looking to see what one can do with breath. And for this you need a Patsy, you need an Ammanur Madhava Chakyar, you need an Ambu as your foundation. At each moment when you work, you need to use breath freshly in your own way for each fresh situation, with all these learnings lurking around in the background.

When I observe myself I find that at every new movement, every new thought, every time one wants to focus when observing something, I hold my breath. It's almost like another language that is running simultaneously, underpinning everything.

It has its own rhythm and that rhythm breaks, gets textures, and changes according to what is happening around you and inside you.

Day 4

GANDHI: We've talked a great deal about questions of form. Let's turn to script and scripting. From your first forays into theatre, you've been drawn to archetypal stories and characters. We've talked a little already about your interest in Greek texts. But you've moved away from those to the South Asian epics, the Mahabharata and the Ramayana, in that order, and as a source for your own scripts. Any thoughts on the uses of archetype, myth, epic for the kind of theatre practice you do and also on the expediency of evolving new scripts out of these earlier core sources?

CHAWLA: I believe that there is a kind of eternal quality about epic texts. They seem to be forever and do not only represent the moment. That of course is because they are mythic. I believe myth expressed as metaphor is the finest expression of theatre because then the myth yields multiple simultaneous interpretations. And that is when you can be original.

GANDHI: What you call an open text.

CHAWLA: Yes. And I have always wanted to have my own voice in a text. I suppose because I am not entirely satisfied with what it is saying. Both with *Oedipus* and *The Trojan Women*, I intervened by editing and rewriting certain parts and by closing both plays differently from the way they closed originally. And since then I have felt the need to write my own scripts. It was again Sri Aurobindo who showed the way. In the writing of *Savitri*, he took a myth and created a metaphor.

GANDHI: And the Indian epic materials that you are engaging with now already have such a rich history of that sort of continuous intervention, editing, reworking, and interpolation.

CHAWLA: Yes. A myth is like a secret portal which allows the knowledge in the cosmos to pour into our expressions. It is a myth precisely because it is something that can resonate for ever and ever. It includes within it not only things of the past, of when it was created, but also of future times. It resonates into future times, and there is that in it, a wisdom, which allows for contemporary intervention. And here I am not talking about using it as a peg to hang current ideological preoccupations on. I am talking about the myth in itself, having qualities which can be unpacked in the light of contemporary time, or for any possible future time. And that is what is exciting. You take what exists and that which already has many layers of interpretation, which are the result of other interventions in history, and you carry this bulk of the history with you and add your own, so you have a thick, rich feast for the audience.

GANDHI: What is at the heart of some of the characters and metaphors you've fleshed out yourself—*Bhima, Ganapati, The Hare and the Tortoise?*

CHAWLA: Bhima is the archetypal hero, a man of physical strength and prowess. But how far can you take such a hero? What possibility does he have for growth and movement? I wanted him to go beyond just brawn and guts. So in *Impressions of Bhima*, at the end of the play, the battlefield shifts to his interior spaces, where alone, real victory is possible.

Largely, *Impressions of Bhima* was my reaction to a novel— M.T. Vasudevan Nair's *Randamoozham*, which gave a brilliant psychological and realistic portrayal of the character and made him the wronged but essential hero of the Mahabharata. It portrayed him as having a troubled relation with almost every other character in the Mahabharata as an angst-ridden, bitter second eldest. I personally have always found Bhima endearingly comic because of the emphasis on his brawn. In a reaction to the novel, I emphasized the comic element and made it highly stylized. This allowed me to bring out the latent tragedy of such a persona at the end.

Impressions of Bhima was the first time I attempted to experiment with dramatic structure. The highly stylized scenes in form were realistic in narrative, and were interspersed with storytelling episodes which, on the other hand, were natural in form but overblown and bizarre in narrative. This allowed me to take the relationship between Duryodhana and Bhima beyond the realistic into a kind of archetypal domain in the main body of the play.

Brhannala begins and ends with two different, though related, moments of crisis in the life of Arjuna, two liminal moments of transition and critical choice about how to be in the world. The choice is between a binary view of the world and of 'seeing with the eye of complete union'.

Ganapati explored the different stories relating to the birth of the figure. And these parallel different kinds of creativity. The essential thought behind this, was to see creative energy as a power inherent in all life and not just the prerogative of the talented few. For, on impact, all life synthesizes, creates anew, and gives back more than it receives. Non-life only reflects, as do mirrors, or repeats, as does an echo, and gives back just what it receives.

The Hare and the Tortoise was inspired by an essay written by Nolinida on Arjuna and Hamlet.

GANDHI: What does he say?

CHAWLA: He talks about the similarity of their crises and the dissimilarity in the outcome; that both have reached a point of sensitivity which makes them alive to the horror of what life really is behind its painted mask. And they are so steeped in depression that they cannot act. However, while Hamlet goes round and round in his mind, futilely looking for a solution, Arjuna finds it through another way of knowing. In the production, however, both processes are given validity. In the economy of the universe, both Hamlet and Vishwamitra have a contribution to make.

GANDHI: Your interest in darkness as the potential for light is very consistent.

CHAWLA: Yes, it is.

GANDHI: All this talk of being unfinished and in a state of potentiality brings to mind the lengthy, sometimes almost inarticulate *alap* we have in the ancient musical form, dhrupad, almost as though the raga can only ever emerge out of a primary confusion and uncertainty for performer and audience alike. I bring this up here because, as part of the training in breath and voice, you spent some time learning the form from the Dagar brothers.

CHAWLA: The Dagar brothers, yes. I wanted to learn about breath and the larger project was about developing a vachika, a style of speech, for contemporary theatre. I did not succeed in that entirely, although I did find a way to work on the text of *Savitri*.

The gurus taught me Raga Bhairavi. But I was taught only the *sargams*, permutations, and combinations of the note patterns of Bhairavi. But you know, I was depressed at that moment because I thought I had not learnt anything. But much must have come to me on the margins of the formal classes; because as with everything I learned in those years, I am still unpacking the learning. I am still unpacking everything which I thought was small and banal and trivial or even fantastic. It's been, how many years? Almost 20 years, and I am just beginning to realize what it is that I learned from them.

GANDHI: An important factor in your creative formation is the sheer variety of environments you've worked in. Of these, would it be fair to say that it was especially in the Mumbai milieu that you found a chance to take a life in theatre seriously?

You were officially based in non-theatre worlds as a school-teacher and a doctoral student. Nonetheless, even in these worlds—and so differently from somewhere like Delhi, say— doing theatre was a real option and also, intellectually, a very rigorous undertaking. People looked to Naseer not just for craft but also to think about a bridge between art and politics. Khalid Mohammad was engaged in an exemplary type of film criticism, almost a new kind of writing for newspaper consumers. Then there was Shanta herself, of course, for whom the work of theatre and thought were and continue to be inseparable. Reflections?

CHAWLA: First of all about Shanta. I met her very early. I met her because I went to observe rehearsals of Pearl Padamsee's *Sita*, written by Snehalata Reddy who, as you know, died in prison during the Emergency. The play was for the inauguration of Bookpoint, an Orient Longman's outlet at Ballard Estate. It was a play-reading rather than a performance. Shanta, Victor Banerjee, Sohaila Kapur were involved in it among others. Shanta was reading Sita and Victor, Ram. Subsequently, the interaction continued, first by accident and then by design. I invited her for my rehearsals and she came for even the kiddie plays. She saw the kiddie *Rosencrantz and Guildenstern Are Dead* that I had done and then the later one. And consistently she's been with me, with each play, observing it before performance, giving feedback, reviewing it. Over the years, the interaction has enlarged to include a dialogue about everything under the sun. A rich resource and a rigorously ethical being.

Then there was Khalid whom I met when I joined Bombay University for my master's in political philosophy. He started writing about film while he was still at university. And then he joined *The Times of India*. He was, as you mentioned, responsible for making the world of cinema available to me. I had of course, as a student in Delhi University, been a member of a film society; but Khalid made this journey possible in Mumbai. He opened me to regional cinema, to Malayalam cinema in particular. I remember writing a review of a Malayalam film. Of course today my conversation with Malayalam cinema is very different. It is more intimate. It feeds my nostalgia for Kerala. But also, I love the actors—Mohanlal, Manju Warrior, Nedumudi Venu, Thilakkan, and the new Prithviraj. They are some of the finest in the world. And I find the narratives fresh, bold, and engaging. Khalid made me see commercial cinema seriously. He made it possible for me to meet different kinds of people and interview them. The most important was Naseer. I also interviewed Hema Malini, Moushumi Chatterjee, etc. And he pushed me forever to get an interview with Amitabh Bachchan. Finally, we were at dinner at Kishore Kumar's house for his birthday, and Amitabh was there, and I walked up to him and said, 'I want to interview you for *The Times of India*.' He indicated someone who was with him and said, 'Talk to him.' Khalid followed up on this and got his interview. Those were the days there was a war between Amitabh and journalists and he had refused to talk to them.

Another person from the world of film I met through Khalid was Amol Palekar who roped me into his Marathi production of *Roshomon*. I played the medium. And I experienced travelling with a theatre company from town to town for the first time. Travel at night after one performance and perform the next night in another town. And travel again. Above all, through Amol, I met Deepa Lagoo, who was the one who gave me the confidence to direct *Oedipus*. She kept company with me through that production—she played a superb Jocasta—and for years after that, as a friend and confidante. Deepa took me further into Marathi theatre and through her I met, among others, the playwright Mahesh Elkunchwar. It was because of a conversation with him that I started exploring live music in my productions after *Oedipus*.

Another big influence was Alaknanda Samarth the actor. She was a legend, the actor who could have changed the face of Indian theatre had she not left India. While casting for *The Trojan Women*, I had dared to contact her for Hecuba. That did not happen. But we kept in touch. And it was because she wrote to the voice coach of the Royal Shakespeare Company, Cecily Berry, about my desire to work with her on voice and vachika that I got to work with Patsy Rodenburg. Alak herself works with Patsy periodically now. But in 1986–7 we got together to work on two solo pieces for Alak. One was *Kunti* by G. Sankara Pillai, the playwright, theatre director, and the then director of the Trichur School of Drama. The other was Cocteau's *The Human Voice*. What was most exciting was watching Alak in action, her processes and her responses to performance situations. I am still discovering and unpacking what I picked up from my observation of her then. One was the 'tension' she experienced between the word and the action which Kumar Shahani, the director, asked her to perform. This 'tension' is something I always try to look for in my work when dealing with different signifiers. Alak continues to be a great source of creative stimulation.

Rustom Bharucha also entered at some point to observe the process. Later I was to discuss Sri Aurobindo's *Savitri* with him, as a potential performance piece. Recently, we collaborated on creating the Ramayana Festivals at Adishakti. And today our conversation continues, stimulating and provoking.

I discovered Chandralekha close up from this production of *Kunti* and *The Human Voice*. And what struck me in this working situation was the honesty of her commitment to supporting other women in difficult situations. With Kumar I learned about the relationship between money and art. I was the producer and it was my first experience in a professional set-up. Although I believed I was now doing theatre professionally, my attitude to its economics remained that of an amateur. We had little money for this production and everyone had to get a fee. But no one did. Because the money went into paying for lights, and transport, etc. My argument was that as we all enjoyed what we were doing, we did not need to be paid. But the man whose survival came from renting his lights should be paid because he probably hated his business, yet had to do it. Kumar told me I was supporting a petit bourgeois view of the world, and that everyone should be paid. Artists more so.

I've had much opportunity to put this through the test of experience and reflection. In the utilitarian world we occupy today, it is difficult for the community to see the very critical contribution that artists and creative persons make because it is intangible. Some scientists have, however, argued that major scientific discoveries or shifts in scientific thought have followed in the wake of the revolutionary visions of artists and that the artist is really the advance guard of society, a forerunner of a new way to look at reality. Be that as it may, I personally believe that the processes of artistic creation are the result of alternative ways of knowing, and one has to guard and nurture this way of knowing as much as one does the more conventional ones.

GANDHI: You met Jennifer Kendal at this time too, didn't you, who had such seriousness of purpose. You became foyer manager at Prithvi theatre for some time.

CHAWLA: I was inspired by Jennifer's parents when I saw them in school, both at Nainital and at Dehradun. I think I got this excitement for theatre then.

GANDHI: And Prithvi itself became a schoolroom for performers, no? I recall actors going to watch a good performance again and again, no matter how different it might be from their preferred style or medium.

CHAWLA: Yes it was. As foyer manager I was allowed to watch every performance that happened at Prithvi. That was a privilege. And there were all kinds of theatre happening— Gujarati, Hindi, English, Marathi, drawing-room farce, avant-garde, the works. I remember seeing Naseer's *Waiting for Godot* five times, and each time it was different and a new learning experience.

I have been lucky in that I have had the opportunity to see so much performance. In London, I was lucky to have a similar privilege, courtesy Patsy, who spoke to some theatre managers she knew and I could watch a performance almost every day. In Kerala, I travelled across the state to catch rare traditional performances. And now, I have the privilege of seeing performances from all over the world at Adishakti and the Adishakti actors performing there as well.

GANDHI: There's also Anmol Vellani. Perhaps a great resource for you and many others besides was the theatre laboratory project that he pioneered for Ford Foundation. He also supported your own research in other non-metropolitan parts of India?

CHAWLA: Anmol was enabling in many ways. I met him after a performance of *The Trojan Women* which he came to watch. He has been a nurturing and stimulating force since then. He was the one who suggested the stint at Barba's Odin Teatret. Although I was not a part of the theatre laboratory project, I think somewhere that notion must have percolated into me from his exercise. And of course it helped, that he was more than familiar with the arts and artists of Kerala and knew G. Sankara Pillai who opened Kerala for me.

And so we come to Kerala, and my experience of living outside a metropolis. But much before Kerala, I experienced the interiors of Orissa, Bengal, and Bihar. I took this journey to experience the three kinds of Chhaus in that region. It was very difficult being there. That world was so different from anything I had known, that I would have had to transform myself completely to be able to live there. I finally learned the form from Orissa, the Mayurbhanj Chhau. But I learnt it in Delhi at the Bharatiya Kala Kendra from the great guru Krishna Chandra Naik. I was introduced to him by the dance critic and scholar Sunil Kothari, who gave me remarkable advice. He said, 'Don't try to learn dance items. Learn the grammar. That will be more useful for the work you want to do.' That was the most brilliant advice I have received, it has helped me in my approach to the learning of all traditional forms.

Kerala was more accessible than the interiors of Bihar, Orissa, Bengal. Accessible because of the egalitarianism, which was also shocking in a way. For I had not experienced this degree of it even in the metropolitan cities. It was both contemporary and traditional, and for that reason, also creatively stimulating. There were other things about it which made it so attractive. Lots of young people learning the traditional performance arts, making a lifetime commitment to performance despite the meagre monetary returns that it would bring. And I joining their ranks with a discipline and austerity I had never thought myself capable of! Above all, what was seductive was the integration of life and the environment and the arts. And I was overwhelmed by the natural environment.

GANDHI: I'm sure these interiors were extraordinary. Yet, you reacted very strongly and very productively against the traditional and the non-metropolitan settings that you were so relentlessly immersing yourself in. In a way, Adishakti bears the marks of your revolt against pure tradition; yet, and I guess this is crucial to emphasize, one that does not result in reformist or patronizing metropolitanism, urbanism, or 'modernism' either.

CHAWLA: I agree with you entirely. At the end of the day Kerala was not truly cosmopolitan. It could have been, it had the ingredients but somehow it did not make it. And that disturbed because it was a wasted potential. You talk about finding my roots in Kerala. At one point I asked myself, 'Wouldn't it be wonderful if I were a Malayali?' And I immediately thought, 'No'. Because my root is somewhere else, not in a geographical or cultural location, but in a different way of seeing things—in the Aurobindonian way of seeing. That is the root. And I can be anywhere and this is my root. It is about being constantly radical with oneself. Which, by the way, is what I did with myself in Kerala. People who visited me while I was there and learning all these difficult things at the age of 40 plus, asked, 'How is this going to help you with your work?' I just felt that I needed to learn again and to learn and know with my body. To learn again with my body and not just with the brain.

GANDHI: The body is a sweet instrument, thankfully. It learns quickly.

CHAWLA: Yes, it learns by imitation, mind you, and then it falls into habits which have to be knocked out.

GANDHI: You mean it learns very quickly but forgets less easily?

CHAWLA: That is exactly it. One has to constantly displace. Perhaps be uncomfortable.

Let me give you the example of working on *Bhima* with Vinay. Here was a body, Vinay's, which had internalized all these forms because it was familiar with the culture of the region. Magical forms that make you fly and make you do other wonderful things. But this body was asked to drop its habits of performance. It was difficult. Vinay will vouch for it that I had to constantly interrupt him and say, 'No, no, you are falling back into habit.' And then, after the habit was erased, the body, honed by these wonderful forms, started to create spontaneously. And instead of taking the external, visible elements of all that it had learnt, it started being prompted by deeper impulses at the root of the dynamics which underscored the forms.

Four

Theory and Practice

VEENAPANI CHAWLA has been frequently called upon to share her ideas about the theatre she practises in various forums. The following selection of papers which she has presented at different times and at different venues articulates her theory and practice of theatre. Certain key concepts she returns to frequently include the idea of hybridity, the idea of the actor impacting the audience by a contagion of consciousness, and the idea that the actor is at all times in the process of becoming. Chawla emphasizes time and, again, the vital features that distinguish theatre from the other performing arts and cinema—the live presence of the actor, the 'hereness' of the space which the actor inhabits, and the possibility of using elements like music and lighting as vital signifiers, greatly enriching the meaning of the whole.

Theatre Research and Laboratory outside the Urb

Problems and Possibilities*

VEENAPANI CHAWLA

Adishakti is located 200 kilometers from the big metro of Chennai. It is 10 kilometers from the town of Pondicherry. It is in a rural area. And I am told, 'artistes who move away from the city may get an opportunity to focus more on their craft, but at the same time they have to balance the reality of being away from where the action is—in the cities.'

* Excerpted from a paper presented at the Ranga Shankara Festival in Bangalore, held in 2004.

I must clarify right away that the work of the Adishakti Laboratory for Theatre Arts Research is not merely about developing a craft of performance as an end in itself. The work that we are engaged in at the Laboratory, tucked away in a remote part of the country, is in response to certain needs which emerge out of the larger world. Our research in laboratory conditions towards evolving a language of performance and a new aesthetic, must be seen in this context.

The Validity of Theatre

In 1996, Eugenio Barba, the director of the Odin Teatret, Holstebro, Denmark, wrote to me lamenting that, 'in Europe, theatre is dying like the epidemic'. In India too, both contemporary and traditional theatres were facing a decline.

Some part of the fading appeal of traditional theatre, within its own spectator-communities, was not so much due to the corruption through urbanisation, etc., of audience taste, as is commonly assumed; but rather, to the historical attrition or paralysis of the forms themselves. As for contemporary theatre, its need was to reinvent itself in the face of the art of the times—cinema.

The crucial difference between cinema and theatre is that in theatre, the only reality is the live presence of the actor, while cinema accommodates every other reality except that of presence. At one level, therefore, the work of Adishakti has been aimed at re-establishing the validity of theatre around the notion of the live presence of the performer; and our work has been to equip the performer with tools whereby she can impact her audience through an enhanced and vibrating energy, both physically and psychologically.

Much of this work has been accomplished through dialogue with traditional theatre practices. The traditional forms and practices too, use performance languages which have a sensorial impact on the spectator. Of course, although these encounters have aided our own formal and imaginative directions, they have, equally, stimulated the traditional artists to discover old forms anew. Within our understanding, the contemporary performer is privileged as a critic whose task it is to reinterpret and, as it were, fill in the blanks within specific traditional forms. The encounters were thus premised upon a powerful recognition of mutual worth and capability.

Adishakti has also endeavoured during this time to widen the scope of theatre, trying to make it do more than it has done so far, or making it evolve beyond where it has been so far. In line with the tradition, we have looked at using the different perceptual arts as signifiers or texts; but, unlike the tradition, these signifiers do not act as illustrations of each other, but in tension with each other, to create a metaphorical wholeness of the *mise en scène*. In our view, the contemporary mind is not satisfied with an aesthetic of repetition, and prefers multiple layers and multiple views of the same thing.

Culture and Post-coloniality

Adishakti's aesthetic practice and philosophy of the theatre has emerged out of a considered examination of the three approaches to culture that existed in post-colonial India. In the first, Europe still remained the cultural metropolis, and modernist, rationalist, scientific thought was the only way to view the world; in the second, the world was viewed through the prism of an original, uncontaminated, pure Indian culture, to be resurrected by obliterating the intermediate past; in the third, a marriage was envisaged of all that India had experienced historically, and continues to experience.

For Adishakti the first approach was problematic because it was derivative. Eurocentric epistemology excludes a whole range of knowledge systems and ways of knowing, which are an essential part of the genius of the Indian tradition. The second approach was equally problematic. The attempt to try and move back to a 'pure Indian' way of seeing existence, did not recognise the change that would inevitably have taken place between 'then' and 'now', rendering the past impossible to return to. (Although the tradition talks about the nature of Brahman as being eternal, it also says it is *avinava*, ever fresh, never static.)

Rejecting the exclusions and rigidities of the first two approaches, Adishakti chose to practise the third, the marriage of all things. Today, it venerates the 'mixed' space which acts as a bridge between a range of diverse realms not normally or visibly seen to be in communication with each other. It seeks out the subtle interconnectedness between disparate peoples, localities, knowledges. It accommodates multiple inputs across time, space, and other cultures.

Our work has been the consequence of dialogue between traditional performers and contemporary performance; between theatre practitioners and urban architects; between physics, philosophy and religions; between Dalit performers and Sanskrit pundits; between Vedic chanting, Koranic chanting and Koodiyattam *vachika*; between the needs of the contemporary actor's body and the resources of traditional medicine; between music and the language of the stage; between music and *Nada Yoga*; between South Asian performance traditions and histories, and East Asian performance traditions and histories. Ardhanariswara, the half-man, half-woman form of Siva, and Ganapati, with his animal head and human body, resonate with the idea of 'mixed' spaces and strange marriages. It is with the creation and fostering of such spaces that our aesthetic concerns itself, and offers itself to the world.

The Global Consciousness of Sameness

Such hybridity stands firmly against the sameness perpetuated by the globalised world. This sameness or homogeneity, is being reinforced by the democratisation of knowledge, the information technology revolution, etc., of which one of the vehicles is the urban or city culture. We fear homogeneity because it can lead to the loss of plurality, alterity and specificity. We could lose countless alternative systems and processes of knowing, and therefore many knowledges, due to the emergence of a mainstream, homogeneous, global culture. It is important to guard cultural specificity, because it is the expression of individuality, of uniqueness, of originality, in a group and in the individual. It is this individuality which provides an aggregate or group with variety. This, in interaction with others, stimulates creativity through the shock of difference.

Culture is a living organism. As such, it has a double action, a self-development from within and a reception of impacts from outside, which it has to accommodate and make into material for its self-growth. Nothing grows by pure self-development from within, and in isolation. External impacts stimulate the force of self-development. It is only when there is a perpetual traffic of ideas, and perpetual transitions in thought, that newness enters the world.

In each of Adishakti's bridges with difference, we have scrupulously maintained that the proper site for 'new creativity' is the bridge itself, such that it does not require either participant in a creative interchange to cross over to the other side. Our endeavour has always been to reinforce the awareness and appreciation of the uniqueness of the 'other'.

In the process of our work, we have been confronted by two simultaneous though contrary movements, which seem to resonate in every field world wide. One is an impulse towards larger wholes and the other towards atomism. I believe that in art practice, the movement towards larger wholes or hybridity is an attempt at communication, while the movement towards the specific and atomic, is a quest for meaning. We have to have faith in and acknowledge both; for they hold within them the possibility of a more complex and healthy cohesiveness than ever known before.

The City as a Cultural Metropolis Today

I would now like to contend that the metropolis is no longer relevant as a cultural metropolis in a world where the spread of knowledge and culture is more or less equitable. In today's situation, the question of a centre and its margin/periphery, or of the provincial and the metropolitan, ought not to arise, at least culturally. In a world such as ours, the proliferation of small organisations like Adishakti, living away from the metropolis and forging multiple connections with other communities at the local, regional, national, and global levels, acquires greater relevance.

Collective life is easier, more varied, more fruitful, when it can concentrate itself in small spaces and simpler organisms. In larger collectivities, the individual dwindles and weakens, and is over-powered by the huge organism of the State. Consequently, life loses its colour, richness, variety, freedom and impulse towards creativity. Not only the individual, but also the city and the region, sacrifice their independent life and become mechanical parts of a machine. Collective life seems to lose its productiveness if it gets diffused over very large spaces.

At the same time, the global consciousness we are moving towards today, makes it possible for us to enjoy the benefits of both the large and the small aggregates. Today, we can have a number of small communities within a larger aggregate. While polity takes care of the business of administration, security and economic well-being, these small aggregates can take care of the cultural health of the community at large. This is possible because we can live anywhere today, and still absorb the thinking and psy-chological movements occurring in other parts of the world. It is no longer a necessity for creators/artists to live in the city to find their inspiration.

Adishakti's experience of living away from the 'city', or 'the urb', the so-called centre where 'the action is', and yet responding to the cultural needs of the times, is a case in point.

Adishakti and Its Performance Techniques*

VEENAPANI CHAWLA

I once asked Koodiyattam guru Ammanur Madhava Chakyar what 'satvika' meant. What was it like to experience as a performer. He answered, saying,

> This will come to you after you have spent seven years learning *angika* (body expression), and *mudras* (gestural language), then seven years learning *netra abhinaya* (eye expression), then seven years learning *vachika* (vocal expression), then seven years learning *abhinaya* (facial expression) and *bhava* (emotion), then 30 years

* Presented as a talk at the National School of Drama, New Delhi, in 2009.

practising these together in performance. Then, after you are 60, you might experience *satvika* and begin to understand it a bit.

I quote this to illustrate the kind of rigour, related to the craft of the performer, that traditional theatre demands. It explains the hypnotic power of these forms. Contemporary theatre pales in comparison, when all that is needed for it is some natural talent and four years in training school.

Inspired by the rigour of training in the traditional form of Koodiyattam, as well as by the distinction that exists in its aesthetics between *natyadharmi* (performance behaviour) and *lokdharmi* (daily behaviour), Adishakti has evolved techniques for the training of the contemporary performer for lifelong practice on a daily basis.

Physical Training

Natyadharmi implies an energy which is different from that of daily life. It suggests something larger than life. Training is required for developing the capacity for this energy, for making the body more conscious, more transparent and expressive, and less inert and dull. A first step towards achieving this is by doing all physical actions of daily life with a greater awareness and consciousness in the body. A second step is by carrying out certain movements on a daily basis, which employ a larger energy and break the automatisms of the body. Thus, at Adishakti, the performers practise Kalaripayattu every day, they swim, they do *asanas*, they practise at the gym, they play badminton and they try to learn new physical forms as often as they can. This is important because the continued practice of routine forms leads to the creation of another kind of automatism.

Natyadharmi actually means a particular kind of performance behaviour or language. So the next step in the process of the physical training of the actor, is to equip her to develop a language with the body which would enable her expression. Most traditional forms in South Asia have very defined and identifiable performance languages. A contemporary performer cannot use these languages, as they carry associations with them. She will have to create afresh, so that the language reflects her contemporary sensibility.

Over the years we have found Kalaripayattu, a neutral form that does not have a performance behaviour which carries associations, to be suitable for our purposes. We have discovered that this martial art was a foundation for many other performance forms of Kerala. For example, many Kathakali postures and movements have evolved from stances and postures of Kalaripayattu. Its basic stance has emerged from a modification of the *amarcha* posture in Kalaripayattu—the squat position used in fighting with a short stick. The *pranam* or the movement for ritual worship in Kathakali, is constructed from such movements and stances from Kalaripayattu as the *chadi keti* (jump with crossed arms), the *amarcha*, the *hanuman* posture, the first leg exercise, and the *choriche* (turn on the opposite side). The transformation of these elements from a martial art form into the performance form of Kathakali occurred when a new principle was introduced into the Kalaripayattu form. This new principle was a fixed and unchanging balance axis, a fixed stance and a fixed energy centre. In Kalaripayattu, stances, postures and centres change freely and all the time, so as to serve the functional needs of combat.

Using this experience as an example, we began our intervention into Kalaripayattu, by introducing other patterns of breathing than the functional one that it uses; and we were rewarded by a wealth of new movements and body behaviour. Additionally, just the internalisation of the form gave the performer material which emerged in new ways in the course of improvisation.

Over the years we have discovered that the practice of Kalaripayattu secretly nurtures, and makes the practitioner aware of, the centres in the body named *chakras* in the Tantric tradition. What is the relationship of these centres/*chakras* to performance practice?

Each of the *chakras* is a centre for body dynamics. For example the *swadhishthan chakra*, located below the abdomen, is the centre for balance. Correctly used, it can facilitate standing on one leg, swimming, etc. The *swadhisthan*, the *mooladhara*, the lowest *chakra* at the base of the spine, and the *manipura* at the navel, are the centres which facilitate the typical half-sitting posture with knees pointing outwards of South Asian forms.

Awareness of the centres leads to the creation of a new vocabulary. For, with the ability to flow from centre to centre, the performer acquires such a control over body dynamics, that it allows her to do things which she may have found difficult to do earlier.

Interestingly we discovered, that the centres/*chakras* are also centres of psychological expression, and that their location in the body corresponds to the location of the voice resonators. By getting into certain bodily stances and structures, the performer can reach or stimulate emotional states of being, as well as impact the voice and its expression.

Emotional Expression and Breath

Western methods of acting use Stanislavski's process of emotional recall for psychological expression. We found this inadequate for our purposes. To begin with, the process of emotional recall takes real time, and it is not unfailing in performance night after night. The sharpness of recall seems to wear off after some time. It was Ammanur Madhava Chakyar who pointed in the direction of an unfailing physical craft—breath. This was a few years before our discovery of the centres as a potent force for the stimulation of emotion.

Breath is the physical expression of thought and emotion. In daily life we find that the way we think and feel determines our breath. If we experience shock or fear, we find ourselves drawing in our breath sharply, and holding it at the back of our throat. If we feel sorrow, we find our breath locked in the centre of our chest, etc. This implies that a particular emotion has a particular pattern of breath. In Koodiyattam practice, there existed the knowledge of eight codified patterns of breath, corresponding to the eight emotions mentioned in the classical Sanskrit treatise on performance, the *Natyashastra*. It is apparent that this codification emerges from a study of breath behaviour in everyday life.

Adishakti's contribution to the Koodiyattam craft, was to extend it. To begin with, we modified the large stylised patterns of breath as given to us by Koodiyattam and made them subtle, such that while emotions were internally experienced, they did not necessarily have to spill out externally.

Our discovery that the resonators of the voice, the centres of body dynamics and psychological expression are located in related regions of the body, in addition to the knowledge that each emotion has a breath pattern which is located in a *chakra* unique to it, led us to demonstrate that all three—psychological, vocal and bodily expression—were united by a common breath.

By way of example, the same breath used in expressing *karuna* or sorrow in Koodiyattam for *mukha abhinaya*, was used by actor Vinay Kumar to express anguish through his voice and body in *Brhannala*, when he cries as Arjuna at the death of Abhimanyu. In Koodiyattam, *karuna* is expressed through the face by a process in which the breath energy is pulled up from the base of the spine and stored in the chest region, while the breath energy from the neck is compressed down on this concentration in the chest. The concentration of these two energies coming from physically different parts of the body, results in the feeling of a load in the heart. It also creates an expression of extreme pain on the face and a contortion of the body, because it is struggling in the absence of breath. This expression of pain feeds the emotional centre and arouses real emotional pain. It is akin to watching yourself cry in the mirror, which makes you then cry more fiercely.

In the case of the voice, the breath, which is concentrated in the chest, emerges with extreme difficulty in a strangulated sound. This is a physiological replication of what happens to breath in a real life situation of emotional pain. The shock of tragedy robs the body of breath, and the cry that emerges then is almost a plea for oxygen. Here again, in the performance situation, the sound the actor creates feeds the emotion and helps the performer to take the expression of the emotion further.

The performer at Adishakti is encouraged to master the Koodiyattam patterns of breath and apply them in performance. But she is also encouraged to observe her breath in daily life,

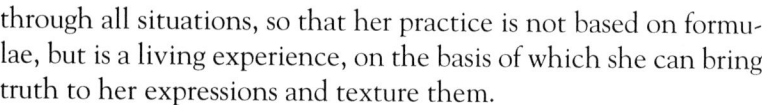

through all situations, so that her practice is not based on formulae, but is a living experience, on the basis of which she can bring truth to her expressions and texture them.

Rhythm, Expression and the Inner Text

If the logic of thought has been replaced by breath, then how do we deal with the question of the unwritten or inner text of the actor which runs right through her performance without break? This is important, because the inner text provides a continuity, an emotional graph to her performance.

Again, Koodiyattam was the source of our inspiration; for while breath was the Koodiyattam performer's craft to stimulate expression, rhythm was the impulse underlying all her expression. The rhythm in Koodiyattam is behind the performer as an unwritten or unspoken text. And the actor performs against a backdrop of constant rhythm. Each breath, each emotion, each gesture, each transition is fed by corresponding rhythms. These feed her performance, they feed her inner rhythms. And we see that the nature of life, as of performance, is a series of rhythms. We are born with the rhythm of the heart-beat, each word has a rhythm, each thought has a rhythm, each line of text has a rhythm, the structure of performance has a rhythm. We could go on infinitely about this.

As with breath, the performer at Adishakti is encouraged to observe herself at all times and notice the rhythms and graphs which underlie the events and experience of her daily life. Indeed breath and rhythm are related, for rhythms emerge out of the changing breath. The performer at Adishakti is encouraged to express narratives and experiences purely through rhythm; to step back from the thought and the word and replace these, internally, with rhythms which correspond.

As rhythm is so important to us, all performers at Adishakti learn to play a percussion instrument. Mainly it is the *mizhavu*, the Koodiyattam percussion instrument. And there is a daily practice of the craft so that a sense of rhythm is internalised by them. Apart from that, each one of the performers is encouraged to learn new rhythms and to create new ones. This facilitates the application of unusual rhythms as a running inner text through performance.

There are other benefits which come from the playing of rhythms on a daily basis. We know that there are 27 bones in the hand, 1300 nerve endings per square inch, 17000 tactile receptors, which is neurological evidence that playing a percussion instrument would fire brain development. One of the *mizhavu*'s virtues is that both palms of the hands are used to beat out the rhythms. The rhythms of Koodiyattam encourage the equal use of both the right and left hand simultaneously, so that this is really an exercise for firing up both sides of the brain.

The Performer's Voice

The body and voice of the performer are her two main physical and external means of expression. The voice requires as much training as the body for it to become a flexible, pliant, strong and clear instrument of the performer. Of the two, the voice is far more sensitive and reflective of the performer's psychological condition. So at Adishakti, an effort is made to understand vocal issues both at the physical and psychological level.

Exercises for vocal development are preceded by relaxation processes through swimming, *asanas*, *pranayama* and meditation practices, where the practitioner switches off emotional and mental preoccupations and concentrates on the breath at her nostrils. This is followed by further loosening up exercises for the body.

Voice work is based on an understanding of the physiology of voice production and the body's anatomy. The parts of the body involved are the diaphragm, the breath, the lungs, the vocal folds, the upper palate, the six nasal channels, the cranium, the facial bones and the other resonators in the body.

The diaphragm is important because it is the sheet of muscle which, like a trampoline, propels the breath with focused force up through the voice box, slightly strumming the cords but not attacking them, towards the upper palate. Without this force, the breath generated for the voice would be weak and manufactured by the upper lungs, creating tensions in the neck, shoulders and chest, and thereby distorting the voice. To really understand the role of the diaphragm in vocal production, the practitioner runs, builds up a breath, and then stops and tries to speak normally and evenly, without a hint of breathlessness. This effort makes her realise that it is the diaphragmatic control which gives her an even breath and helps her utilise the little breath she has; and that, because her breath comes from the diaphragm, her voice has power, strength and richness. It somehow roots her voice into her body. The daily use of voice, which is careless in its attention to diaphragmatic control, seems on the other hand to root her voice in her head. So as to strengthen the diaphragm and make it flexible, the performer does the *Bhastrika* and *Kapalbhati pranayamas*.

Additionally she practices two different ways of exhaling breath when speaking or singing. One practice involves the continuous pushing out of her abdominal muscles while exhaling/ speaking or singing. The other involves the contraction of her abdominal muscles while exhaling, etc.

With this work the performer begins to understand the importance of building the capacity for breath in the lower lungs and the back of the lungs. The kind of breathing which athletes engage in, where the upper lungs store the breath is not for the performer, as this creates tensions near the voice box. With the two kinds of exhalation practices mentioned above the practitioner begins to create breath capacity in the lower lungs and develops the muscular ability in the lower rib cage to expand so as to store breath in the lower lungs. Other exercises which enable this are Yogic breathing and breathing into the back in the *Ardhakurmasana*.

Lengthening the capacity of the breath is another important aim. Swimming enables this, if the breath is taken straight to the lower lungs and the swimmer tries to breathe out into the water, for longer and longer durations while swimming.

To create sound the breath has to bypass the vocal folds, touching them lightly. To physically apprehend this, the practitioner breathes out on an 'S' sound and then on a 'Z'. In creating the Z, she finds the vocal folds have been activated. She is encouraged then to focus her breath on the point of articulation, that is between her tongue tip and the back of her upper teeth; allowing the sound to emerge without any tension in the vocal folds. To further strengthen this experience, she articulates 'V' and lowers and raises her pitch in a siren sound, sustaining the energy of breath at the point of articulation while keeping the vocal folds free of tension and relaxed.

A relaxation of the vocal folds can be additionally achieved through the *Sarvangasana* and the *Halasana*. Swimming and breathing out into the water on a vowel, the *Khechari Mudra* (pranayama), and the *Simha Kriya asana* are additional ways of achieving relaxation and strength in the vocal folds.

Next for amplification of the sound, the breath and sound have to hit the upper palate, the cranium, and the facial bones. For once resonance starts here, it can then travel easily to other resonators in the body. The practitioner explores breathing in through the six nasal channels and exhales first through each and then through all on a hum. She learns to observe how this can set off vibrations in her cranium, facial bones, and in the upper palate. She learns to orient her palate and nostrils to achieve this. The upper palate has to learn to arch upwards like a vaulted ceiling to set off this resonance. Imagining a ball in the mouth arching the upper palate is one way, yawning and singing on the yawn, another.

Activating the other resonators in the body is possible also through the postures and stances of Kalaripayattu. Singing or saying text while getting in and out of these postures helps to activate them, for as I mentioned earlier, the vocal resonators lie in the same place as the centres for physical dynamism. The *Bhramari Pranayama* is another way for exercising these resonators.

Apart from singing, Adishakti has interacted with practitioners of sacred chanting from a number of different traditions like *Sama Veda*, *Yajur Veda*, Koranic chant, and Koodiyattam *vachika*/speech. This is not only for training the voice, but also to develop, at some point, a *vachika* or *natyadharmi* speech style.

During our interactions with the *Sama Veda* practitioner, we discovered that a vowel has many sounds and these can be released by modifying the position of the head and thereby its location in the mouth. The change in sound also triggers a change in emotional expression. These discoveries have great significance for the creation of a *vachika*.

A last word. The physical training of the performer actually supports and enables the vocal training. Much of the vocal training depends on elements also provided by the physical training— a relaxed physique, breath capacity, strength in the upper back thighs to support the back so as to prevent tension, and an awareness of the resonators/centres.

Approach to Text

As a preface to the work on text, I would like to mention that at Adishakti, we made a choice to use English as our verbal language, but an English as Indians speak it, which is usually an eclectic mixture of other Indian languages and speech rhythms. For training, however, we use principles from the *Chhanda Shastra* (the science of prosody), and western techniques and texts, which include Shakespeare among others. When training those who do not use English but other languages, our attempt is to understand their needs, hear their language, and allow broad principles of our knowledge to guide us.

Like all the performance elements mentioned above, the techniques used for an approach to text also have a physical basis. Fundamentally, we focus on the physicality of the word, and we start work on text by a physical experience of the vowels and consonants in the mouth. Work with a *Chhanda Shastra* expert led us to the assumption that vowels and consonants are located in specific points in the mouth, and to experience them correctly, one must feel them rather than hear them. Breath must hit the exact point of articulation in the case of the consonants, and bounce off the specific place on the tongue or the upper palate in the case of the vowel. In speaking the word, it is important to experience the movement of the breath as it goes from point to point in the mouth.

In our understanding, it is more important to sensuously discover the word in the mouth, than to understand it cerebrally. For in the origin of language, it was sound which preceded the word and conveyed significance; and it is sound which stimulates the emotional imagination more than the significance.

The word is onomatopoeic. In its spoken form, it has content locked into its physicality. 'Take' for instance withdraws into our mouths and stops on the *k*—unlike 'give' which moves forward and goes on and out with the *v*.

Such an approach by the performer to her text gives her an immediacy of emotional and imaginative understanding quite lacking in a cerebral approach to the text. In the latter, while the critical analysis would provide information, it would hardly result in an immediate emotional response, which is what the performer needs for expression.

Additionally, such a physical connection to the word, helps the performer to stay in the moment on the text. Patsy Rodenburg in *Speaking Shakespeare* says, 'If you do not stay on the text, you miss the acting clues written into the physical word constructions— the most basic of which is that if something is difficult to say, the situation itself is difficult or uneasy.' She goes on to give an example by quoting Paulina from Shakespeare's *The Winter's Tale*: 'What studied torments, tyrant, hast for me?'

The line is difficult to speak because of the number of '*t*'s and '*d*'s—consonants very close to each other in the mouth; so Paulina has to force herself to speak clearly. And it seems as though she is close to tears or controlling her temper.

Additionally, with the sensuous experience of the word, there comes a clear sense of its rhythm, which is the result of the combination of long and short vowels and the quantity or quality of consonants; for some consonants will cut the vowel short, and some will allow it to resonate. By way of example are the words '*put*' and '*puss*'. Consequently the rhythm of a whole line will emerge out of a sensuous experience of the sound of the words in

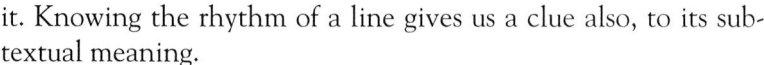

it. Knowing the rhythm of a line gives us a clue also, to its sub-textual meaning.

Breath too plays a very important part in the work on text. Earlier we discovered, that breath is the physical expression of thought and emotion. In our work on text, we try to express one thought on one breath. Patsy Rodenburg spoke of Shakespeare writing his text in a manner in which the breath and thought were so linked, that the performer need only honour the principle to perform with emotional truth.

By way of example, here is a passage from *Othello*, when he is convinced that Desdemona has been unfaithful to him.

OTHELLO: O, blood, blood, blood!

IAGO: Patience, I say, your mind perhaps may change.

OTHELLO:
Never, Iago! Like to the Pontic sea,
Whose icy current and compulsive course
Ne'er feels retiring ebb, but keeps due on
To the Propontic and the Hellespont,
Even so, my bloody thoughts with violent pace
Shall ne'er look back, ne'er ebb to humble love,
Till that a capable and wide revenge
Swallow them up. Now, by yonder marble heaven,
In the due reverence of a sacred vow
I here engage my words.

The sentence which begins with 'Like to the Pontic Sea', and ends with 'Swallow them up', is one thought. Said on one breath, Othello will express the violence of his emotions through his behaviour and words. But said with the breath honouring the grammatical pauses, which are many, it will sound as though Othello was explaining his feelings to Iago in a reasonable manner.

There are other traditions we have discovered, that have in their texts, such markers for breath so as to enhance emotional expression. Noh performer Wakita Haruko told us about such markers in Noh poetry. The *Chhanda Shastra* expert has told us about the *yeti* in Sanskrit poetry. There are interesting consequences of this. The thoughts in a passage will, through their corresponding long and short breaths, create a rhythm for the passage, which will again communicate a sub-textual sense of the passage.

Conclusion

We have spoken relatedly about *angika* when we discussed body expression, about *abhinaya* and *bhava*, when we spoke of emotional and psychological expression, about *vachika*, when we spoke about vocal expression. But we have not discussed that with which we began—*satvika*. For many years I believed *satvika* meant the truth of emotion. But it seemed too pat a response, especially when gurus would shake their heads and say, 'too difficult to explain'. Today I believe *satvika* to be the expression of that mysterious subliminal element which Sri Aurobindo calls the psychic—our best evolving self. For this, there are no techniques at hand. One just has to hope that, as promised by the Chakyar, a lifetime of dedicated work to one's craft and performance will enable this to emerge.

Space and the Actor*

VEENAPANI CHAWLA

Space, time, light are three preoccupations common to the mystic, the physicist and the artist. They are three ways of knowing and interpreting reality, and of expressing it. For the artist, they are central to her formal expression.

In general, mystics agree that 'objective' spatial reality is not the only valid reality; that the 'subjective' reality of the 'in here' space is as valid as the 'out there' objective space of physical reality. They also agree that space is fluid; that there is no sharp dividing line between the 'in here' space and the 'out there' space.

* Presented at a seminar 'Spaces for Theatre', organized by the India Theatre Forum at Ninasam, Karnataka, in 2012.

One can float from one to the other, or be in both simultaneously, giving even objective reality the colour of the 'in here'. Sri Aurobindo, a contemporary mystic, explains this philosophically when he says, 'Space and time are our names for the self-extension of one reality.' They are 'fundamental conditions of the spirit itself, which assume different appearances or status according to the status of our consciousness and even different movements of time and space within each status.'

In the early 20th century, Einstein's concepts of the relativity of space-time totally displaced the concept of the inert, logical, continuous Newtonian space, characterised by the distances of 'here' and 'there', and violated commonsense notions of it every day. Gertrude Stein's description of her hometown 'There is no there, there', could apply to Einstein's condition of space at the speed of light. There is no 'there', because it is all 'here', as all the points in space along the path of observation occupy the same place simultaneously.

This view of reality came to be expressed in art for the first time when Cubism fractured objects and rearranged them so that their front, back, sides, top, bottom could be seen by the viewer simultaneously, rather than sequentially, as in real life.

We come now to theatre. Is there a vision of space parallel to this in theatre today—a 'hereness' that the contemporary mystic, physicist and visual artist share and know?

In South Asia there co-exist two differing notions of aesthetic space. One perceives it as an objective three-dimensional 'extent', in which objects and events occur. Emotional events translate it into a dramatic space; fictionalised events translate it into an abstract space of the imagination; and the gestural space created by the actors and their movements, modify the surrounding space. As this notion of space is about the relative position, distance and direction of the objects in it, it is seen as the objective container of actors, events, emotions, etc.

The other notion comes from traditional theatre, and it recognises three kinds of space. There is the inner psychological space of the performer, the external 'real' space, which she shares with the audience, and a larger cosmic space. All these spaces are fluid, without sharp dividing lines between them, anticipating the aesthetic space of 'hereness'.

In Koodiyattam performance, the performer expresses her inner psychological space through *mukha abhinaya* (facial expression). She reinforces this expression through her *mudras* (hand gestures) and *netra abhinaya* (eye movement), recognising the necessity of communicating to the objective space shared with the spectator. Her *vachika* fills and communicates with cosmic space.

Let us try to demystify this third cosmic space. In one of my earliest experiences in Kerala, I attended the flag hoisting ceremony at a temple. The flag-pole rested on a sculpted tortoise and the flag at the other end carried a bell. Material space was connected to etheric space by sound. Sound is said to be the substratum of space. It is said to have created space, whether through a mystic sound, or through the big bang! Space is extent, sound is pervasive. The third cosmic space of the Koodiyattam performer reflects precisely this idea, that sound creates its own space through pervasiveness.

My work in the theatre can be divided into two phases. In the first phase I viewed theatre as the performance of a literary text; a text which had an aesthetic existence independent of its performance. In the second phase I believed theatre could be anything and everything so long as we recognised that it could be nothing without the primacy of the live presence of the performer. Inherent in these two positions were the two different aesthetics of space.

In the first phase, text was a determinant with regard to space. It needed a defined locus. It needed to be situated. This gave primary focus to space as an objective container of the text. For it accommodated the action and behaviour demanded by the text. It was its existence field. However, when I started giving primacy to the live presence of the actor above all other elements in the theatre, then my use and understanding of space changed. This needs a little elaboration.

The performer acquires primacy when she cultivates a qualitatively different presence on stage from that of daily life, a presence which has an enhanced energy and an enhanced consciousness.

An enhanced energy emerges from the honing of her physical instrumentality. But this is not enough. For a focus only on the body as a performance tool enables the performer, at the most, to have a sensorial impact on the audience. During the period of my work when text was the primary element in theatre, I did employ, at times, an enhanced physical behaviour in performance; but my aesthetic of space remained unchanged. The performer's behaviour in relation to the given three dimensional objective space, was determined by the needs of the text. Her behaviour of movement at the most modified the space around her such that it yielded greater significance.

So, apart from honing her physical instrumentality, the performer must also expand the peripheries of her consciousness. Energy becomes consciousness when it moves from the physical to the psychological realm. The actor must expand her inner focus progressively to increase her inner awareness. This is not done so that the performer can bring a kind of Stanislavskian psychologism to her performance, but because it enables her to bring a concentrated, multi-layered simultaneity of consciousness to her performance. A quality of 'hereness'.

For we have a multiple consciousness, or diversified spaces within us, each possessing a different quality and degree of subtlety, often pulling in different directions. We conveniently cover all these spaces under the blanket of 'mind', to provide a cohesion or homogeneity to these differing movements within us. We flow from one space to the other like water without control; and sometimes, like water, we are in all the spaces simultaneously, but in a kind of haze. The conscious, energised performer will, through a daily practice of self-observation, bring to her performance a concentrated consciousness of her multiple inner spaces, as well as and as much as to her external space—her body.

An outcome of this process of self-witnessing and one relevant to today's theme, is that the performer gets experiential evidence of the many spaces and times that she occupies. It informs her that her reality is not only that of the logic of the external and sensorial world. That she is the container of realities, the space that can express all things.

She is the space which reflects her inner spaces and conditions. She becomes the space on which the dramatic expression occurs. She is the space that the text is situated in. Under these circumstances, the external, circumambient space, becomes a tool for her to extend her inner intentions and conditions. For example, when the Koodiyattam performer, through her gestural behaviour and her eyes, describes an imaginary tree or suggests the distance she needs to walk, the circumambient space transforms to accommodate these suggestions, and then goes back to neutrality.

Because presence is the one reality in theatre, imparting reality to the other elements, the external space itself becomes fluid and transforms into whatever is demanded of it. It is not fixed. The notion of space as something logical or continuous, gives way to something more fluid which can then reflect many different realities in an aesthetic of 'hereness'.

Apart from transforming the circumambient space, the performer's body can also image concepts, ideas and other realities which can then be sensuously experienced by the spectator. In other words, it can create visual metaphors in which the metaphor itself reflects a 'hereness', because it can be apprehended in an all-at-once manner. Simultaneity is a spatial way of knowing, as distinct from the temporal way of knowing, which is sequential.

Many Adishakti productions have opened with visual metaphors. In *The Hare and the Tortoise* for example, the performer is contained in a small box or square of light, and his behaviour within it images the dilemma of Hamlet caught in the box of his mind, the main flavour of which is 'doubt', the essential quality of the reasoning mind.

However, manifesting this particular visual metaphor would not have been possible without the play of light. Thus, although the live performer has primacy in the theatre, there are other signifiers which aid the performer's spatial expression, or enable her to extend her intention, or even perhaps, complicate and layer it. These signifiers can be the word, the light, the music, and many others.

In Koodiyattam performance, the accompanying rhythm extends and fulfils the actor's intention. It is a critical signifier.

For example, if with her gestures, the posture of her body and her eye movements, the performer indicates a presence with height in front of her, the music stretches in tension to provide the aural image of length and height. If the space of her face reflects an inner turmoil, the music will provide an aural dynamic movement to the turmoil. Indeed, the music in this instance provides the temporal element to the space, which is the performer. It temporalises or dynamises this space, providing it with movement.

Temporalising space, however, can be achieved by other signifiers as well. In Adishakti's *Brhannala*, there is a scene where Drona is teaching the Kuru children. He expresses, through the space of his body, the temporal processes of knowing, as distinct from the spatial ways of knowing. He does this through gestures, eyes, speech rhythms, content of word and movements. The aural images by the musicians extend and add to the temporal nature of the thinking mind. And the light, by sequentially lighting up segments of the circumambient space which the character occupies sequentially, dynamises it, temporalises it, and provides it with additional movement. Talking of light providing movement brings to mind the shadow puppet performance tradition of Kerala, where the static puppets acquire spatial mobility because of the mobile flame lamps.

In 2001, Adishakti produced *Ganapati* so as to explore the possibility of using music/rhythm as the prime signifier. Let us recall here the traditional view of sound as space, as pervasiveness. It is space beyond the visual space of the Koodiyattam performer, seen through a keyhole vision by the spectator. Its vibration is experienced at a subtle level. It is universal in another sense too. It is pre-verbal.

Let me expand this thought. Like the physical image, rhythm embodies a pre-verbal stage in the process of our coming to grips with reality. When words supplant images and sounds, we not only lose contact with a direct and fresh experience of reality— for it begins to be provided to us through the indirect agency of the constructed word—but we also acquire cultural specificity. As rhythms come out of a more fundamental space within us, they touch that same fundamental space in the spectator. To my mind, this seems to be a way of looking at the notion of the universal (cosmic?) space of sound.

A final word about signifiers. All signifiers in theatre exist because they extend the performer's intention and reveal significance. All reveal meaning in their own unique way, such that a dimension or layer is added to the performance which provides it with different angles of view. As the angles of view are provided simultaneously, not sequentially, the actor's spatial intention reflects a 'hereness'.

Back again to space. Another aesthetic space which Adishakti has explored, is the in-between space, or the space of transition. My interest in it was aroused when I explored it from the point of view of the actor's craft. How, for example, does she make the transition from one emotion to another, from one character to another, from one movement to another, one state to another? What happens in that moment of transition? What occupies it?

Then came *The Hare and the Tortoise* which was an exploration of what happens to Shakespeare's Hamlet offstage, before Act V. What happens to him to make the transition from 'to be or not to be' to 'let be' in Act V? Shakespeare does not explain the process of change. It is a space left unexplained.

However, even beyond this focus on the unexplained moment of transition, of liminality, there is an exciting aesthetic possibility, in allowing the main markers of a narrative to be portrayed as frames to the transitional moments, which would then become the main space of the narrative. Were we to frame these and focus on them, what would be the implications for an aesthetic of 'hereness'?

A last word. I believe there can be no conclusive definition of space. Each genre has its own take on it. Thus the film-maker, the architect, the mystic, the philosopher, the physicist, the visual artist, the theatre practitioner, the poet, the musician and the psychiatrist would each have their own notion and use of space. And even the aesthetic space of 'hereness' would find a different expression and manifestation in each of these.

Five

Performance Texts,
Reviews, Interviews

Impressions of Bhima
Performance Text

VEENAPANI CHAWLA

Veenapani Chawla's *Impressions of Bhima* was first performed at the Vasanthabba Festival at Nritya Gram, the dance institution located on the outskirts of Bangalore, founded by the dancer, Protima Bedi. The play was produced on a grant from the Department of Culture. It did 21 shows between 1995 and 1997. Besides Puducherry, Mumbai, Pune, Chennai, Ahmedabad, Kolkata, and Delhi, it was invited to Théâtre du Soleil, Paris, Asia Society, New York, and Schoenberg Hall, UCLA.

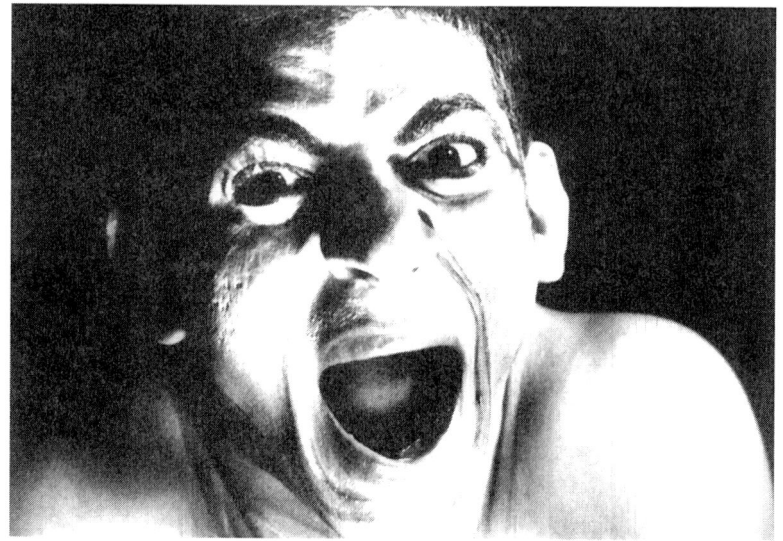

Vinay Kumar in *Impressions of Bhima*. Photograph courtesy of Gautam Mitra.

Scene 1

(*Darkness. In the manner of the Suprabhatam, a voice sings the many names of Bhima in praise and description of him.*)

Achuthanuja,
Anilatmaja,
Arjunnagraja,
Arjunapoorvaja,
Vallavia,
Bhima,
Dhanvavu,
Jaiya,
Kaunteya,
Kaurava,
Kurushardula,
Marutatmaja,
Maruti,
Pandava,

Partha,
Pavanatmaja,
Prapanjana Suta,
Vayu Putra,
Vayu Suta,
Vrigodara.

(*When the song ends, there is a beat on a drum, and a faint light comes on stage to light up a figure in silhouette. It is a man in the vajra asana or Japanese posture, but the knees are spread outward and his body is bent forward towards the floor. His fists are resting on the floor in front of him, elbows pointing outward and head lowered. As the light grows, the play of muscles in his shoulders and arms becomes apparent. The image is of a man of great physical bulk and strength. Slowly he raises his torso without raising his head, his arms straighten and hang in front of him. Then his hands slide upwards. With a jerk he rests them on his hips, sits back on his heels and jerks up his head. As he reveals his face there is the sound of a new-born baby's cry from the musicians' pit. The face revealed is that of a small child. The actor has reoriented his face in a mask. The eyes are round and wide. The lips are curled upwards in a stylised smile. The mouth is open but there is no show of teeth. For some time he examines the world in front of him, blinking his eyes and angling his head this way and that. Then he slowly brings one hand forward and places it on the floor before him. He pauses and then brings the other forward, as though he were crawling. He pauses a while then rises to sit on his haunches, knees facing outward, hands back on hips. He continues to examine the world in front of him and then rises slowly on his legs. He stands there for some time, hands on hips, knees slightly bent and body inclined slightly forward.*

We have seen the birth, the infancy and now the childhood of Bhima.

Tentatively Bhima brings one foot forward. The movement is a stylised tiptoe. He then brings the other forward. He has seen something ahead and, like a thief, he moves slowly forward towards it, hands on hips, eyes focused, body inclined with intent, the walk a stylised tiptoe. When he reaches centre-stage, he pauses and examines the object of his interest. Then slowly he brings a hand forward towards his focus and licks his lips. The hand goes forward hesitatingly and when it reaches the extreme, it searches for the object of Bhima's focus. It hovers for a suspended moment and then withdraws sharply as though stung. Bhima's face expresses extreme shock. Then this mask dissolves and shifts as the face crumbles slowly into a soundless crying. The actor's chest heaves. Then slowly the eyes clear, the face lightens and the first mask of the happy child is back in place. Bhima sighs with happiness.)

BHIMA: Yesterday Arjuna killed his first animal.

(Drum beat) A deer. *(Drum beat)*
(At the second beat, Bhima jerks his head to his right. Then, keeping his gaze fixed on this focus to the right, his body turns slowly and gracefully in the opposite direction, till it can no longer take the tension and he has to complete his turn quickly with a jump to get back to his point of focus again. He has just described an anti-clockwise movement so as to suggest going backward in time to 'yesterday'. A percussion instrument has been following and marking the movement. After the jump, the actor mimes driving a chariot. The percussion gives an aural description of this movement. Occasionally he slows down and smiles at his invisible companion. At one point...)

BHIMA: Serious eh Arjunan? *(He stops the chariot. Then, mischievously)* Did the elders give you a bow and arrow?

(He then leaps and shouts 'kabbadi' and starts playing the game. He does this comically and in extreme slow motion. The musicians join in with the shouting. At the end Bhima leaps and collapses centre midstage.)

BHIMA: *(Shouts)* A deer! Arjuna has killed a deer.

(He moves smoothly out of his prone position into the Kalaripayattu amarcha position.)

BHIMA: Yudhishthira told Arjuna...

(The actor becomes Yudhishthira. He slowly reorients his face into the mask of a toothless old man, shoulders raised and hands and fingers used with finicky precision to emphasise his words. The voice too is that of a toothless old man.)

BHIMA: ... 'When a Kshatriya kills his first animal, he gives it as a bali—to the gods—and says thanks to them.'

(*The mask of Yudhishthira dissolves into that of Bhima.*)

BHIMA: I felt very proud. (*With great joy and rising excitement*) And I looked forward to the feast!

(*In an expression of his excitement, he drops his hands forward onto the floor and levers his body up almost into a headstand before coming down to sit cross-legged on the floor. He then sighs with pleasure and looks around at the feast of food. He reaches out for a ladoo and throws it into his mouth. As he does so, his hand masks his face. When he withdraws his hand slowly, we see that his face has become sad and petulant.*)

BHIMA: (*Sadly*) I too killed my first animal. Yesterday. (*Brightening up and then excited*) A wild boar. (*He levers himself off the floor into a semi-headstand to fall back into an amarcha.*) A single wild boar. (*He makes a quick transition to the posture and mask of Yudhishthira, crossly shaking his finger at Bhima.*)

BHIMA: Yudhishthira said to me, 'Manda, why did you do this? If Ma knows about it she will be very angry!'

(*Bhima drops Yudhishthira's mask and slowly assumes his own.*)

BHIMA: (*Conspiratorially*) For Yudhishthira I am still Manda [Stupid]. For the Kauravas, Vrigodara [Big stomached].

(*Bhima makes an incantation of the words Manda and Vrigodara. And the musicians repeat them in different voices suggesting that he is being called by people from many sides. His body responds to these voices like a puppet, jerked around by them. Then the sound and the rhythm subside.*
Pause.
The rhythm starts slowly building up again as Bhima begins to rise, his arms turned up like one showing off his physical strength. When he reaches maximum height, he speaks. When he speaks of his achievements in the following passage, he reinforces his victory posture.)

When he speaks of Arjuna, the posture is held but now it acquires a languor.)

BHIMA:
I love Arjuna.
Yesterday he killed an animal.
Yesterday I killed an animal.
He killed a deer.
I killed a single wild boar.
He killed in the game of the hunt.
I killed in self-defence.

(*Bhima in his victory posture. He turns anti-clockwise on one leg and goes into the amarcha with one hand resting on the floor in front and the other held behind his back, his head up and looking straight ahead: the stance of a boar.*)

BHIMA: (*Low, intense and serious*) A single wild boar had come out of the rocks. It took my smell ... (*increase in tempo and tension*) ... and ran towards me like an arrow. (*The body describes the action of the boar taking the smell and running like an arrow with a stylised gesture.*) I was afraid. (*He covers his face with his arm.*)

BHIMA: (*Still in amarcha*) The hunters say (*calling out*) 'You must fear the single wild boar, fear it more than a lion'. (*Bhima hides his head in his arm.*) I was afraid. (*Slowly Bhima's face emerges from behind his arm, and he makes a slow physical transition. His tone is adult and full of self-disgust.*) What stories would the sutas sing of me? Bhimasena, son of Vayu, born to be the strongest man, died on the tusk of a boar—before killing his first animal. (*A short percussion piece during which he effects a physical and emotional transition, moving from high seriousness to a lighter mood, and back to being a child.*)

BHIMA: (*With greedy delight*) Bali! (*Another musical transition and Bhima moves from glee to petulance.*) I offered no Bali. (*A third musical transition. Bhima moves from the petulant to the heroic, puffing up his chest and spreading his knees apart.*) But when you kill the single wild boar, you become a man.

(*And the musicians whistle at Bhima. One says Ay hai! And then they break into a vaitari [vocal expression of rhythms], which is teasing in tone and carries the tenor of roadside Romeos describing the seductive walk of a woman.*)

ACTOR: (*Shushes them*) Don't you have mothers and sisters at home?

(*The musicians gasp and subside. The actor has lit a fire in a pot on stage and he sits before it in readiness to tell a story. The physical stylisation of the last scene is broken by this* lokdharmi *mode—relaxed, easy, everyday. But the narration goes over the top. This is a tall story. And the actor is free to ad-lib and introduce everyday topics for satirical comment.*)

ACTOR: When I was a little boy, my grandmother told me, 'Never sleep on a tiny little mat'. So I asked, 'Why grandma?' So she said, 'My dear, if you go to sleep on a tiny little mat, your legs will stick out of the mat and the next morning, when you wake up, all your strength will be drained out of your body.'

Now very often, my grandmother would make up a story and say 'this is history'. But this time I realised immediately that this one was not history, but her story, passing from generation to generation from the time of Bhimasena and Duryodhana.

Now our Bhimasena and Duryodhana, even as small, tiny, tiny, little children, were always fighting and quarrelling, and quarrelling and fighting, to prove who was the strongest man. (*With assumed modesty*) Every time Bhimasena won. Even though Duryodhana had some skill, Bhimasena had lots of strength. So Bhimasena won!

One day fed up of being defeated, Duryodhana ran to his uncle, Sakuni, and called (*crying*) 'Unkil, Unkil, Unkil, Unkil! That Bhimasena, today also, beat me!'

Now this particular Uncle had lots of cunning and tactics to defeat an enemy. What he did was to think for a while, walk across the room twice and then go into a corner, think again for a while, and laugh (*sinister laugh*). Then he went into another corner, picked up a packet and said, 'Duryodhana, this is a packet. Give this packet as a present to Bhima.'

(*Sinister laughter.*)

So Duryodhana took that packet and started to walk towards Bhima. When he met Bhima, he called, 'Bhima, Bhima, Bhima, Bhima.' So Bhima came. So Duryodhana said, 'This is a packet, no, a present from me. Take it, take it.'

So Bhima took that packet. Why? Because he loved presents! Also Bhima had no ego problems, no professional jealousy and no other existential problems. So he took that packet and said to Duryodhana, 'Thanks.'

Sunset.

That night our Bhimasena opened that packet and what did he see? A TINY LITTLE MAT! Bhimasena, son of Vayu, not a fool. What did he do? He spread out the mat, put his legs on top of the mat, put the rest of his body outside the mat. And then went for a Good Knight's sleep.

(*The actor sings the advertisement jingle for Good Knight mosquito coils, and puts out the flame. The musicians start singing a nursery rhyme in Malayalam, and with each repetition, it increases in tempo. When it reaches top speed, they start shooting each other with their fingers and instrument beaters. The light fades on them and they shut up.*)

Scene 2

(*A small light, left stage, reveals the back of a man who rotates, and as he faces the audience, the facial mask reveals him to be Bhima. He continues his rotation smoothly, and when he next turns to face the audience he is another. The mask is different. It is the face of an adult man, dissatisfied, clever and sarcastic. The rotation continues, sometime revealing Bhima, sometimes the other. This is accompanied by percussion music. Each of the two characters has a special pattern of rhythms which signify him. After the fourth rotation, the other man, who is Duryodhana, lifts his leg and places it forcefully on a stool in front of him and slaps his thigh.*)

DURYODHANA:
> The first animal
> The first enemy,
> The first woman.
> All are precious.

(*He opens his mouth wide, crinkles up his face to give a huge soundless, devilish laugh. Then jumps onto the stool and sits in amarcha*) But when you killed the single wild boar, you became a man. (*At 'man', he jumps off the stool to fly in the air and land on the stool with his feet on the floor, his head and torso lowered. When he looks up, he is Bhima.*)

BHIMA: In my mind I feel love for Dhritarashtra's son; he, the single wild boar, is my enemy and a part of me. (*Bhima gets up from the stool in the Kathakali posture, his arms up in a victory posture. He slides forward on his feet as Kathakali actors do.*) Today, at Pramanakotti, we are friends! (*With 'friends', the actor changes his posture and mask sharply, to become Duryodhana. The transition is punctuated by a drum beat.*)

DURYODHANA: Mone [son] Bhima. The first drink is also very special. (*Quick transition to Bhima with a transition beat.*)

BHIMA: (*Flattered and trying to flatter*) My friend Duryodhana is very wise. But at my age? (*Transition to Duryodhana.*)

DURYODHANA: (*Sarcastic and provocative*) If you are afraid, don't. Drink is for those who are men. (*Quick transition to Bhima.*)

BHIMA: (*Confused*) I don't want to lose Duryodhana. (*Quick transition to Duryodhana.*)

DURYODHANA: (*Pleased and flattering.*) Your brother Yudhishthira is not brave; nor is he courageous. (*Goes down onto the floor to talk to Bhima as though he were two inches tall*) You are more capable. (*Quick transition to Bhima standing in his victory posture.*)

BHIMA: (*Flattered into speechlessness*) !!!!!!!!!!!!!!!!!!!! (*Transition to Duryodhana.*)

DURYODHANA: (*Slyly provocative*) Balarama is going to teach me the *gadha*. (*Quick transition to Bhima.*)

BHIMA: (*Delighted to begin with, then confused and upset*) Balarama is *my* mother's brother's son. (*Quick transition to Duryodhana.*)

DURYODHANA: (*Warming up and getting more provocative*) Do you know who is the strongest king? (*Quick transition to Bhima.*)

BHIMA: (*Happy and confident that his response is correct*) Jarasandha! (*Quick transition to Duryodhana.*)

DURYODHANA: (*Openly aggressive now*) No, my father Dhritarashtra. He has the strength of ten thousand masti elephants. (*Pause. Then quietly and with sinister intent*) I will get that strength. (*Quick transition to Bhima.*)

BHIMA: (*Singing out his words happily and with confidence, and dancing to their rhythm*) My father Vayudeva *is* strength. I will grow into that. (*Transition to Duryodhana.*)

DURYODHANA: (*Duryodhana takes his time to respond, then says quietly*) Do you believe these stories? (*He gives an evil, soundless laugh. Quick transition to Bhima.*)

BHIMA: (*In an aggressive posture*) Don't laugh! I am Bhimasena! Son of Vayu. (*Quick transition to Duryodhana.*)

DURYODHANA: (*Starts dancing and then, still dancing, says the following in time, rhythmically*)
For Yudhishthira, Dharma
For Bhima, Vayu
For Arjuna, Indra

(*Pause. Then in an abusive tone and with an aggressive stance*)
Your mother—could she find no better stories?
(*Quick transition to Bhima, who gasps and assumes the mask of horror. It stays for some time. He is in a chauk [half-sitting posture], and his torso sinks slowly into an amarcha after which he bows his head. He speaks to himself in an adult voice.*)

BHIMA: Duryodhana poisoned me. He tried to drown me. (*Raising his head to look at the sky and with tears in his voice*) Achindeva! When will I offer you my *bali*? (*Blackout and music.*)

Scene 3

(*Music from the end of the last scene. Ghatam and bells for a dance. It fades and the light comes on to show an amiable man, quite feminine, ready to dance. He has two dandiya dance sticks in his hands. It is Arjuna, or rather, Brhannala. He speaks of Bhima with great reverence and about himself with quiet modesty.*)

ARJUNA/BRHANNALA:
I love Bhima
One day he killed an animal
One day I killed an animal
He killed a single wild boar
I killed a deer
He killed after the game of hunt.
I killed during the game of hunt.
He killed in self-defence.

ARJUNA: (*Starts singing and dancing. He is joined by the musicians. He begins by singing a Gujarati folk tune, doing the steps of the dandiya ras.*)
Hey! Duryodhana
Don't play with Bhima!
He has come back from the Nagas
From the Nagas he has returned
He is my brother
He is our strength
Returned from the Nagas
With the strength of ten thousand masti elephants.
To protect his family
To protect his friends
To protect his people
He killed:
Hidimba,

Baka,
Jarasandha,
Anshuman.

(*At Anshuman, Arjuna runs out of steam and also forgets the next name on the list. So he goes to the musicians to check the script. Having located the next name he runs on to stage singing Anshuman. Then throwing away his sticks, he sings Dirghalochanan and starts up a Kathakali dance movement and number, singing the following names. He is joined by the musicians. The Kathakali includes the Kailashudharana at the end.*)

Dirghalochanan
Susena
Bhanusena
Keechakan
Kuntedi
Charuchitran

(*After the Kathakali piece is over. Arjuna turns to the audience and says*)

My brother Bhimasena killed these people also.

(*And he starts dancing in the Ottan Thullal style, singing the following names*)

Anuvindhan
Shukradeva
Bhanuman
Durjaya
Angan
Abhayan
Rudrakarma

(*Arjuna then pauses and exhaustedly calls out*)

Dushasanan

(*He collapses and sings the last name*)

Duryodhanan

(*And says with awe*)

Bhimasena is the strongest man on earth.

(*This announcement is followed by drums. There is a blackout during which the drums make a transition to Kathakali music. The actor returns to the stage with his pot of flame and scolds the musicians to make them stop. He then prepares to tell another story.*)

ACTOR: Our Bhimasena and Duryodhana, even after they grew up, never stopped their fighting. Every morning they would put on their alarm for five o'clock and as soon as they got out of bed, they would run towards each other and start fighting. But today they introduced some cathartic improvisations into their fight. Oooo! What is that? Today, while they were fighting they started to walk also. In their walk-fight they travelled all over the world. London, Paris, Amsterdam, New York, Punjab, Sindh, Gujarat, Maharashtra, Dravid, Uttkal, Vanga. When they reached Anga, D looked at B, B looked at D and they said together, 'Let's take a break.' So they broke.

After some time D started singing. (*The actor does a sarcastic rendering of the Bhima Suprabatham.*) So Bhima looked at Duryodhana and said, 'Duryodhnana, don't take a risk.' So D fell silent.

After some time they saw someone coming towards them. As they looked, the person came nearer and nearer and nearer. (*The actor's voice becomes more and more awestruck with each 'nearer' and he mimes seeing a very, very tall and big person, who he has to look up to.*) They saw a poor woman going towards the paddy fields. They said, 'Hey, hey, hey, you woman, you poor woman, you must tell us who is stronger. Is Bhimasena stronger than Duryodhana (*the actor points to himself as Bhimasena and the other as Duryodhana*) or is Bhimasena stronger than Duryodhana (*the actor points to the other as Bhimasena and at himself as Duryodhana*)? And the poor woman looked at them like this (*amused*). 'Aha! So you too want to know "who is the strongest man". (*Suddenly curt and serious*) 'I am very sorry. I have no time to waste on answering such trivial questions. (*At breathless speed*) Because, I have to go to the paddy fields and give this food to my husband, go back home and look after my children and my cows. I have no time. (*Pause.*) But I can do you a favour. You two get onto my palm and stay there. (*An easier rhythm for the following.*) I will go to the paddy field, give this food to my husband, when he has finished eating, I will repack the food basket and when I am walking back home I can tell you who is the strongest man.'

Now B was tired, D was tired. So they looked at each other and said in chorus: 'Agreed. Show your palm.' And the woman showed her palm. (*The actor stretches out his arm on the floor, with his palm facing upward.*) Now this is the palm. And here are Bhima and Duryodhana. (*The actor marks the distance between the palm and B and D, with his other hand. Two fingers of this hand stand for B and D. And when the two fingers move on the floor it is to show B and D walking.*) And they started to march towards the palm.

'Red salute! Red salute! Red salute! Red salute! Don't push. B first. B first. Red salute! Red salute! Red salute!' (*The actor shows B and D marching onto the woman's palm.*)

In this way the poor woman carried B and D and the food basket and started to walk towards the paddy field.

While she is walking towards the paddy field, let's have a look at what's happening on her palm. B and D can't stand each other. D looked at B. B looked at D. D gave a kick. B gave a bash. D took B's *gadha* and threw it out of the palm. (*Pause.*) The war began.

In the meantime our poor woman reached the paddy field, opened her food basket, gave the food to her husband, and while he ate, she looked around the paddy field and found lots of left-over jobs. She finished *all* these left-over jobs, came back to sit with her husband and started to talk to him about the global slow-down, economic cutbacks in the UK, double digit inflation in India, the corruption problems, environmental problems, nuclear energy problems and countless other problems. (*The actor ad-libs here using the current issues of the day.*) And she sorted out all these problems, repacked the food basket and started to walk back home.

While she was triumphantly walking back home, there was a call from her palm. 'Hey you cheat. You silly woman, you told us that you would tell us who is stronger. Is B still stronger than D, or is B still stronger than D?' So our poor woman looked at them like this (*amazement and contempt.*) 'You two are still stuck on that old problem? You have nothing better to do in your life? I am sad. I am furious. Do one thing, get out of my palm and stay off.' (*Actor mimes the woman wiping her palm of some filth.*) 'I have no time to waste on such issues.' (*The actor strikes a heroic pose.*) And in this way she walked towards her home. But what happened to B and D? As usual they continued their fight.

(*The actor puts out the flame and war drums take over. They continue even after the light comes on for the next scene.*)

Scene 4

The fight between Duryodhana and Bhima mimed in Kalaripayattu and accompanied by war drums.
   Duryodhana dies.
(*Blackout.*)

Scene 5

(*Light comes on to show a man in victory posture. He slowly crumbles and collapses to kneel on one knee. It is the adult Bhima without a mask.*)

BHIMA: I am the strongest man in the world

(*He jumps to face front still on one knee and speaks forcefully. But his hands are behind his back as though tied.*)
   I am the strongest man in the whole world.
(*He looks away, and then front again. He mimes the playing of a flute and says in a sinister voice.*)
   Krishna said to me, 'You killed all the sons of Dhritarashtra. Now you must kill Duryodhana.'
(*He drops his arms helplessly.*)
   And I killed him.
(*He mimes Duryodhana's posture in death. From there he rolls into the cross-legged sitting posture and mask of Yudhishthira.*)

YUDHISHTHIRA:
Manda!
That was unfair
That is not dharma
Remember he is a king.

(*Bhima in despair. His face takes on the mask of a soundless cry and his hands are together as though in prayer.*)

BHIMA: But I won the war for my brothers!

(*He drops his head and slowly his arms go behind his back again.*)
The night I killed Duryodhana—I felt a big emptiness in my mind.
(*He gets into a low amarcha, the posture of the boar. As he says the following lines, his head moves up to look ahead*)
The enemy who made me
The enemy who made me stronger
My first enemy
Was gone
I was very happy.

(*His face takes on the mask of a huge soundless cry. A musician gives voice to the cry musically. Bhima does a funeral dance, his face and body contorted in pain. At the end he sinks slowly onto his heels, his knees turned outward, his arms still behind his back. Slowly he looks up.*)
In my mind I feel love for Dhritarastra's son.
I won the war for the kingdom.
He won the war inside himself.

(*He rises slowly in a serpentine movement. His arms behind his back. When he reaches near standing position, his voice, face and body expressing anguish, he says*)
I am still Manda
I am still Vrigodara.

(*A slow inner transition from anguish to horror to intense focus. The transition is enabled by a light change.*)
Arjuna does not sleep at night, because he killed Karna

(*The focus is sharper, expressed through the energy of a fierce whisper. Then the energy gets overwhelming and expresses itself in the voice rising and ending in a shout. Then as the energy disperses with the rising voice, the arms loosen from behind the back and slowly spread out and then rise upward on the last line.*)
I too cannot sleep at night
Because Ashwathama still runs in the forest
Because Ashwathama still runs in the forest
Because Ashwathama still runs in the forest

(*Then the energy slowly fades into despair. And this expresses itself in the mask of the cry, the slow collapse of the body and the arms miming the taking on of a burden. Bhima walks with this burden on his back, barely able to move. He speaks as he walks, goading himself on.*)
I must kill my next enemy
I must prepare for the next war
I must always be the strongest man on earth

(*He pauses for a long time, looks slowly ahead and then asks, almost in a whisper*)
That is my dharma?

(*Blackout. The mizhavu plays a rhythm signifying preparation.*)
(*The actor lights the flame, sits in the Kalaripayattu Hanuman posture on the floor and tells a story. The mood is quieter and more serious than the previous two stories.*)

ACTOR:
Many years after the war, Bhimasena wanted to meet Vidura.
But Vidura had hidden himself away in a forest,
And every time Bhima tried to meet him,
He would escape into a more secret and mysterious part of the forest.
This game of hide-and-seek went on for a long time,
And the desire within Bhimasena grew stronger and stronger.
Then one day Bhima went deep into the forest,
Very deep

Into the heart of the forest.
There—
In a clearing
Naked and still
Stood Vidura,
Against a tree.
The two looked at each other silently for a long time.
The man of Knowledge and the man of Power.
Then Bhima stepped forward, and Vidura embraced him.
The man of Power fainted.

(*The actor puts out the flame. A conch is sounded three times.*)

Scene 6

(*Light comes on to Bhima. He is in the same posture as at the start of the play. But there is an angavastra on his shoulders and he is old. He straightens slowly. There is an equanimity in him.*)

BHIMA:
The Mahaprasthana.
In heaven, the second chair will remain empty,
I am not Jeetendriya.
I do not have a right to sit on that chair.

(*Slowly, as he speaks, he looks up towards the direction of the sky, his head turning sideways to take in all of it.*)
My eyes are turned to the green valley of the earth in front of me.
My eyes are looking for the wild boar inside the forest.

(*Slowly he lowers his head and turns his gaze to look straight ahead.*)
My eyes are looking for the wild boar inside myself.

(*Slowly, ritualistically, he takes off the angavastra, and holds it before him.*)
I must offer now the *bali* of the wild boar.

(*Still in ritual mode, he gathers the angavastra and places it on the floor before him. He pauses there for some time. And with a smile in his voice he says*)

No I am not Jeetendriya

I am not yet ready for the Mahaprasthana

(*The conch sounds. Bhima takes time to complete his ritual. When he is done, he picks up the bundle which was the angavastra, deliberately steps over the ritual space, walks forward and slowly offers up the bundle in his hands, holding it skyward and looking in that direction. There is a slight pause. Then he brings his head down and looks ahead.*)

The sutas say—stories never end!

The End

Impressively Funny

A Review*

KEVAL ARORA

Veenapani Chawla's theatre company, Adishakti, recently gave at the IIC (India International Centre, Delhi) a single performance of *Impressions of Bhima*, with Vinay Kumar K J as Bhima, Gautam Mitra the vocalist-percussionist, and M Natesh on lights.

When Adishakti last came to Delhi in 1992 with *A Greater Dawn*, a dramatisation of Sri Aurobindo's epic poem *Savitri*, the thin audience at the Kamani had been mesmerised by its

---

* Earlier published as 'Impressively Funny' in *The Pioneer* on 25 April 1996.

austere, yet vibrantly graceful combination of music, chants, stylised movement, physical presence, rhythm and colour. The media too had celebrated in tones of awe the eclectic array of performance systems that had gone into the production: Kathakali, Kalaripayattu, Koodiyattam, Buddhist and Gregorian chants, Manipuri death music, T'ai Chi, and quite a bit else.

It was obvious that Veenapani's interest in these systems, for all the rigour evident in training and rehearsal, was neither arcane nor scholarly. Appropriating, modifying, and improvising upon elements from within these systems that fit into her vision of theatre, where a 'new movement vocabulary' challenges the traditional primacy of the spoken word, Veenapani works by an intuitive rather than a learned feel of the theatrical act. The synthesis that her theatre effects in its best moments, can of course be theorised, but such theorising is the consequence of the project and not its intention.

And yet there is a real danger of her production's impressive genealogy setting up barriers to one's enjoyment. It is unlikely that her audiences are equally conversant with the several traditions from which Veenapani borrows fluently, a discomfort that can be only compounded by the production's tendency to flaunt its pedigree with sonorous self-consciousness.

It is in this context that *Impressions of Bhima*, an hour-long show with just 10 minutes of text, sprang a delightful surprise. The reliance on traditional performance systems was still there, but these were encased in a puckish humour that coloured the performance with a mischievous lightness which was totally unexpected.

The humour was superbly paced—stealing in craftily, then going over the top in improvisatory abandon before returning to the solemnity of the opening. The absence of a prefatory note on the production helped. Much of *Bhima's* sparkle derived from the fact of an unprepared audience having to discover its way by itself.

Bracketed by an invocation in Sanskrit of Bhima's lineage and qualities (Mitra modelled his chant on Subbulakshmi's *Suprabhatam*), the play is a montage of five episodes. Each provides one impression to a deconstructive portrait of the Pandava whose 'strength' is so enshrined in popular perception that it seems to have set the seal on interpretations of this warrior hero. Veenapani recovers from beneath this mask of masculinity a sensibility that, both in spite of and because of its simple and zestful view of life, is capable of experiencing tortured agonies of conscience and loss. Of the three rites that mark Bhima's initiation into manhood ('my first animal, my first enemy, my first woman'), she fleshes out only the second, while completely ignoring the last.

'Fighting and quarrelling, quarrelling and fighting' with Duryodhana comes so naturally to Bhima that, having vanquished Duryodhana, he is less troubled by Yudhishthira's accusation ('you killed a King') than by 'the emptiness in my mind'. Bhima's assertion of happiness is searingly undercut by the gnarled tension of his arms and his cry of pain hauntingly echoed by the singer, as he wanders away, 'looking for the wild boar inside myself'.

This simple tale acquired its theatrical energy partly from careful selection of Kalaripayattu and Kathakali elements, but primarily from the deployment of humour at various levels. Bhima's insightful commentary (impersonating Yudhishthira as a gumless old moralist, and swiping at Delhi's 'subaltern theory people' being 'like this only'), or a confused one (mixing up his role with Duryodhana's); Vinay Kumar's incompetent narration/ acting (forgetting his lines, scolding the musician and the lightsman), or wicked tongue-in-cheek dancing (flinging his finger out to get the *hasta mudra* right, complaining of pain in his feet with all that leaping); Mitra's scatting of the phrase 'Bhim Boy' to the tune of *Ek do teen*; and above all, Vinay's hilarious mix of contemporary phraseology with a dysfunctional syntax were some of the reasons why *Bhima* pulsated with gay, irreverent energy.

This was entirely Vinay's and Veenapani's doing. In M.T. Vasudevan Nair's novel *Randamuzhan*, which is said to have inspired *Bhima*, the comic tone is so completely absent, that the relation between the two works is more a story of origins than influences.

'I wanted to break through laughter the sanctity that surrounds everything, the theatre, even the subversive element itself. So for Delhi we chose subaltern theory. In France it was structuralism and Barthes,' explained Veenapani. However, humour, especially subversive humour, needs both a vantage point and a tangible thrust to work effectively. With its near-anarchic swipes not consolidating into a coherent critique, *Bhima* lacked both. Scattered in several directions, its humour was theatrically funny, but it had neither the polemical nor the textual rigour of subversion. The best that can be said of *Bhima*'s humour is that it embodied, through sheer performance energy, the *joie de vivre* of the eponymous hero.

Is this a momentary phase in Adishakti's theatre, or will we see more experiments in a lighter vein? With its latest production titled *So What's New*, the answer seems obvious.

Brhannala

Performance Text

VEENAPANI CHAWLA

B*rhannala* was first performed in June 1998. It did 24 shows over the next seven years in all the Indian metros as well as in Germany, Singapore, New York, London, and Edinburgh. This play and *Khandava Prastha Agniahooti*, which could be performed only once for unforeseen practical reasons, were the outcome of the grant Chawla had received from the India Foundation for the Arts in 1997 for a project entitled 'A Dialogue between Koodiyattam and Contemporary Theatre'. Her collaborators in the project were Usha Nangyar and Vinay Kumar.

Vinay Kumar in *Brhannala*.
Photograph courtesy of S. Anwar.

Scene 1

Savyasachin and Brhannala

(*The stage is largely bare except for the musicians, who sit on the left and right sides of it. At the back, barely visible, there is a black puppet stand.*

Softly, the rumblings of a gong. A light comes on slowly, lighting up the left side of a semi-naked man sitting with his back to the audience in the centre of the stage. He looks armless. The rumbling gong grows a little louder. A single melodious note is struck softly on a xylophone. The man's left shoulder heaves and his arm seems to grow out of his shoulder, first as a stump and then the forearm is seen opening out in a sinuous, undulating, curved movement. From the beginning, the heaving of the arm is accompanied by the sound of a clarinet which emphasises, aurally, the breath pangs/birth pangs of the arm. The arm moves upward. The sound of the gong, clarinet and xylophone fade as the arm starts plucking the invisible strings of a vichitra veena. *Soft sound of strings being plucked. Then the arm falls down. The stage darkens and the rumbling gong starts off again, gathering volume incrementally, as the light fades on and illuminates the right side of the figure. As his right arm appears, the clarinet joins the gong and follows the angular, linear movement of the arm in its show of brute strength. Both arms then rise up together as though carrying an object offered up towards the sky. They mime the action of discarding the object/the throwing off of Gandiva, the bow. A top light comes on to light the seated figure. The gong and clarinet are silent, but there is a crescendo of cymbals on a higher treble note than the gong. As this fades, the strings are heard again. The man's arms slowly come down on either side and pause, outstretched from side to side. They figure a single ripple which runs from his left to right, uniting the two arms in a single movement. The entire visual expresses Arjuna as Savyasachin, who is ambidextrous.*

The man's arms drop and he turns his head slowly to look back towards the audience.)

ARJUNA/SAVYASACHIN: Give me something to hold.[1]

(He turns back. His movements are marked by beats on the mizhavu. There is more light. Through a series of undulating snake-like movements, he rises to stand. Then he turns very slowly and gracefully, as would a dancer, towards the audience to face it in a three-fourth profile and looks at them coyly from the corner of his eye. Brhannala has entered the court of Virata. The light suggests a doorway.

Brhannala raises her hand as though to smell an invisible rose and sneezes violently. The sneeze alerts a sleeping guard, played by the same actor, who is shocked out of his wits. He leaps in fright and looks at her in horror. Brhannala's movements on stage are sketched by the gaze of those observing her on stage, as well as by the sound of anklets throughout this scene. A haughty courtier spots her and expresses disgust at her appearance. Bhima who is there already, sees her and waves out to her. As Brhannala sways forward, she is spotted by Uttarakumar who is smitten. He dances her into the court singing the following song accompanied by the sound of Brhannala's anklets.)

---

[1] Dharma means literally that which one lays hold of and which holds things together—the law, the norm, rule of nature, action, and life.

UTTARAKUMAR: (*Sings*)
    She came into my father's court
    Like the leader of a herd of elephants.
    Of enormous size and exquisite beauty
    And hips as large as the banks of a river.

(*Music continues into the blackout and opens the next scene. The sound of anklets increases and is joined by the playing of a ghatam. Brhannala sings a song in the darkness.*)

Scene 2

Brhannala Tells a Story in the Court of Virata

BRHANNALA: (*Singing in the dark*)
    I sing, I dance, I play music
    I tell stories
    I am Brhannala, Brhannala, Brhannala
    I am Brhannala
    Son nor daughter
    Without father, without mother,
    I am Brhannala, Brhannala, Brhannala

(*By the last line of the song, the stage lightens and she is seen centre-stage, with her back to the audience, singing and dancing. When the song ends, she turns slowly and walks forward in a modified Chhau chali.*)
    Pandu, pandu,
    Once upon a time, there was a tiger (*Brhannala takes on the Kalaripayattu pose for a tiger*), and one day he met someone on the road. (*She sways to the right and morphs into a dog, who whines and barks and then raises one leg to pee. A dog whistle reinforces his whines. Then with a leap, the actor goes from the dog posture into the tiger posture, essentially a Kalaripayattu amarcha. The tiger stretches voluptuously to the sound of two sticks being rubbed together. He has a very happy and contented look on his face. He sings and giggles to himself as he settles into a squatting posture. Then he sees someone whose attention he tries to catch with hand gestures and waves. He calls*

out, speaking in a feminine voice. Both the dog and the tiger reorient their faces. They have characteristic facial masks which identify them, as well as different voices. The tiger has a high, feminine voice and the dog has a deep voice.)

TIGER: Hello, hello ... dog? ... hello dog, dogetta look me, look me, dogetta look me, look me, look me, look me, look me ... (*Each repetition of 'look me' becomes more insistent. The actor leaps into the dog posture. All transitions are accompanied by musical flourishes or beats.*)

DOG: Yare ... tigera ... hello tiger how are you? How, how (*the 'how' becomes a howl*), how, are you?

(*The actor leaps into the tiger posture.*)

TIGER: (*Laughs*) Discontented. (*Slides into the dog posture immediately.*)

DOG: Why ma, why discontented?

(*Transition.*)

TIGER: (*Sighing sadly*) Dogetta, life is making a bonsai out of me ... cutting and chopping all my creative expression.

(*The tiger looks up at an imagined tree, tries to clamber onto it, then leaps back into the squatting posture.*) All I want is a little bit of growth.
(*Transition. The dog leaps happily and laughs loudly.*)

DOG: Tigere neengaluma [You too? He sings an old MGR song which means 'There is no team like you and me'] ... Neeyum nanuma, kanna neeyum nannuma! Tigere you and I, very good team. (*Laughs and does a little jump on the spot. More seriously*) Tigere, *athu enna sonna?* Where were you coming from, ha?

(*The dog leaps and transforms into the tiger, who laughs hysterically and uncontrollably. The music pit goes berserk, blowing whistles and pipes and drums and other ridiculous instruments. The tiger stops laughing suddenly, looking very confused and dazed.*)

TIGER: Where am I ... What am I (*looks down at his genitals*) ... Who am I ... I ...

(*Light dawns on him as he connects the sound of I to Chennai.*) ... Chennai! (*Said with rising confidence and then mad joy*) Dogetta, Chennai! Dogetta Chennai! (*He leaps across the stage and becomes the dog on landing. He looks puzzled.*)

DOG: Chennaia? Kekkaveilliye ... *leftile pona Kovai, rightile pona Madurai*, where is Chennai? Never heard about it. (*He turns to the tiger*) Mm, route *pathukkalam*? [Should we see the route? He turns back to his calculations.] A square is equal to B square. Square *ille Sachin*; then Sachin should take 4.3 per over, then India can beat Australia, Zimbabwe, New Zealand, Pakistan ... Pakist. (*With that, he knows how to go forward in his investigation and he asks the tiger excitedly*) Tigere, which countries did you pass on the way?

(*Musicians go berserk again as the tiger jumps into place, hysterical with laughter.*)

TIGER: That is so easy—that is so easy ... bullatta ... bullate ... royal enfield machismo. (*He mimes riding on a bike, and makes it look like a dance.*)

First I walked down the mountain ... on the other side of the mountain is the Kanafussi forest na? There I met some of my old friends they called me for lunch ... but I tiger stayed on for tea. (*Then, as though in response to a query from the audience*) What? (*Disgustedly*) Nothing much—we all just went behind Mary's little lamb ... and here I am on the road.

(*He rises up on his trembling hind legs with great excitement and collapses into the dog's posture. The music goes berserk again. The dog is hysterical with laughter as well.*)

DOG: (*Congratulatory and admiring*) Tigere that is quite a distance you travelled. Very nice, very nice, in fact very ni ... (*The dog suddenly hears a whistle and he sways onto his hind legs, back to audience and gets into Brhannala's swaying walk. He then dissolves into his normal posture, howls and whines. The tiger is then shown watching him with alarm and interest.*)

TIGER: I say dog, what is it like being a dog?

DOG: (*The dog gets into posture with a wail*) Horrible! Horrible! Tigere, there is no variety, no prospects—today pup, tomorrow dog, day after tomorrow dead dog. Dead dog. It's a dog's life. (*A dog flute wails. The dog leans confidingly towards the tiger*) Tigere, do you know man? No? Wonderful creature. It stands on its hind legs. Not only that, man has prospects.

TIGER: (*Very excited, but then realises he doesn't know the meaning of prospects.*) What are prospects?

DOG: That is when your right eye looks straight ahead into the future.

TIGER: (*The tiger leaps with excitement.*) Let me look into my future ... I have never seen my future. (*He goes cross-eyed trying to see his future.*) Nice nose. Dogetta, I can only see my nose (*His nose twitches*) ... lambs, lambs, Mary's lambs! (*Excitedly*) My nose can smell my past!

DOG: (*Leaps into posture. Very excited, laughing uncontrollably and singing nonsense*) So can I, So can I, So am I, So am I, So do I, So do I!! My memories have a wonderful smell.

TIGER: Is that so? Dogetta please sing me your memories; please, please.

DOG: (*Trying to shrug off the tiger. Very irritated*) Ha tigere, don't force me.

TIGER: (*Begins by pleading and then getting ferocious.*)

DOG: (*Extremely irritated with the tiger*) Tigere *please*! Don't do that! Stay there.

(*Uncomfortable pause during which the dog thaws and tries to placate the tiger.*)

I can't smell very well these days Tigere ... my memories are all mixed up with Man's memories—(*Pause. Then giving in completely*) If you want I can sing you Brhannala Sir's Memories. Brhannala Sir's? ... Memory? ... Can I? ha ha ha!

(*He makes himself comfortable centre-stage, and asks the musicians to join him. They sit around him. There is play and conversation between them. He gives them instructions on the taal and then starts howling/ singing. The musicians play on the ghatam, sticks and the stage floor.*)

DOG:
There was a god called Prediction.
Time was his father,
Space was his mother
Memory was his sister ... and she looked back in time.

'Creation is the proof of our parent's hand
From chaos they made something terribly grand.'
Prediction looked ahead into the future—
And saw the great need for a brand new creature.

He used rainwater, rich loam and fertile sand,
And called this confabulation Wo An Man.
He gave it two big heads, four arms and four legs,
And then sat down and had ten Patiala pegs.

But the king of gods was terribly afraid
Of this potent creature Prediction had made
'Split it down, split it down the middle!' he cried,
'Call one half man and the other woman!' he sighed.
'Let each half waste its time and its energy,
Seeking the other, endlessly, fruitlessly.'

So Wo An Man became a divided creature,
With one head, two legs and two arms in the future.
But Prediction loved his new creation.
He tried to help in its evolution.

He taught it 123-ABCDE;
Special gifts not shared by any other kind.
They came from an appreciation of Time.

(*Dog rises on his hind legs and starts dancing.*)

Then there was a great leap in evolution,
A divided brain caused a revolution,
Wo An Man's brain was now split in two,
Out sprang Wisdom, a goddess new.

She had strategy, skill and military head,
She could look behind she could look ahead.
She could use the past to deal with future threat.
Though from a divided creature she had come,
She herself was both Woman and Man in One.

(*Pause. The dog gets irritated with his audience of musicians. He barks at them and chases them away. A very faint slow beat starts up and another joins it in an off-beat. The dog starts speaking, honouring the rhythm of the percussion.*)

But because Wo An Man's brain was now in two
Each part developed a different hue—

(*He moves his body languorously, he speaks languorously. The light has changed and his body's movements try to break the expanse of space thus exposed.*)

One was about—

The moon, muse, music, magic, madness, memory, myth and metaphor,

(*The dog sits erect. The body's lines clean. He speaks his lines into a rhythm he establishes by slapping on his thighs. This rhythm is an off-beat to the musicians' rhythm*)

The other about—

The sun, science, speech, sentence, sequence and seriousness;

And in this state of division and duality,
When half was left and half was right,
One side was rooted in space and saw everything *all-at-once*

(*Softly into the already existing rhythm, a snare drum starts playing a war march.*)

The other side was rooted in time and saw everything *one-at-a-time.*

(*The war beat gets overwhelming, and the dog rises in horror and turns his back to the audience to hear it more clearly. He covers his ears and shouts.*)

Brhannala, there is a war!

(*The war music builds up, continues through the blackout, connecting this scene with the next.*)

Scene 3

Drona and His Students

(*War music from the last scene peters out and there emerges from under it, the sound of a metronome ticking away the time. Light fades on to a figure in the right backstage corner. He is an old man in silhouette and his back is to the audience. A drum rolls and the musicians start off a double rhythmic* vaitari *[vocal expression of rhythms], which gives the sense of thoughts rumbling in the old man's mind. He uses his hands and fingers rhythmically as though working out a problem in his mind. He jerks to face the left side of the stage with a drum roll. There is another roll and he faces front, continually waving his hands to the* vaitari *and the metronome. We see his face now and his eyes are moving rhythmically to the beat of his thoughts, giving the look of a man working out problems in his mind. Then the* vaitari *stops abruptly and the old man speaks, with the rhythm of a teacher underlying his speech. He continues to use his hand rhythmically. At one point he summons a student and evicts him from the class in this manner.*

This is Drona instructing the Kuru children in the science of war.

In the course of the scene he moves forward one step at a time, almost dance-like in his movement. By the end of the scene, he has crossed the stage space to the left downstage corner. The light changes with his movement, lighting up only him as he moves across the stage. The aim in this scene is to bring out the temporal processes of the left brain.)

DRONA: In the course of evolution, the eye of the bird developed into a spectacular organ of vision. Living too high, off the ground, the bird could no longer find its food through smell.

(*Drona moves a step forward*)
So—retina.

The retina of its eye developed cones in its centre. (*Drona, looks around at his students, focusing on each one by slightly squeezing his eyes in a squint. This is accompanied by a rhythm slapped out by the musicians on their thighs. Drona moves a step to left as though facing a student there.*) Nakula, cones allow a creature to see colour and to see details.

(*He moves forward one step with the next word.*)
Birds.

Birds can abstract a single detail from a whole picture and scrutinise it separately from the rest.

(*Pause. Metronome stops as does everything else. Drona looks up with his eyes, as though observing something on a tree in front of him. Then he turns to his left side and looks down at someone sitting near him. He makes a sound in anticipation of catching a student off-guard with his next question.*)
Arjuna what can *you* see in that tree, ha?

(*An explosion of light and sound as Arjuna leaps into a typical martial arts posture. His eyes move with rhythmic focus like a bird's, up the imaginary tree, and he calls out joyously.*)

ARJUNA: The eye of the bird.

(*There is an explosion of drums as before. Arjuna leaps in sync with these and shoots the bird's eye. He falls back into the earlier posture. Drona rises up from that position and his head is moving in time to a vaitari, as though he is really enjoying his thoughts. His words break into the vaitari and halt it. He moves forward.*)

DRONA: If the nose played a part in the discovery of the past, the eye gave birth to the future. It saw the world in sequence. It moved from what *was*, to what *is*, then demanded, *what next?*

(*With each of the phrases, he moves a step in the direction of the left side corner of the stage. The transitions are accompanied by the roll of a drum. At 'what next' his right leg remains suspended in* mid-air. Then he turns to his left again to address an imaginary seated Arjuna)

This is how the future was born.

(Again there is an explosion of drums, and Arjuna leaps into position and shoots an arrow. He waits for it to hit its target. It takes a long time and he gets impatient and disappointed. He collapses into a sitting position on the floor. After his arrow hits the target, he turns with urgency and addresses an imaginary Bhima next to him. His words are accompanied by rhythms slapped by the musicians on their thighs.)

ARJUNA: Bhimettan, if my arrow had an eye like the bird, it could find out its prey and chase it into the future. (He turns respectfully to Drona) Acharya, what was Ekalvya's secret?

(A gong sound fills the air and a didgeridoo accompanies it. Drona rises in slow motion and describes a circle with his arms. His movement and voice anticipate that of Siva's in the next scene. So far, he has spoken in the voice of an old man. Now it is young and strong.)

DRONA: Your arrow must hit its target at the moment it leaves your hand. Time must stand still for your arrow, then it will have power over the future.

ARJUNA: How can I make time stand still?

DRONA: (Drona becomes himself) That is a question you must ask Siva.

(The musicians play a damaru and other percussion instruments join in.)

Scene 4

Arjuna Goes to the Himalayas to Get the Pasupata from Siva

(A deep gong interrupts the fading damaru. It strikes three times and resonates into the scene which follows. A blue light comes on off centre-stage on the right hand side. Siva is seen balancing on one leg and assuming the Nataraja posture of dance in slow motion, his movement flowing. Light fades and there is a roll of drums at the end of which *a yellow light comes on in the same place to show Arjuna with his back to the audience doing a rhythmic martial dance accompanied by percussion. The light, movement and sound of both scenes are in sharp contrast, and the two scenes seek to establish extremes. The light fades on Arjuna and the gong resonates again, the blue light comes on Siva again, rising up and playing cricket in very slow motion as he speaks the following lines.)*

SIVA:

When you can see the three faces of time, with the eye of complete union
Time will stand still and you will have power over the future.
Your arrows will fly at the speed of light, but they must be as light as light.
For that you must explore the formula, which can convert mass into energy.

(Blackout, roll of drums. Yellow light comes on to show Arjuna facing audience and doing his staccato, rhythmic dance to percussion. He pauses abruptly to ask)

ARJUNA: How do I see with the eye of complete union?

(Blackout. Gong again. Blue light fades onto Siva standing in a languorous posture. He starts dancing in slow motion, with a flowing, non-rhythmic motion. The gong fades into strings and, as he dances, he says)

SIVA:

Savyasachin, you shoot arrows with your right hand and your left hand,
Use your left-hand knowledge, which makes you Brhannala, to understand time through space. Become me—Ardhanariswara.

(The strings take over completely from the gong, and Siva continues to dance, his movement slowing and deepening whenever a string vibrates for a longer duration. At irregular intervals, the chime of a manjira is heard. Slowly, almost imperceptibly, a rhythm enters it as it does Siva's dance. Unobtrusively, a yellow light enters. The audience must

witness the middle ground of slow change as the dance moves from one extreme to the other. Then the rhythm becomes clearer, heavier, and the flowing feminine dance gradually becomes a martial dance. Arjuna turns his back to the audience as he continues Siva's movements in their martial extreme. At the crescendo, he takes on the posture of one doing penance and a conch cuts through the rest of the sound. Blackout. The gong strikes five times through the blackout.)

Scene 5

En Route to Kurukshetra

(*The light falls on the tiger who looks like his head has been mounted on a wall. He has a hibiscus flower behind one ear. After the light settles, he starts giggling, then speaking, then moving. And we realise that, but for the head, the rest of him is hidden behind a puppet screen.*)

TIGER: I am not dead! I am cheating!

(*Laughs and dances with his head. Music starts up and he sings*)
    Many, many, years ago, a tiger always had the choice
    Of colour he would like to be;
    Some choose black others choose yellowy…!

(*As the song ends, the tiger hears a distorted dog bark. He is startled.*)

TIGER:
    Who is that?
    That is who?
    Who is that?

(*He disappears behind the screen and the dog comes up barking. He does not have a hibiscus flower behind his ear.*)

DOG: Who's that who is saying 'who's that' to me? (*Familiar music which the dog associates with the tiger.*) Tiger? Tigere, where have you been?

(*He transforms into the tiger, flower and all.*)

TIGER: Mm, where are we now?

(*Ducks behind the screen and transforms into the dog. This happens throughout the scene, the dog changing into the tiger behind the puppet screen and vice versa.*)

DOG: Smells like Delhi, it really has a bad smell.

TIGER: Oh what a mess! What a mess! Dogetta how did we get here?

DOG: Tigere, you said you like travelling, so enjoy it now!

TIGER: I will and I want my prospects. (*Speaking like a politician at a rally*) Remember we tigers are becoming an extinct species, so we want our prospects! (*Turning on the dog ferociously*) And once again remember, I am discontented.

(*The two disappear behind the screen and there is much sound and fury and we can see bits of the dog being thrown up. Finally a toy dog is flung from behind the screen and it lands on a musician's instrument. The dog pops up from behind the screen, his head covered with toy stuffing.*)

DOG: Oho, Tigere you want your prospects ha?

TIGER: Yes I think there is a future in that.

DOG: OK then let's go and find Wo An Man.

TIGER: The creature which stands on its hind legs? I love it. Dogetta, hold my hand and talk to me while we walk.

(*Light fades. A ghatam starts playing a rhythm, and we hear a song sung by the tiger. The words consist of abuses in Tamil: pati/female dog; thendi/beggar; naye/dog. Finally light comes on to show the tiger sitting front left. Close by is the toy dog, on top of a percussion instrument. Tiger address the toy.*)

TIGER: Dogetta I am in a singing mood, may I sing you my memories? Yes?!

(*Addressing the musicians*) All of you, come and sit around me— like in the last scene remember? And then I'll sing. Ok, start. (*The tiger starts clapping a beat. After some time he realises no one has joined him.*) What is the matter? (*Looking around*) What is the problem? (*Shocked and angry whisper at the silent uncooperative musicians*) What are you doing? The audience is waiting! (*The musicians are silent. Then, one by one, they respond with offensive music.*)

TIGER: *Please* come. *Please.* Alright don't come! I'll sing alone. (*Threatening*) And then if I sing two times, it is like five times. (*Giggles.*) So better I sing one time only. (*Does a voice warm up.*) That's enough. (*A soft beat begins, and he starts singing*)
One young tiger we are told
Got tired of being yellow gold
He concentrated all day long
And sang the tiger witch's song
He practised till he learned the knack
Of changing yellow fur to black.

Very nice! Very nice! (*Applauding himself. The musicians mimic him. As this dies down the sound of the metronome is heard. Pause. The atmosphere changes. There is a sense of dread and anxiety in the air.*)

TIGER: (*Troubled*) Dogetta, how long is it since we started remembering again?

DOG: (*Pause*) As long as the road from Delhi to this place.

TIGER: So what is this place? It really has a bad smell.

DOG: This is the place where Man plays with his prospects.

(*The tiger is overwhelmed. He speaks with rising excitement.*)

TIGER:
Will I meet Man?

(*The tiger starts rising with each question, till he is standing on his hind legs*)
Will it stand on its hind legs?
And the prospects?
Will I meet my prospects?

(*Starts dancing and jumping*) I want to see my prospects—(*Gasps as he catches sight of someone in front*) I can see. I can see Man. I love you Man. I want to become you. I am coming—(*The sound of a shot. The metronome halts. The tiger is hit and collapses slowly. He dies. Lights fade. The dog howls. Blackout. Soft crying and wailing flutes.*)

Scene 6

At Kurukshetra

(*Faint light comes on to a figure sitting where the tiger was, in the last scene. He is sitting in the dog's posture, crouched over in grief. He raises his head slowly and he is howling soundlessly. We realise it is Arjuna when he speaks.*)

ARJUNA: (*Dazed*) Abhimanyu dead. (*Remembering*) Beautiful smiling eyes.

(*Arjuna jumps into the tiger posture, sticks his tongue out cheekily. He is Abhimanyu now. Then he gets back into the dog posture as Arjuna admonishes Abhimanyu for playing cricket near the railway track. A flashback.*)

ARJUNA: Abhi vedu po. Venda Abhi. Railway track—cricket—venda. Abhimanyu.

(*Arjuna gets up to chase Abhimanyu. He goes into slow motion in the chase. Lights change. A flute starts playing. Arjuna's hand drops onto Abhimanyu's shoulder, he morphs into an old man happily being led by a little boy. He moves thus towards the left stage. Suddenly, a strong drum beat, and Abhimanyu disappears, leaving Arjuna with seeking and outstretched hand. Arjuna comes back to the present and turns front looking at his hand. He is front stage, left.*)

There is no future. (*Agonised*) The heroes of tomorrow, they died,
So that five old men could live.

(*The mizhavus start up. Arjuna goes into a grief-stricken martial dance, and then bends as though to pick up a very, very heavy object with his right hand. He lifts it up with difficulty above his head. Waits. Then throws it over his head with ease. The percussion stops abruptly. Bereft, he squats and addresses someone in front of him.)*

Give me something to hold.

Gandiva has slipped from my hand.

(Sudden shift into a laughing child.)

They call me Savyasachin.

I shoot arrows with my right hand and my left hand. (*Pause. Voice becomes that of a man.*) Which hand was it that killed Karna? (*Pause. He starts shaking his finger at the figure in front of him and builds up to a violent emotion*)

My mind has no belief in Gandiva.

Give me something *else* to hold.

(Distracted by the sound of fire, he looks towards it.)

On the banks of the river, someone puts fire to the torn clothes of a soul.

(His gesture questions the why of this. He faces front and reinforces the question through the gesture and then puts it into words)

Why this world of battle? Of each breath, which is a breath of death? Why at every step forward something is crushed, broken— (*He howls the dog howl. Light changes and the sound of anklets is heard. Arjuna turns to look over his shoulder and sees Brhannala, hips swaying with her back to the audience. She calls out as though to a child who is crying. She turns and bends forward, from waist down, to match the child's height, the one she is addressing.*)

BRHANNALA: Arade? Arjuna kutti? Va, va. Arra ru, ru.

(She takes the child in her lap and starts singing a lullaby. At the same time, a musician chants the 10 names of Arjuna, sung to children when they are frightened, to give them his courage. Both the lullaby and the 10 names come to an end simultaneously and Brhannala speaks to the child in her lap, telling him a story.)

Arjuna. Three birds, mother, father and their baby flew over the ocean to a warm country for the winter.

In the middle of their flight, baby bird grew tired and fell into the waves.
The parent birds cried out to it, they tried to help it, but there was no sight or sound of it. So they flew back to the shore from which they had come, and stood there. Paralysed with grief.
After some time, they started to dig a hole.
When the hole was big enough to their minds, they went back to the ocean and picked up a few drops of it in their beaks.
Then they came back and emptied the water into the hole.

They went back and came, went back and came.
Trying to empty the ocean.
And their action was full of power.

Then one day they went up,
high,
very high,
higher than they had ever been.
From there,
they saw with the eye of complete union—the eye that sees everything-all-at-once.
Time stood still.
And they had no grief.

(*Strings played by musicians.*)
So joyfully they went back to their task of unveiling the ocean.
And their action was full of creative power.

Arra ru-u-u.
(*Strings. Blackout. Strings continue through the blackout.*)

Scene 7

The Union of Polarities

(*The same spot at which the play began. Light silhouettes an armless man standing in* chauk *with his back to the audience. He turns and opens his arms out. There is a ripple through them before they fall to his side. He moves forward one step at a time in a Chhau chali to the front of the stage as he speaks. He pauses now and then. The light changes at each step.)*

ARJUNA:
They call me Savyasachin,
And I have something to hold.

I was asked at Kurukshetra;
'Savyasachin, do you want the wealth of a thousand cows with gold rings around their horns,
Or do you want existence beyond Time and beyond Space?'
But what do I chose?
For the two are one.

Krishna said to me
'Let it be known Savyasachin, you are one half of my body,
We two are one.'

I become in Time and Time is a Man,
I exist in Space and Space is a Woman,
The two are one.

(He squats front stage and speaks intimately to the audience)
The world is born at each moment,
And each moment is one still moment of now.
I hold this moment carefully in my hand, for it is Vasudeva,
And there is no grief in me.

The End

Brhannala

Two Liminal Moments*

VEENAPANI CHAWLA

There are two moments in the *Mahabharata*, related by a concept and its impact. The concept is Brhannala and the impact is Arjuna's experience at Kurukshetra. How are these two moments connected? How does the concept of Brhannala impact Arjuna at Kurukshetra?

At the outset I would like to draw attention to the liminality of these moments in Arjuna's life. Both are periods of transition,

* Previously a paper presentation at 'The Conceptual World of the Mahabharat' seminar held at the Indian Institute of Advanced Study, Shimla, in June 2011.

where known rules of behaviour have been abandoned; and both are periods pregnant with the potentiality of alternative modes of being and becoming.

What are these potential alternatives to the old, which lie inherent in the concept of Brhannala and which impact Arjuna at Kurukshetra?

At Kurukshetra, Arjuna is forced to confront the universe as it really is without the veil of ethical illusion, and he is terrified. The vision of the *Vishwarupa* or the World Spirit as Time the Destroyer, which comes as a response to his search for an alternative, is initially even more terrifying. For it reflects his particular problem. He sees its destructive form—the very aspect he is running away from. And the World Spirit says to him, 'I, as Time, have come to destroy the old structures and build up new ones.'

And ultimately Arjuna is soothed, for he can accommodate the World Spirit's intention within himself. He can see himself as a part of the *Vishwarupa*, who has no beginning, middle and end. He can see reality with the eye of complete union.

In 1998, I created a theatre production called *Brhannala* in which my attempt was to show that Arjuna's ability to see with the eye of complete union came from his Brhannala self. Through a discussion of the play I shall indicate how I arrived at this conclusion.

The performance opens with an image of Arjuna as Savyasachin translated simply as one who is ambidextrous and can use both his left hand which is the feminine in him, and his right hand, which is the male in him. Thus the image created by the actor, with his back to the audience, was of a man who grows first his left arm and then his right arm. The left arm appears sinuously in a feminine *lasya* movement and moves upward to mime the act of playing on a string instrument, perhaps the veena. The right arm emerges in a *tandava* movement, which is geometric. The actor then lifts both arms and casts off an imaginary object held in his hands, and turns in profile to say, 'Give me something to hold', which in effect implies, 'which of these two rules should I hold on to so as to live by/walk by'. Obviously, at this stage, the implication of being ambidextrous is a potentiality and not yet fully realised.

I would like to pause here and say a few words regarding this implication, and about the related concept of Savyasachin. Contemporary brain liberalisation theories talk of the right-hand/left-brain as the male/temporal, and the left-hand/right-brain as the female/spatial, and ascribe the functions, capacities and processes of knowledge to different sides of the brain, right and left. Art, intuition, metaphor, music are the functions of the older left-hand/right-brain, because they process information spatially. Physics, rationality, words, logic, war, are functions of the younger right-hand/left-brain, as they process information temporally. One side of the brain, the right, sees everything all-at-once, and the other sees everything one-at-a-time.

Metaphor and sequence are the two important characteristics of these two sides of the brain. The majority of people are left-brained-right-handed. A few are left-handed-right-brained. A few are ambidextrous, and they enjoy the capacities of both sides of the brain. We know from history, that Leonardo da Vinci was ambidextrous and his many scientific inventions, along with his art, are proof of his capacity to use both sides of his brain and to see space and time differently.

The concept of Savyasachin is similar. For Savyasachin knows how to unite his left (female) side to his right (male) side. The folklore of the Draupadi cult in Tamil Nadu suggests that the reason why Arjuna was able to shoot the eye of the rotating fish by looking at its reflection in the water below it at Draupadi's *swayamvara*, was because he was able to unite the left with the right in himself/use his left-handed knowledge.

Brhannala and Savyasachin are related concepts in that they indicate the union of binaries/polarities. But Brhannala stresses the right brain and the ability to see everything all-at-once more than Savyasachin.

Let us proceed now with the performance of *Brhannala*. After asking for something to hold, almost as a response, the actor turns to face the audience as Brhannala—Arjuna as the female impersonator and dancer who enters the court of Virata incognito. What follows in the scene is a mimed response of the courtiers present, to Brhannala's entry—disgust, delight, awe, etc. Uttarakumar then sings a song describing this entry. And the scene ends here. There is a certain absurdity and light-heartedness to this scene which is reminiscent of the humour in Book IV of the *Mahabharata*.

Additionally because this is a solo performance, it is possible to keep the style from becoming representational, and to allow the *mise-en-scène* to communicate metaphorically. Brhannala's presence on the stage is established by the sound of anklets, in a kind of live surround sound, and through the direction of the actor's gaze.

Although the production keeps the story of the *Mahabharata* always in mind, it is more a skeleton that provides a frame for other concerns. It does not follow a linearity in the events it refers to. The structure of the production attempts to reflect metaphorically one or the other side of the two hemispheres of the brain. Thus the first scene reflects the sensibility of the right-brain in its characteristics of metaphor, pure being, absurdity, feeling states, music and song.

The second scene continues to reflect the right-brain. Here, Brhannala dances and sings at the court of Virata, and, as a story-teller, goes on to tell the story of a dog and a tiger (binaries of the canine and the feline). The absurd conversation and relationship between them reveals the cerebral dog as male and the emotional tiger as female, although the tiger is actually a male.

In the middle of Brhannala's narrative, the dog sings a song called *Brhannala Sir's Memories*, which is based on the Greek creation myth and describes the birth of the two hemispheres of the brain with the birth of Athena, an androgynous figure, warrior and artist, a possible reflection of Brhannala. It also describes the functions and capacities of the two sides of the brain, giving space and time an important role in the processes of each side. The song is interrupted by a cry which declares that there is a war. Probably the Goharan, which came at the end of the 13th year of exile.

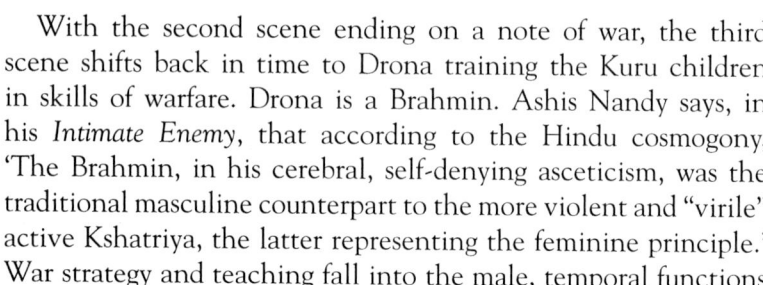

With the second scene ending on a note of war, the third scene shifts back in time to Drona training the Kuru children in skills of warfare. Drona is a Brahmin. Ashis Nandy says, in his *Intimate Enemy*, that according to the Hindu cosmogony, 'The Brahmin, in his cerebral, self-denying asceticism, was the traditional masculine counterpart to the more violent and "virile" active Kshatriya, the latter representing the feminine principle.' War strategy and teaching fall into the male, temporal functions of the left brain.

This scene therefore is a metaphor of the left brain. And so a metronome and a rhythmic verbal set of sounds/*vaitari* dominate the sound-scape, seeking to make the temporal grumblings of thoughts audible. As Drona speaks/lectures, the pulse of thought dominates his speech rhythms. He gestures rhythmically as he speaks, using his eyes in a highly stylised, rhythmic manner, to express thought. He moves across space one step at a time, covering the stage from one end to the other by the end of the scene. The madness and playfulness of the earlier two scenes is gone and even the text reflects the analytical processes of the left brain. The scene begins with Drona saying, 'In the course of evolution, the eye of the bird developed into a spectacular organ of vision.' It ends with Arjuna asking, 'How can I make time stand still?' Drona answers, 'That is a question you must ask Siva.'

Time enters the production late, as it did in evolutionary history, where apprehensions of space came earlier than apprehensions of time. And even then, early mammals had an apprehension only of the present and the past. The sense of the future came with *homo sapiens*. In the second scene the dog tells the tiger that man has prospects and the tiger asks, 'What are prospects?'

In the scene with Drona, not only does the apprehension of the three dimensions of time get established, but a fourth is anticipated. When Drona says, 'Your arrow must hit its target at the moment it leaves your hand. Time must stand still for your arrow, then it will have power over the future', he is anticipating the appreciation of Time in Einstein's space-time continuum—a dimension where space contracts and time dilates to include past, present and future in a single moment of now.

In the fourth scene, where Arjuna and Siva meet, metaphors of the male-female, brahmin-kshatriya, space-time polarities are created through movement, light, words and music. Thus the slow motion cricket movement and science-speak by the male Siva, is juxtaposed with the warrior movement and ambition-driven queries of the female Arjuna. Finally, Siva unites these polarities through his dance, which moves from one polarity to the other by exposing the middle ground between them. The polarities thus become one single seamless loop. Indeed, this scene is the key to the concept of Brhannala—the union of polarities.

This fourth scene is contextualised within Arjuna's pilgrimage to the Himalayas, where he performs austerities towards acquiring weapons, most notably the Pasupata from Siva. In the play, however, when he goes to meet Siva, the conversation is different. He wants to know how to make time stand still and see with the eye of complete union.

Siva's response is, 'Savyasachin, you shoot arrows with your right hand and your left hand,/Use your left hand knowledge, which makes you Brhannala, to understand time through space. Become me—Ardhanariswara.'

I have mentioned Savyasachin and his use of his left-hand knowledge earlier.

Ardhanariswara is Siva whose left side is female and right side male. In the Veda it is mentioned that the polarities of the male and female are symbolic of all the polarities in existence. We can conclude therefore, that a union of the polarities of the male and female in the body of Siva, Lord of Time and Timelessness, is a metaphor with gigantic consequences.

That Brhannala is related to this metaphor can be gathered from the etymology of her name. She is referred to as Brhdnata and also Brhdnara. 'Nata' is dancer, which she is. But what about 'nara'? Arjuna is often referred to as Nara (Man/Human) in his relationship with Krishna who is Narayana (God). Here God and Man/Human are a binary pair who become seamlessly one when referred to as Nara-Narayana. Professor Robin Zaehner, scholar of Eastern religions, hints at this when he says, 'Krishna is the God whom Man became', indicating the potential in the human to become God. But Brhdnara, which means Great Man or rather Male, can only refer to Siva, who is Purusha (Great Man/Male). In a sense then, Brhdnata and Brhdnara both connect Brhannala-Arjuna to Siva as Ardhanarishwara, both being dancers and the epitome of maleness.

So both Brhannala/Arjuna and Ardhanariswara are great dancers, both combine feminine and masculine elements, both have extremely erotic natures, but can be ascetics, both have strong cerebral brahmin characteristics as well as the warrior moods.

In this fourth scene Arjuna is referred to as Savyasachin and is encouraged to become Brhannala through Savyasachin's left-hand knowledge. For it is only as Brhannala, a manifestation of Ardhanariswara, that he will see with the eye of complete union and therefore experience motionless time.

The right brain, as mentioned earlier, has the ability to see everything all-at-once. Visionaries, mystics and artists have frequently said that their insights occur in a flash of intuition—an epiphany which is inexplicable rationally. Is this what is meant by the left-hand knowledge? Maybe.

At Draupadi's *swayamvara*, Arjuna shoots the eye of the rotating fish by looking at its reflection in the water below. He is able to see beyond maya/illusion/water, even while looking into it, and pierce the reality above, not the image in the water. It is said that his left-hand knowledge enables him to do this. In a flash, his vision takes in the entire picture, and he knows intuitively what is required to be done. Is this what is meant by seeing with the eye of complete union? Maybe.

Someone who can experience space-time would see that all events that in our three-dimensional world appear in a linear fashion, occur simultaneously, that is all-at-once, in this fourth dimensional world.

Exploring the Many Levels of Theatre

A Review*

GEETA DOCTOR

'Give me something to hold!' The voice is Arjuna's. It fills the auditorium at the Museum Theatre with a low growl at the beginning of *Brhannala*, a theatrical performance, written and conceived and directed by Veenapani Chawla. As performed by Vinay Kumar K.J. during the last evening of the eight days of The Other Festival at the Museum Theatre, it is a vital piece of theatre that combines dance, mime, music and philosophy. The actor-dancer's back is turned to the audience.

His muscular body is all but naked as he stretches out his hand from which the bow, Gandiva, has slipped, and asks for

* Previously published in *The Economic Times* in 1998.

something to grasp. From the back he looks like a warrior, but against the backdrop, the shadow appears to be that of a female, sensuous and curvaceous. The hand, now stretched out, is asking to be held.

In a powerful invocation of the spirit of Brhannala, the male-female form of Arjuna during the one year that he is in disguise at the court of Virata, Veenapani's vision acts like an arrow. It soars on the wings of a magnificent performance by Vinay Kumar who has the Kerala Kudiyattam training running through his veins. It sings through the air with the music from many cultures as a quartet of musicians create the atmosphere of a Kerala temple performance during the first 20 minutes of the presentation. It shatters the expectation of the audience.

From moment to moment the atmosphere changes, even as Vinay leaps into the air, becoming a dog, a tiger, a story-teller, a pair of birds, a man-woman, a warrior, a temptress, an ascetic, a god, in the intake of a breath. The sheer physicality of his presence reaches out from the stage and knocks you over.

He is in turn a comic, who has the audience rolling with laughter; a mimic with a Malayalee accent, who makes you believe in the high caste Dog who gives advice to Tiger riding on an Enfield Bullet; an acrobat who leaps in the air like a Chhau dancer, a mother crooning to her infant in Malayalam; and an Einstein who bowls the famous equation about energy being transformed into matter like a cricket player on the pitch, no less than a philosopher explaining the essence of the Bhagavad Gita.

The transitions are so quick and questions come so suddenly—for example when Arjuna turns around and asks Bhima, 'What was Eklavya's secret', or when he turns to Krishna and asks him the question that brings forth the Bhagavad Gita, or when he becomes just another human being, a father, who has just seen his young son killed before him and howls with pain—that the audience is transformed at the end of the performance.

Every moment of the play has a different twist. It is as though Veenapani and Vinay have devised a new way of knocking the centres of our perception open, until we too are made alive and aware. As a piece of theatre, it is a tremendous experience.

In Search of the Enigmatic Arjuna

A Review*

SHANTA GOKHALE

Veenapani Chawla and Vinay Kumar presented their latest work, *Brhannala*, on December 6, at The Other Festival, held in the beautifully maintained, colonial style Museum Theatre in Chennai. The entire police force was out that evening, random-checking vehicles for bombs; but a sizeable audience turned up for the play, nevertheless, and Vinay Kumar rose all the way up to their expectations.

Chawla had been mulling over Arjun as Brhannala for many years. Reading and thinking around the subject, she soon arrived

* Originally published in *The Sunday Times of India* on 20 December 1998.

at the exact focus of her preoccupation—the duality at the centre of Arjuna's life and being. He was Savyasachin, one who could shoot with both right and left hands. Although acknowledged as the greatest archer, the unacknowledged Ekalavya proved to be even greater. Arjuna was the perfect man; but in the 13th year of the Pandavas' exile, he chose to be a woman. Or neither man nor woman, but totally integrated into one being, like Ardhanarishwara.

In *Brhannala*, the essential oneness of other dualities is revealed, forming patterns around the magnetic force of these central dualities. There is the space-time continuum, the separate but complementary faculties of the right and left brain and bhoga and yoga as the two equally balanced paths to self-knowledge. Chawla's script, characteristically elliptical, metaphoric and anecdotal, encompasses them all within its brevity, while leaving unarticulated spaces open for Vinay Kumar to fill with gesture, posture, movement and dance.

Brhannala is framed by an outrageously funny cover story of a tiger and a dog. They underline yet another duality, the rational and the irrational. At one point the tiger asks, 'I say, dog, what is it like, being a dog?' To which the dog's gloomy response is, 'There is no variety, no prospects. Just pup-dog-dead dog. A dog's life'. Both animals are played with elastic virtuosity by Vinay Kumar transiting from one to the other with leaps. These animals secure the foot of the ladder to ultimate knowledge firmly on earth.

Vinay Kumar uses his magnificently tuned body and voice, aided now by the Kudiyattam technique of breath imbibed from Usha Nangiar during a collaborative project at Adishakti. One notices a greater self-awareness regarding this technique in Vinay Kumar's embodying of *Brhannala* than was apparent in Adishakti's previous production, *Impressions of Bhima*, which also Vinay Kumar performed solo. As before, here too, his partners in performance were musicians—the master mizhavu player from Kerala, V.K. Hariharan, Aurelio, a French instrument maker from Auroville, Arvind Rane and Suresh Kaliyath. Between them they played something like 40 instruments to create never-before heard sounds which added up to exciting music.

Ganapati
Performance Text

VEENAPANI CHAWLA

Ganapati premiered at Auroville in August 2000. Between then and 2005, it did 14 shows all over the country—Chennai, Delhi, Heggodu, Trichur, Bangalore, Kolkata—and Berlin. *Ganapati* marks the end of Chawla's push towards assigning an increasingly bigger role to music till it became the text itself in this play, with the spoken word almost entirely absent. The trigger for looking at the role of music in theatre came with a remark made by musician and composer Joseph Celli, after he saw a performance of *Impressions of Bhima* at the University of California, Los Angeles in August 1997. While he confessed to having admired the production and performance, he wondered why more thought had not been given to the possibilities of music in the piece. Chawla's explorations in this direction intensified when she discovered how rhythm not only supported, but often dictated, the performer's moves and expressions in a Koodiyattam performance.

(L to R) Suresh Kaliyath, Vinay Kumar, Nimmy Raphel, and Arvind Rane in *Ganapati*. Photograph courtesy of Anoop Davis.

(*The performance is an interpretation of the birth stories related to the myths of Ganapati, the elephant-headed god from the Puranic cycle, and Martanda from the Vedic cycle. It is structured in a recurring cycle of creation, celebration, destruction and return, which parallels the motif of the birth stories. The return is suggested by a re-telling of the myth repeatedly and from different points of view. The aim is to allow its main concern, that of creation and creativity, to be interpreted at a variety of different levels.*)

Act 1

Creation

1

As rituals commemorate myths, the performance opens with the ritual creation of an image of Ganapati for the annual festival, by a group of artisans. In the dark, four small round surfaces glow with light, seeming to float mid-air. They run diagonally across the stage, upstage centre to backstage left. Above one surface, a hand appears and rises slowly in the shaft of light illuminating it. Then it falls to hit the surface and creates a sound. The ring of a beat. Both hands then appear above this surface. Other hands appear above the other three surfaces. They slap the surfaces, creating a rhythm which gradually increases in tempo. These opening beats replicate the sounds and rhythms of fashioning something materially. Likewise the visual image with its focus on the hands working over the surfaces, communicates a steady physical labour of work.

The rhythm played is the 3-beat Koodiyattam 'Ta Ki Ta' in increasing tempos. All four percussionists play together on their *mizhavus*. They progress from the 1st tempo into the 4th tempo. (See Score 1 of Percussion in Appendix II.)

2

The rhythm stops abruptly. The hands are withdrawn momentarily, and four disembodied and distorted faces appear, floating above each instrument. They image what each of the percussionists has been shaping under their hands.

VOICE: *Ye to adha hi bana hai!* (This is only half done!)

The faces disappear simultaneously, and all four pairs of hands start playing the three-beat rhythm again. The tempo is moderate at the second speed and then it speeds up from the 2nd to 3rd to 4th in a staggered manner. The hands on the 1st and 3rd surface play together throughout. While those above the 2nd and 4th start together and then have their own journeys, giving an uneven and textured sound of labour and individualistic progress in work.
(See Score 2 of Percussion in Appendix II.)

3

During the sequence mentioned above, a light slowly illuminates more than the surfaces. It reveals four percussionists, each playing on an instrument which resembles the belly and torso of Ganapati. It is the *mizhavu*, the main instrument in Koodiyattam performance. A string hangs down its centre. Originally meant to tie the leather surface to the body, it signifies here the trunk of Ganapati.

The percussionists on stage are actually artisans and they are creating images of Ganapati for the annual festival. The act of crafting these images is portrayed visually and aurally through the rhythms that they play.

The focus on their work is total.

As they reach a crescendo, the rhythm changes seamlessly from the 3-beat to the 3½-beat. But the tempo shifts gear and slows down dramatically, creating a shift from the exterior to the interior landscape. The light goes off on percussionist 1, who has slumped in his seat and looks like a shapeless mass. The other three remain illuminated. We see them slowly raise their heads from their work and look as though they were searching for something in their minds. The 3½-beat at that slow tempo, mirrors the slowing down of active thought and the search for something so far unthought of and unheard.

The tempo slows further and their concentration moves more and more inward as they look for inspiration for their creative work. A point is reached when, with the slowing tempo, their hands become still and the moment is suspended on a breath, as they go inward, into a world of their own imagination. (See Score 3 of Percussion in Appendix II.)

4

As the three come to the end of their playing, light falls on percussionist 1. He looks like a shapeless mass behind his instrument. When the 3½-beat stops, he assumes a defined shape with a quick circular flick of his head and torso: Ganapati.

Silently he marks the 3½-beat on his body, by moving one shoulder, then the other to it. He jumps backward from his seat and continues to do this for another eight rounds. (See Score 4 of Percussion in Appendix II.)

5

The others are holding their breath as they see this in their mind's eye. One of them, percussionist 3, in her excitement, beats out a fast roll in preparation for getting back into work mode, so as to give shape to her vision. And then she slips into the 3½-beat, which the others join her in.
(See Score 5 of Percussion in Appendix II.)

6

In the meantime percussionist 1, their muse/teacher/Ganapati, is dancing in the space behind their backs. He picks up a baby version of the main instrument called a *kutti*, and dances towards percussionist 3 and plays into her ear. Immediately she looks up, inspired and starts an improvisation on the 3½-beat rhythm. The others continue to play the original 3½-beat. The muse dances behind her, a shadowy figure, and when she falters, he plays into her ear again. Percussionist 3 gets energised and continues with the intricacies of the improvisation. The muse dances around her and leaps into a sitting position in front of her, layering her improvisation with one of his own. The other two continue to hold the original 3½-beat which binds the totality of this textured rhythm.
(See Score 6 of Percussion in Appendix II.)

7

Light fades on percussionist 3 as she completes her improvisation and lights up percussionist 2. The muse now leaps to stand next to him and inspires/prompts him to explore a new improvisation. Then the two play a duet for a while, taking the energy to a new high, before percussionist 2 plays a solo improvisation of his own. The improvisation ends.
(See Score 7 of Percussion in Appendix II.)

PERCUSSIONIST 2: (*Shouts in Malayalam*) *Kitee!* [Got it!]

8

The original 3½-beat held by the others in the company has increased in tempo by now. And the muse leaps across the stage to join percussionist 4. A frenzied improvisation by this percussionist follows. As in the case of the others it is layered by the muse's own inputs.

(See Score 8 of Percussion in Appendix II.)

9

Each one of the percussionists has played an improvisation on the prevailing rhythm, indicating a variation in vision and inspiration. At the end of the last improvisation, the rhythm is in high tempo, when the muse leaps across the stage to the other side. As he lands, all become still.

Slowly percussionist 3, a young woman, gets up to face the muse in the space behind the instruments. She starts clapping a tabla bol with her hands and then with her feet. The muse moves slowly towards her, observing her carefully. Then he responds to her by tapping his feet and clapping his hands to another tabla bol.

The other two percussionists behind whose back this is happening, have a stylised dialogue, using the words: *ardha* (half), *ardha kunja* (half elephant), *ardhanarishwara* (half man and half woman), *ardha kunja narishwara* (half: elephant, man, woman, god).

Thus, along with the other varied visions of Ganapati, another is added.

As their dialogue concludes, the two percussionists, the second and fourth, start playing the 3½-beat rhythm gently on their instruments. The muse and the woman then layer their respective tabla bols with improvisations. Together they tap these out with their feet and hands, interspacing the beats with leaps and other movement figures. These improvisations are based on the 9-beat and 12-beat cycles of the tabla.

(See Score 9 of Percussion in Appendix II.)

10

The muse ends the sequence with a circular leap, which transforms him back into Ganapati. The woman joins the others and they all play the 3½-beat rhythm at an increasing tempo. As they do so, the muse dances towards a *ghatam*, picks it up and holds it to his belly: a pot-bellied Ganapati. The others turn to look at him. He then dances forward and towards the other percussionists in a typical Ganapati dance. He halts before them abruptly. They all stop playing. Ganapati holds them in thrall for a moment, and then sits down near them. As he does so, they beat out a roll on their instruments.
(See Score 10 of Percussion in Appendix II.)

11

Ganapati echoes the roll on his *ghatam*, then starts playing the joyful 2-beat rhythm of Koodiyattam. As he plays, the others look up, as though with dawning realization. They seem to see another aspect of Ganapati. They respond to this with happy affirmation, marking it with a beat on their instruments so that it falls harmoniously within each unit of the 2-beat played by the muse on his *ghatam*. They call out 'that's it!' in different languages, as they play.

The muse then stops playing and the other percussionists take on the 2-beat rhythm on their instruments in a slightly quicker tempo. The muse reinforces their rhythm with an off-beat on another instrument, the *chenda*, and then goes on to play a variation of the 2-beat on this other instrument. The other percussionists support this enthusiastically, doubling their affirming beats as the muse's improvisation speeds up.
(See Score 11 of Percussion in Appendix II.)

12

The muse stops and allows the others to play the 2-beat on their own, so that they can further explore and internalize this detail for the creation of Ganapati. As they internalize their visions, they slow down and go inwards, into themselves, and finally come to a stand-still, their eyes focused only on their hands on the surface of their instruments.

They are ready to give form to their inspiration.
(See Score 12 of Percussion in Appendix II.)

13

The muse has been inspecting their work all this time. When he thinks they are ready, he sits down on his seat and all of them get ready to give form to their creative inspiration. They swing their arms up from one side to the other in a synchronized movement and, in the process, beat their instruments with a single beat each time. Next they use each arm singly to swing down to hit the surface of their instruments as though they were beating clay.

The image communicates the labour required in the process of crafting a work of creative inspiration.
(See Score 13 of Percussion in Appendix II.)

14

As the tempo increases, the percussionists move into the 4th speed of the 3-beat Koodiyattam rhythm, their hands now close to their instruments.
(See Score 14 of Percussion in Appendix II.)

15

The image, both aurally and visually, is of artisans at labour on their material, totally absorbed in it and getting the hang of it.

So as to provide detail of the process, one percussionist is brought sharply into focus. After six rounds of this 3-beat rhythm, percussionist 2 suddenly goes into a cartwheel, jumps high and lands in front of a baby instrument a little way off from the others.

There is a dramatic shift in rhythm. As he lands, the others shift seamlessly into a 4-beat Koodiyattam rhythm at the slowest tempo. This balanced rhythm at the slowest tempo communicates a mood of relaxed enjoyment in work, as the artisans give expression to their inspiration. Light too shifts dramatically at this point, falling largely on percussionist 2 and his baby instrument. The other percussionists are in the background, only their hands and the surfaces of their instruments are illuminated.

Percussionist 2 examines the *kutti* (baby instrument) in front of him. It signifies his image of Ganapati. He picks it up ritualistically, and displays it to the others, each giving him his/her opinion of it through the language of rhythms. He then leaps into a sitting position on the ground and starts examining it, sounding it, tinkering with it, before getting on to crafting it lovingly into the image he wants. He conveys all this through a relevant attitude of his body and by playing improvisations of the 4-beat rhythm, which the others have continued to play in slow tempo. As percussionist 2 gets into his stride, percussionist 1 improvises on his improvisation. The combined sounds that emerge, simulate the sounds of activity in a workshop, although more musically.

The percussionists then slow down to indicate that they have come to the end of their work. Percussionist 2 mimes the sprinkling of water on the image he has been creating. The others create water sounds from their instruments.

(See Score 15 of Percussion in Appendix II.)

16

As percussionist 2 takes his work and puts it in the sun to dry, percussionist 1 starts playing the 4-beat rhythm in its regular tempo. He is joined by percussionists 3 and 4, one after the other. Each is lit up when s/he joins in. All of them texture this rhythm by playing on different parts of the surface of the *mizhavu*. In the meanwhile, percussionist 2 has been looking proudly at his work. He fiddles with it a bit, arranging the image, allowing the trunk/string of the instrument, to be displayed prominently, pulling at the side skin of the instrument to draw attention to the elephant ears of the image. Then he joins the rest in his usual place and is lit up.

The time has now come to complete the image by putting its head in place. While playing the 4-beat rhythm, the four percussionists close their eyes. With rhythmic movements of their heads, they create a stylized image of a head being fitted onto a body. Finally, to an unsounded rhythm, they make a circular flourish with their heads and torsos and open their eyes.

The Ganapati image is ready for the annual festival. (See Score 16 of Percussion in Appendix II.)

Celebration

As the music and the figures freeze, there is a pause as short as the intake of a breath. But the open eyes of the four are full of excitement. Then the light floods the stage and the celebration for the festival begins with a bang.

Percussionist 1 starts off by playing the 2-beat rhythm in fast tempo on the *chenda*. He is joined by percussionist 3 and then 4 on their *mizhavus*. Each one plays an improvisation of the 2-beat through the celebration that follows.

Meanwhile, percussionist 2 has started dancing. He moves towards the baby image of Ganapati he has created and dances around it, saluting it. Then he moves back to his instrument and, with his back to the audience, swaying like an elephant, he starts playing it.

As he does so, percussionist 1 plays a roll on the *chenda* and then gets up to dance towards the baby Ganapati. He picks it up, dances to the opposite side of the stage, and places it in a strip of light, indicating a threshold. Percussionist 3 in the meantime has picked up a *tappu*. She plays a 2-beat from the Tapattam tradition on it, and dances towards the image. As she does so, percussionist 1 mischievously occupies her vacant seat. She carries on towards the image regardless. On reaching the image, she dance-salutes it and occupies percussionist 1's seat. In the meantime, percussionist 4, playing a small djembe, has danced up to percussionist 3, who is now playing a big djembe. They play a duet. At the end of it, percussionist 4 pays passionate homage to the image and dances back to his place. Percussionist 2 dances to the far left corner to call unseen others to join them in the festivities. He then dances back to the image, leading an imaginary crowd, represented by

a corridor of light to salute the image. After the salutation, he dances back to his place. As he does so, the 2-beat reaches a peak in tempo. Into this, percussionist 3 plays a long roll on the *chenda* as though giving a call. The others fall silent. A sombre mood replaces the so far joyous one.
(See Score 17 of Percussion in Appendix II.)

Destruction

Percussionist 3 sounds a transition beat on the *chenda*. This beat in Koodiyattam signifies the passage from one sequence to another or its conclusion. The entire sequence which follows, is based on this beat as it draws attention to the passing away of Ganapati from this world to another.

The percussionists look up in the silence and slant their bodies such that they are all looking at the image of Ganapati/the *kutti*. They look at it sadly and follow the departing image with their eyes. They indicate the passage of its departure by playing the transition beat repeatedly. Each time they play it, the interval between repetitions is reduced, as is the volume. The sound seems to recede gradually. The light on the Ganapati image, standing on the threshold, fades and goes out.
(See Score 18 of Percussion in Appendix II.)

Return

1

The percussionists sigh as the icon is taken away. Then they straighten up and start playing the 4-beat rhythm in a moderate tempo. Balance is restored. Ganapati will return the next year.

The performance now goes into story-telling mode, narrating the myth, which the festival celebrates. It signals the 'return' of Ganapati after his 'destruction'.

After a few rounds of the 4-beat rhythm, percussionist 1, now sitting in the third place, dances forward, chanting a *vaitari*. He uses the Ottan Thullal form for his story-telling. His words have an underlying rhythm to them. The others in the company support his *vaitari* quietly on their instruments.

PERCUSSIONIST 1: The woman made the boy ... he points to the kutti on his right, the threshold light comes up on it ... from the dirt of her body and a few drops of water. (*Sound of water played on the* mizhavus.) He breaks from the narrative and dances away, chanting a *vaitari*. He returns and claps.

PERCUSSIONIST 1: 'You are my own,' she said. 'And you have no one else to call your own.'

(*He returns to vaitari mode. While doing so, he mimes the argument between Siva and Ganapati. This time the chenda supports him and at the high point of the disagreement between the two, the timpani enters as does the mizahvu. At the gesture of rejection by Siva, the action and the music stop abruptly. There is silence.*)

PERCUSSIONIST 1: The man felt his power broken.

(*He now mimes the fight between Siva and Ganapati and dances across to the kutti on his right. The other percussionists support his performance on the* chenda, mizhavu *and* timpani. *As the music reaches a crescendo, percussionist 1 sits before the* kutti *and, with one flourish of his hand, cuts off its head. The* kutti *rolls across the stage. There is silence. Percussionist 1 mourns the moment with his body.*)

PERCUSSIONIST 1: He cut off the boy's head—

(*The* chenda *plays two rounds as percussionist 1 remains motionless on the floor. Then on its stress beat, he rises triumphantly. He is an elephant and the music on the* chenda, elethalam *and* timpani *creates the aural image of an elephant walking. The percussionist walks across the stage like an elephant to this music. He turns swaying like an elephant.*)

PERCUSSIONIST 1: And then embraced the young man like a father.

(*The scene ends with a beat on the* elethalam.)
(See Score 19 of Percussion in Appendix II.)

2

A group of traditional musicians is startled when one amongst them breaks away from the accepted form and opens himself up to new outpourings of his spirit. They are angry to begin with, but soon accommodate these new outpourings within their tradition.

The percussionists return to playing a moderate 4-beat rhythm. Percussionist 2, however, does not join them. He persuades a reluctant percussionist 3 to change places with him, so that he has access to the wide variety of instruments lying near her. Percussionist 2 wants to join the others but with something different and new. However, the rhythms of the majority are too overwhelming. So, like a child, he interrupts their playing by not allowing them to touch the surfaces of their instruments and beating out nonsense on their instruments to drown them. They stop and look at him. He has danced his way to percussionist 4, who gets charged by this madness and starts beating out the jazz shuffle with his brushes on a cymbal. Percussionist 2 enters the swing of the shuffle with a rhythm of his own. As he plays a long sequence, the other two percussionists observe and discuss this improvisation and calculate the beats on their fingers. Suddenly at a crescendo, percussionist 2 stops and the two traditional musicians, 1 and 3, enter with the 4-beat at a fast tempo. Percussionist 2 dances crazily across the stage to his earlier position, keeping to this rhythm. Percussionist 4 continues the shuffle with his brushes. When percussionist 2 reaches his position, he plays out sequences of his rhythm both to the shuffle and the traditional 4-beat. The music rises to a crescendo and the scene ends. The light fades.
(See Score 20 of Percussion in Appendix II.)
(*Fade out.*)

(The Ganapati birth stories are, in a sense, the reverse of the Oedipus story. Here it is the father who kills the son, but soon reanimates him. This has some bearing on the nature of the cultural processes in South Asia, where the new, the revolutionary, and the subversive are always accommodated to prevent them from overthrowing the tradition. This gives the tradition its pluralistic/hybrid face. Ganapati images this hybridity.)

Act 2

The light on stage has not faded completely and the percussionists are seen in the dim light rearranging their instruments. Percussionist 1 picks up a *mizhavu* and places it ritualistically front stage in the centre. He puts a seat behind it and carefully arranges the *mizhavu's* string to look like the trunk of an elephant. He flaps the leather near the rim of the surface to remind us of the ears of the elephant. Then he takes up a formal position near it as percussionist 2, chanting nonsense but making the nonsense sound like mantras, approaches the prepared seat. He tousles percussionist 1's hair as he passes and perambulates around the *mizhavu* thrice. As soon as percussionist 1's back is turned, he messes up the carefully arranged string/trunk and then sits down at his *mizhavu* continuing to chant nonsense. Suddenly his chanting is interrupted by the sound of a trumpet. All activity stops. The company look in the direction of the sound and find a gleaming trunk-like shape emerging from the wings. It is followed by a man from another part of the world. The trunk-like shape is a saxophone. To the astonishment of the company, the saxophonist, playing his music, walks confidently towards the seated percussionist 2.

Percussionist 2 and the others listen to the playing for a while. When it stops, percussionist 2 invites the saxophonist to play a duet with him. He draws the attention of the saxophonist to the unique shape of the two instruments. When the duet is over, the saxophonist sits besides percussionist 2 who starts telling a story. It is in a rhythm which the saxophone melody has anticipated. It is also reminiscent of the rhythm in the Koothu story-telling tradition of Kerala.

PERCUSSIONIST 2: Talking about mothers who created their sons single-handedly; there is one. Her name is Aditi. She created eight sons. Seven of them were made with the help of the gods; and as they were quite normal, they went out with her to work in the world. The eighth son was created by her single-handedly.

Aditi delivered a lump of matter, and then gave this lump the shape of an egg ... He beats the mizhavu ... and called it Martanda—which means dead in the egg.

The leftovers of this lump of matter became an elephant. (*He picks up his stool, swings it over his head, and disappears behind the* mizhavu *only to emerge from behind it miming an elephant. The saxophonist rises up to play a trumpeting sound on his instrument.*)

After all, leftovers are always very auspicious.

So Aditi arranged the elephant around the egg (*he disappears again behind the* mizhavu, *and this time rises slowly and majestically from behind it as an elephant. The saxophonist perambulates around him clockwise playing his saxophone, expanding the elephant figure in space through sound*) ... so as to give it a connection with the outside world.

After having done this, do you know what Aditi did with Martanda? She threw him down into the bottom of the earth and left him there. (*He mimes a violent throw into the* mizhavu.) Then Martanda started to be born slowly and endlessly, through the labour of the earth. (*Percussion sounds of birth.*)

PERCUSSIONIST 3: (*In Tamil*) Vinaya, this sounds like the other boy's story.

PERCUSSIONIST 1: (*In Marathi*) Yes, yes very familiar. That was also about multiple births.

PERCUSSIONIST 2: Exactly, you two are right. (*In Malayalam*) Nimmy pick up this *mizhavu* and shift it, and Pascal please go and sit there.

Exactly. Like Martanda, the boy in our play also had multiple births. Multiple births are fantastic because they allow a person to have many, many different points of view of the same thing. But at the same time, multiple births raise the question of intellectual property rights. For example in our play, who should get the highest credit for the creation of the boy? (*To the audience*) Don't know? Let me ask them (*meaning the company on stage. He does so, and they speak simultaneously in different languages. He hushes them up and turns to the audience*) I personally think it should be the person who donated his head. Heads are very important for one's identity. Don't you remember Parasurama's mother's story? Her head was cut off and placed on another woman's body. But she still remained Parasurama's mother.

(*He walks to his* mizhavu, *now placed right stage, and picks up a metronome lying on its surface.*) This is my point view. What is your point of view? Think about it. (*He sets off the metronome.*)

(*Blackout.*)

Act 3

Creation

The sound of the metronome. Soon after that, the sound of a beat. Light falls on two bodies in silhouette, a metre or so apart. They are moving slowly and sinuously. They look like two elephants dancing, their torsos moving sensuously above their large bellies, their trunks and tails waving in harmony, and periodically beating their bellies to create a sound. A pattern emerges slowly. A rhythm.

The image aims to communicate the languor of elephant love-play.

When the light brightens, it reveals the two elephants to be percussionists 1 and 2. They are performing a sensuous, languorous, snake-like movement behind their *mizhavus*. As they dance, one arm waves like a trunk and the other like a tail. As they move in a slow lazy rhythm, they beat the surface of their instruments whenever their movements bring them close to them.

After a few moments, light falls on another pair. They sit further backstage but are visible between the first two. They play a synchronised beat, one on the *chenda*, the other on the timpani. They play in counterpoint to percussionists 1 and 2, and in the intervals between their beats.

The two sets of beats appear to be like a stimulus and a response. In time, the tempo quickens and the intervals between the beats shorten. The aural effect is one of rising excitement. As this excitement builds up and reaches a peak, the elephants pull back somewhat, by slipping into a long continuous 8-beat rhythm without the earlier intervals. In fact, they had been playing the 8-beat so far, but sounding only its 4th, 6th and 8th beats. The second pair, likewise, have been playing the 7-beat so far, but sounding only the 3rd, 5th and 7th beats. They now slip into a continuous 7-beat pattern. The effect of stimulus and response is reinforced by the off-beats between the seven and eight rhythm, which are stressed.

The tempo increases and, as it does so, the aural image communicates the rising excitement of love-play. After it reaches an extreme, the tempo starts slowing down gradually to eventually peter out.

When this happens, the elephant pair in front, disappears behind their *mizhavus* only to re-emerge as dancing baby elephants.

Percussionist 1 leaps out from behind his *mizhavu* to jump around it, playing a 5-beat rhythm before sitting down at his instrument and playing the 10-beat rhythm, which creates the aural image of an elephant walking. While doing this, he sways and waves his arm in the manner of an elephant. Percussionist 2 emerges more languorously. He sways, dances and mimes the elephant walk with his back to the audience, but facing his instrument, which he plays.

The other two on stage have been playing the 2-beat rhythm on the *chenda* and the *mizhavu*. At the first baby elephant's appearance, percussionist 3 starts a 10-beat rhythm and the fourth a 7-beat rhythm.

(See Score 21 of Percussion in Appendix II.)

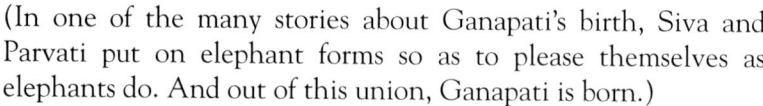

(In one of the many stories about Ganapati's birth, Siva and Parvati put on elephant forms so as to please themselves as elephants do. And out of this union, Ganapati is born.)

Celebration

Percussionist 2 dances and goes off the stage. The light on percussionist 3 fades. Percussionist 1 switches to the 3½-beat and percussionist 4 to the 2-beat. Percussionist 3 has left the *chenda* to sit astride the djembe placed centre stage, such that her back is to us and the image she creates is that of a lingam placed on a yoni. She is Siva. She plays an occasional beat on the djembe.

Percussionist 2 is heard playing a 5-beat rhythm off-stage, on the *edikya*. (*All these rhythms—3½, 2, 7, 5—are played simultaneously.*) He enters unsteadily. An intoxicated baby elephant, waving his head and playing his music, which is an improvisation on the 5-beat rhythm, and varies with the situation and the emotional need of the moment. He weaves his way through those sitting on stage and dances towards percussionist 1, who is playing his *mizhavu* in the manner of an elephant. Percussionist 2 butts him playfully over and over again.

He is celebrating his existence. The music has a joyous, light, playful quality.

Then he dances front stage and spots something/someone in the distance. The volume of his music drops as he tries to get a better view. Suddenly his music picks up tempo and he is very excited. He runs towards what he has just seen. It is Siva, who is sitting behind him.

Through the 5-beat rhythm, he asks Siva a question. Siva responds by playing a sequence on the djembe. (*The others are still playing the 3½ and 2 beats.*) The baby elephant shrieks. In response, Siva plays another sequence on the djembe.

The baby elephant moves sadly upstage again. His music drops in volume as he cries. The Koodiyattam 2 and 3½ beats change to the Tapattam 2 and 3½ beats. Siva punctuates these rhythms on her djembe.

The baby elephant thinks through the problem and then brightens. To the beat of his music, he swings his head as though offering it up. He then hurries off to Siva and offers his head, playing his *edikya* all the while. Siva responds with a thunderous acceptance through the djembe.

Happily, the baby elephant prances off the stage. The music on stage continues.

(See Score 22 of Percussion in Appendix II.)

(In a Buddhist version of the Ganapati birth story, a baby elephant bumps into Siva while he is looking for the head he has chopped off. When the elephant learns that the boy will live only if he gets a head within a specific time, it offers its own head to Siva so as to bring Ganapati back to life. Although the elephant asks for no recompense—there is one. Immortality!)

Destruction

Light falls on Siva alone as she continues playing on the djembe. She plays a roll. In a while, the light fades on her, and falls on percussionists 1 and 2 sitting at their instruments and playing the 4-beat. They chant the word 'custom' many times in keeping with the rhythm they are playing.

Percussionist 4 silences them with a beat on the timpani, saying, 'No! Not custom!'

The other two start playing again and chant 'habit'. Again percussionist 4 silences them by beating the timpani imperatively. He says 'No! No! No! How can it be habit?'

There is a pause. Then the other two happily chant 'choice' as they continue to play the 4-beat.

This time percussionist 4 agrees with them and underlines his words on the timpani saying, 'Yes! Yes! Free choice. The elephant gave his head to the boy. Then both of them went from death to immortality.'

Siva plays on the djembe. She plays fire sounds, signifying the sacrifice.

(See Score 23 of Percussion in Appendix II.)

(*Blackout with a long sequence of music on the chenda and the mizhavu.*)

Return

There is silence. A light comes on. We see only the head and silhouette of a bulky figure. It is Ganapati. (*Actually it is percussionist 2 sitting low behind his mizhavu, so that only his head shows above his tummy/instrument.*)

He raises his eyebrows questioningly. Then his head. The movement of his head picks up in tempo, acquires rhythm, shape, meaning.

Ganapati is trying on the head just donated to him.

Soon he becomes comfortable and assumes superlative powers. In this state he generously offers some seed sounds for further creativity.

He plays these on his *mizhavu*/tummy. Then, with a throw of his arms and hands, offers them to the world. Then one hand moves downward slowly, a finger pointing in the direction of an object lying just in front of him. It is a *kutti*. The light fades on everything else except the *kutti* and the finger pointing at it.

(See Score 24 of Percussion in Appendix II.)

Creation

The light fades and in the darkness the primeval seed sounds offered by Ganapati are picked up variously by the percussionists, each trying to figure out what to do with them in his own way. Then the light comes on, and we see the musicians in a shared act of creativity developing these seed sounds into a complete piece of music. There is a chaos of sound. Each musician creates a phrase or a beat which contributes to a medley of sound. Led by percussionist 2/Ganapati of the last scene, these find place in a larger whole.

The musicians together have created a piece of music. A progression of the beats 1, 12, 123, 1234.

As percussionist 2 has led the previous exploration, he now allows each to explore variations on the theme, through changes in tempo, textures and through different instruments, etc. So rounds of the theme are played by each in turn. Each offers the others and sometimes the audience his/her particular input, for them to take it beyond. They pass their variations around to each other and increase by this sharing. Finally they have created a totality which is another theme altogether.
(See Score 25 of Percussion in Appendix II.)

Celebration

The piece reaches its crescendo and percussionist 2 plays one final long round and then stops. All of them are in a celebratory mood for their creative energy/Martanda, has emerged and inspired them. And they congratulate each other.

Percussionist 2 rises from his seat and addresses the company and the audience.

Percussionist 2: Today when I woke up I had no gloom. I felt very happy.

(*The percussionists play a fragment of the theme they have just developed and he dances to it. He stops. And becomes grim.*) But yesterday was such a bad day for me. You know what happened? I slipped … He shudders downward, but stops halfway to say … into the Sloughs of Despond.
(*Percussionist 2 completes his earlier downward trajectory and falls to the ground. He lies there for some time, till he hears a long note on the saxophone. This makes him rise slowly to full height in a smooth movement. He has a bemused look on his face.*)
(See Score P-5 of Saxophone in Appendix II.)

Percussionist 2: At the bottom of the Sloughs of Despond there is a spring… He leaps up in the air and lands lightly on his feet … Martanda! … He does a slow exultant dance to the saxophone and the rhythm on the percussion instruments. I was inspired to creative energy and output for an addition to the world. (*He points to the kutti lying in front of him. The same kutti that Ganapati had offered the musicians earlier, after wearing his head. Then he moves to sit behind it. He caresses its surface, softly*) And I said to myself: you are not mere matter, which like the echo and the shadow merely repeats and sums up what it receives. You are much more.

(*The percussionists behind him, now in darkness, softly play the 4-beat rhythm. After caressing the kutti, percussionist 2 plays the theme he had played when creating the image of Ganapati in Act 1. The theme images the joy of work. At its conclusion he tells himself*)

PERCUSSIONIST 2: Now that you know the secret of delight, you can grow endlessly and give back more than you receive.

(*Percussionist 1 joins percussionist 2 with a leap. He disappears behind percussionist 2's back, then rises up slowly and powerfully to a long note on the saxophone. He halts the saxophone with a gesture of his hands, and claps out the recently evolved musical theme. The saxophonist responds, taking up the theme and playing it on his saxophone.*)
(See Score 26 of Percussion and Saxophone score in Appendix II.)

Destruction/Creation

The saxophonist enters the space among the musicians. Percussionists 2 and 1 take off to the security of their instruments. The entire company responds to the variations on the theme that the saxophonist plays.

Then he abandons their theme and starts playing his own melody.

An alien sound enters the space and the old music has been replaced by something quite different. The musicians feel threatened.

The saxophonist is aware of their distance and soon goes to each one of them, to build a personal bridge so as to get them to collaborate with him. He does this by playing a few notes, which

each recognizes as a moment from their own personal story. To percussionist 1, he plays a few notes from the latter's narrative about Ganapati. To percussionist 4 he plays notes from his 3½-beat improvisation. To percussionist 2 he replicates the speech rhythms that he had used in his narration of the Martanda story. Then he courts percussionist 3, blowing kisses to her through his saxophone.
(See Saxophone score in Appendix II.)

The company thaw.

Finally the saxophonist goes to the *kutti*/Ganapati standing front stage and plays the sweetest melody to it. The company is completely won over. The percussionists join the saxophonist in his music, providing him with the necessary rhythmic component. A new theme emerges.

Ganapati, with his elephant head and pot-bellied human body, epitomises hybridity.

As the music reaches a crescendo the saxophonist turns again to the *kutti* and starts playing softly to it. The percussionists support him softly. At the end of his melody, the saxophonist plays the old theme of the 1, 12, 123, 1234, developed by the percussionists. This is taken up by percussionist 4, then by the others one by one in the round. They join in a staggered way.
(See Score 27 of Percussion in Appendix II.)

Celebration

They play this new version of the theme, in the round for some time. Then the saxophonist joins them again.
(See Saxophone score in Appendix II.)

The company now play their theme as a support to his melody and percussionist 1 plays a duet with him. The tempo picks up. At the end of the duet, the saxophonist builds sounds with his saxophone that end in the cry and trumpeting of an elephant. He withdraws from centre stage.
(See Saxophone score in Appendix II.)

Now only the percussionists are left, playing their theme. Percussionist 1 builds up the tempo through his improvisation. There is a high pitch of excitement. Then suddenly percussionist 1 leaves off playing and the others seamlessly shift gear into a moderate tempo, but continue playing the theme in the round. After some time, percussionist 1 joins them. And so does the saxophonist.
(See Score 28 of Percussion in Appendix II.)

Destruction

All of them play together for some time.

The music has settled in. The seeds of its destruction sown.

Then, without losing tempo, the music starts getting fainter as though they are all moving away.

Except for the light on the *kutti*, the other lights start fading.

Finally nothing can be seen or heard, and the light on the *kutti* goes off.

The musicians have moved on. So must the music.

Return

It will return in a new form.
(See Score 29 of Percussion in Appendix II.)

The End

Inspired by Tradition

A Review*

LEELA VENKATARAMAN

Veenapani Chawla, writer-director-choreographer has again come out with a clean winner in her *Ganapati*, presented by Adishakti, Pondicherry. Using the myth of Ganapati as a metaphor for the endless cycle of creation, destruction and recreation, Veenapani once again makes a very individualistic theatre statement, inspired by traditional forms of art from Kerala like Koodiyattam for its vocabulary. The beauty of the production is that the main narrative is created by an orchestration of percussion with the brass drum *mizhavu* at its centre.

* Earlier published in *The Hindu* on 8 December 2000.

Interacting with the rhythmic cycle set by the *mizhavu* play, were drums like *ghatam, maddalam, edekka, talam* and a variety of folk drums. With improvised rhythmic permutations and combinations woven into the main refrain of the tala cycle, predictability and dry déjà vu were avoided. With one *mizhavu* expert like Hariharan were other participants like Vinay Kumar, the one-man acting unit with whom Veenapani always works, and Suresh Kumar an Ottan Thullal expert, who had learned to use the *mizhavu* through hard work.

The amazing tonal range in rhythm suggesting the wonder of creation, the pulsating joy of life, the power of destruction and the later re-emergence, was abstract art at its best. One can never forget the dark isolation and despair of 'plunging into the depths of despondency', the entire effect created on the drums. Words were kept to the minimum. The *arbhutam* of creation in Parvati as she fashions a child, the impetuous beheading of the boy by Siva, and the subsequent re-emergence of the elephant-headed identity (it is the head that determines the identity, irrespective of the body that supports it), were shown through a movement vocabulary too. Vinay Kumar as always, showed his imaginative capacity for drama, created through physical agility and an excellent sense of timing—the pauses and silences being as important as movement-oriented passages. Bending down, arms circling the large *mizhavu*, back to the audience, moving sinuously to suggest the rump of an elephant in a majestic walk, with the typical sudden lift and sideways kick of the leg was most creative.

Another touch of brilliance was in an actor, seated on a long drum with his back to the audience, the squatting leg and knee deflection on two sides with the delicately lit hollow in the middle, creating a perfect yoni geometry symbolising creation, the actor playing on the drum-head in front to complete the effect. The saxophone chiming in with its deep notes, became the ideal vehicle for suggesting the trumpeting elephant. Supported by the India Foundation for the Arts, Sir Ratan Tata Trust and the Ford Foundation, *Ganapati* is yet another venture by Veenapani, proving how traditional art forms can help spawn ideas for very contemporary art. The lighting was excellent.

Thoughts on Creativity and Cultural Politics

*A Review**

M.D. MUTHUKUMARASWAMY

erformed at the Other Festival on 3 December 2000 in
Chennai (could I have asked for a more appropriate title
for the festival?) *Ganapati*, a musical drama, conveyed what
millions of words usually fail to communicate on creativity and
freedom. While writing about *Ganapati*, I aspire not to describe
it, but to call it into being. With the fallible light of recollection,
I belatedly accept the seductive invitation of the performance to

* Excerpted from a longer article published in the *Indian Folklore
Research Journal* in January 2001.

explore the aesthetics of interaction: an aesthetics that articulates the religious faith towards the possibility of return to existence, expression, love, and life after total destruction. Readers who hear the echo of Nietzschean eternal recurrence are actually listening to the Dionysian drums of Veenapani Chawla's actors. Abandoning origins, the play, like life, begins in the middle of an unknown celebration. Using the temporality of live musical gestures, the drumming actors suggest the ritual creation of an image of Ganapati with a drum signifying his pot-belly.

Sparsely using words in English, the performance alludes to one of the myths of Ganapati. Ambiguously, Parvati on her own creates Martanda from her bodily dirt. The feminine dirt of a son angers the masculine god Siva when he desires consummation with his wife. Beheading the gate-keeping son Martanda, Siva enters Parvati's chamber. The rigidity of masculine and feminine selves, inevitably results in crime. After consummation, on Parvati's pleading, Siva gives life to the son with an elephant head.

This birth story of Ganapati is enacted again and again in the performance from a variety of perspectives, raising the question, what is this figure all about? Adishakti's actors refer to another myth where the identity of a person is decided by the transposed head and go on to assert that Ganapati's identity is determined by the head.

But then, what is in a head? Or, better still, what is a head? In one of the sensuous retellings of the myth, Ganapati's head becomes a western saxophone and his belly, an Indian drum. Initially, the Indian drummer resists and ignores the invading saxophone, but the interaction is so playfully seductive, that they relate and create incredibly theatrical music and dance. After all, living is hybridisation. Living is creolisation.

In another retelling, an opulent demonstration of the sensorial experience of an elephant emerges theatrically: the flapping of the ears, continuously swaying bottom and majestic walk. One almost feels the mischievous twinkle of the tiny eyes of an elephant. The head, in this theatrical exploration, becomes a combination of the senses. Appropriately. If an innovative combination of the senses enhances the aesthetic experience, it also reveals how the senses constitute the mind and contests the supremacy of the mind over the senses.

By avoiding an Aristotelian catharsis of musical ecstasy and by structuring the play to have cycles from different perspectives, Veenapani Chawla keeps the affective dimension of the play within the conscious realm. In this process, the locus of creativity is rightfully in the collectivity. The collectivity includes the reflective participation of the audience. If this is so, one has to confront the performance's prominent question—who owns the intellectual property right?

Undoubtedly, Veenapani Chawla's *Ganapati* is a radical break-through in the history of modern Indian theatre.

The Hare and the Tortoise

Performance Text

VEENAPANI CHAWLA

The Hare and the Tortoise opened in 2007 with four shows at Auroville, National School of Drama (New Delhi), and Kolkata. It went on to do eight more shows in Bangalore, Heggodu, and Thiruvananthapuram. The play was not reviewed much in the Englsih press. One reason for this erasure was the banishing of reviews from most mainline dailies and other publications that began around the mid-1990s. The other reason could also be the complexity of the themes and structure of the play that made it difficult, even for critics, to comprehend in totality. In his interview with Chawla that appears after the performance text, Anmol Vellani, executive director of the India Foundation for the Arts, questions her about several areas that had baffled him when he saw the play.

(L to R) Arjun Shankar, Arvind Rane, Pascal Sieger, and Suresh Kaliyath in *The Hare and the Tortoise*. Photograph courtesy of Nimmy Raphel.

Act 1

Scene 1

(*The stage is divided in two sections. Three-quarters of it in the front is bare. The rest is covered by three huge puppet screens with two windows between them. Areas on the right and left of stage, are marked for the musicians. On the left is a percussionist. On the right are a saxophonist, guitarist and bass guitarist. In the darkness, a sound of strings played with a bow. Deep, and at times discordant. Slowly, a square of light comes up on front stage left. A figure is seen moving in it, almost dancing, straining to perhaps get out of it. It is Hamlet. He contemplates all sides of the square, getting increasingly frustrated by its limited options. After a while he stands still, thinking. The music trails off.*)

HAMLET: Are there answers outside knowledge?

ARJUNA: (*From the shadows in a gap between the puppet screens at the back of the stage*) That's the mystery, Hamlet!

(*Both tumble towards each other and meet on stage. Light fades and a long note on the saxophone is heard. Arjuna and Hamlet exit in the darkness. The music builds up and Ganapati as a shadow puppet, is seen behind the screen to the extreme right. He sings.*)

GANAPATI:
The world's best pair is Ma and Pa;
Their machinations take it far.
While Ma moves busily in life,
Pa stays still and supports his wife.
But Ma made a stipulation:
'If you want marital station—
With brother Kartik you must race
Around the world, to win first place.'

(*The puppet fades off. The music too fades.*)

Scene 2

(*In a circle of light, Ekalavya plays badminton exquisitely, with an unseen partner. She begins in slow motion. Then the tempo changes and varies. Music accompanies her playing. Occasionally one foot steps out of the light. She seems to be astride two worlds. In the middle of play, she suddenly loses her racquet and the use of her arm. Hamlet appears in a window between the screens. He mimes his quietus—the musicians whisper 'Oh that this too, too sullied flesh could melt', etc. as Ekalavya expresses pain at the loss of her thumb. Light fades on Ekalavya and then on Hamlet after he says—'a dew' or 'adieu'.*

Ekalavya becomes a thumb, then turns to face the audience/'comes before god'/adieu, and resumes play without the arm. She uses her eyes in lieu of the arm. Her movements become a dance. The body moves like a bow and the eyes like arrows. The music rises as she exits and continues into the next scene.)

Scene 3

(*When the light comes on, Ekalavya's space is occupied by one of the musicians—musician 1. He mimes her actions in a hopelessly clumsy manner. The music fades and the saxophone sounds a 'Who?' The musician on stage shrugs his shoulders and looks bewildered and then brightens. He cartwheels towards the saxophonist and sings out.*)

MUSICIAN 1: That was Ekalavya. He lost his thumb.

MUSICIAN 2: (*Walks across the stage saying*) Who? Who lost a thumb?

MUSICIAN 1: Ekalavya. (*He spots Musician 2. They both do a double take*) You! And you lost a race.

(*Disappears behind the puppet screen only to reappear as the Tortoise shadow puppet.*)

MUSICIAN 2: (*Shocked and embarrassed. Then he spots the Tortoise puppet on the screen.*) Who are you?

TORTOISE: Come on stage and I'll tell you.

MUSICIAN 2: I *am* onstage.

TORTOISE: No silly. Onstage. (*Throws the Hare puppet to Musician 2, who catches it and catches on.*)

MUSICIAN 2: (*To the audience*) Showtime folks. (*Dances crazily, disappears behind the screen, and becomes Hare.*)

HARE: Who are you—onstage?

TORTOISE: Don't you remember me? I'm Tortoise! The one who won the race!

HARE: That race ... was not a real race!

TORTOISE: Why not?

HARE: If we race again, you will *not* win.

TORTOISE: I'll win. I'll win every time.

HARE: You know why you won the last time?

TORTOISE: Why?

HARE: Because I went off course.

TORTOISE: Off course? (*Amused throughout.*)

HARE: Of course.

TORTOISE: Of course.

HARE: Off course.

TORTOISE: Of course you went off course. And why was that? Why was that? Why was that? You went off on a magical mushroom trip!

HARE: Don't laugh at me! (*In tears.*)

TORTOISE: OK. Don't cry. I'll tell you what. Let's have another race.

HARE: I love it! Referee *kaun*?

TORTOISE: Referee? (*He calls out*) Ganapati!

(*The race begins. The Ganapati puppet is lit up. He sings.*)

GANAPATI: (*Sings*)
   Then slowest and fastest were gone
   On a race, which seemed all wrong.
   For fast and faster can compete,
   But who can slowest race to beat?
   As for me, old Ganapati—
   The race began simultaneously.
   But I reached my goal instantly.

HARE: (*Returning from the race, tearful*) You won *again*? And what was that song?

TORTOISE: It's called *How Ganapati Won the Race.*

HARE: Ganapati won the race? Tortoise won the race? *Arrey mera kya hoga Kalia?*

TORTOISE: (*Sternly*) Hey! (*He strikes Hare. There is an embarrassed pause. Then Hare waddles up to Tortoise and tries to placate him.*)

HARE: Mr Tortoise, who won the race? What about a Number Chase?

TORTOISE: (*Perking up instantly*) A Number Chase? Gummon!

HARE: (*Sniggers. Aside*) Come *on*!

TORTOISE: Go to the front of the class.

HARE: *Yeh lay, main aya. Pooch.*

TORTOISE: What is 217 multiplied by 49?

HARE: That is too complicated. Give me some zeroes! I love holes.

TORTOISE: Alright Hare, here's your head start. What is 217 multiplied by 50?

HARE: Fifty. Cool. Zero—straight side parking. Five times tables. Cool cool! Thi Ki Tha ka Tha ka Thi ki Tha/Tha ka Thi ki Tha/Tha ka Thi ki Tha/Tha ka Tom Tom. (*Hare starts counting. He does this in a* vaitari, *spoken rhythmic bols which develop in a number of voices and take much time, until he hits a crescendo with …*) … 1085!

TORTOISE: Absolutely wrong! It's 10,850! What about that zero you parked on the side?

HARE: *Ai ga! Visarlo!* I forget the zero! Side parking *mein laude lage.* Never mind. It's my turn to ask you. You go to the front of the class.

(*The Tortoise puppeteer runs on to the stage in front of the screens doing a jig.*)

HARE: *Kidhar gaya?*

TORTOISE: I'm here!

HARE: Go to the front of the class!

TORTOISE: I'm *here*!

HARE: Oh! Sorry! What is—900 (*sniggers*). Gochoo, no zeroes for you—999 multiplied by 1001?

TORTOISE: (*Immediately*) 9,99,999. There. Checkmate! Monkey, donkey, elephant, cow sitting in the bathroom eating palav.

(*The Hare puppet falls and bumps his head from shock.*)

HARE: Accident! (*Then, referring to Tortoise's calculations*) That too was pure accident!

TORTOISE: Try me again.

HARE: (*Desperately and fast*) What is the cube root of 729?

TORTOISE: 9.

HARE: 9 ... 9 ... What is 987654321 minus 123456789?

TORTOISE: 864197532.

HARE: (*The Hare puppet dies of shock. Its puppeteer emerges and tells the Tortoise puppeteer*) Amazing. What speed. *Yeh to mar gaya.*

TORTOISE: Dead?

HARE: Fully dead.

(*The saxophonist plays a funeral march. The Hare puppeteer carries the Hare puppet on his shoulders for burial behind the screen. We see the shadow play. The Tortoise puppeteer does a jig in front of the screen and then disappears behind it. The Hare puppet is seen slowly emerging onto the screen. He turns to find the Tortoise puppet breathing down his neck.*)

HARE: (*Screams*) *Daraa mat. Line bhool gaya!*

TORTOISE: (*Prompts*) Amazing speed.

HARE: Amazing stool?

TORTOISE: Amazing fool! Speed!

HARE: Ya! Amazing speed! How do you do it?

TORTOISE: Intuition.

HARE: Intuition? *Ey Ramanujan ke bacche*, these are mathematics problems. They have to be solved using the principles of mathematics. Where are the intermediate steps, the sequential calculations, the logical conclusions? *Kha gaye?*

TORTOISE: Those are only software subsystems. Besides, they take too long. I love immediacy.

(*Silence.*)

HARE: Love?

TORTOISE: Love!

HARE: *Abe laudoo.* What if you go wrong?

TORTOISE: (*Laughs*) Wrong? Me? (*Suddenly*) Someone is coming!

HARE: (*Excited*) Is it a hare?

TORTOISE: Well, not a hare exactly, just a loser.

HARE: (!!!!!!!!!!!!!) And what's a tortoise kind? A winner?

TORTOISE: Well, Ekalavya who lost a thumb is a tortoise kind.

HARE: Lost a thumb and is a winner?

TORTOISE: Absolutely! Lost a thumb and is a winner.

HARE: And this *yevadiya* sitting here—who is he?

TORTOISE: (*Emerging from behind the screen, the better to see*) That's Arjuna—you remember Arjuna?

HARE: Shankar?

TORTOISE: No no. This Arjuna. Lost to Ekalavya!

HARE: O that Arjuna! (*Emerges from behind the screen.*)

TORTOISE: That Arjuna!

(*They run off to the musicians' pit to the right.*)

Scene 4

(*The actor who plays Ekalavya also plays Arjuna. We see Arjuna now, sitting on stage right, recalling the advice of her/his teacher. A*

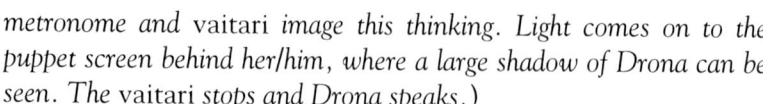

metronome and vaitari *image this thinking. Light comes on to the puppet screen behind her/him, where a large shadow of Drona can be seen. The* vaitari *stops and Drona speaks.*)

DRONA: In the course of evolution, the eye of the bird developed into a spectacular organ of vision. So retina.

(*Drona disappears and Arjuna sits alone, struck by a thought. The metronome and* vaitari *strike up again. S/he mimes eating food in the dark, without sight. Then s/he resumes recalling Drona's words, who reappears as a shadow on the screen behind her/him.*)

DRONA: Time must stand still for your arrow; then it will hit its target at the instant it leaves your hand.

(*Arjuna gets ready to shoot. Drona blesses her/him and disappears from the screen. Arjuna shoots and is disappointed with the result. The* vaitari *and metronome stop. S/he calls out to Ekalavya.*)

ARJUNA: Who taught you Ekalavya?

(*Transition. The actor playing Arjuna becomes Ekalavya. Each has her/his own musical theme, facial reorientation and voice to identify her/him by.*)

EKALAVYA: Taught? (*Teasingly*) What do you mean taught? Taught—us? I taught myself Arjuna.

(*Transition. The actor tumbles across the floor in simulation of a blow received. The scene throws up the rivalry between Arjuna and Ekalavya. There are cheeky responses from Ekalavya and physical aggression from Arjuna. Each transition of character is accompanied by fisticuffs.*)

ARJUNA: Someone must have taught you the three processes at least? (*Transition and tumble.*)

EKALAVYA: Three processes? What are those? Do you mean stringing the bow, focusing on the target and shooting the arrow? (*Transition and tumble.*)

ARJUNA: Don't play with me, *chulla*. You know very well I mean the big three: *Ravana, manana, nidhidyasana*. (*Transition and tumble*.)

EKALAVYA: (*Laughs*) What big, big words. What do they mean? (*Transition and tumble*.)

ARJUNA: Liar! Chulla! You know very well, what they mean. (*Transition and tumble*.)

EKALAVYA: (*Almost in tears*) I swear I don't know! I don't know anything!

(*The stage darkens and the puppet screen lights up to show Tortoise and Hare having a fight. Then the light dims on the puppet screen and the actor is seen onstage, playing on a string instrument—bow/ guitar? Arjuna twangs the bow and Ekalavya makes a melody out of it. This continues for some time. All the while, Arjuna is disgruntled and unsuccessful and Ekalavya is easily competent and teasing, showing off her easy command of the technique*)

EKALAVYA: (*Singing*) I become the bow, I become the arrow, I become the target in a single moment of time.

(*Silence. Transition*.)

ARJUNA: (*Twangs the bow, suggesting the following line*) Is that the difference between us?

(*Transition*.)

EKALAVYA: That is the difference between us. (*Hamlet appears in a window behind her/him. He looks in Ekalavya's direction. Ekalavya gifts her bow to Arjuna and disappears. Music starts up as Hamlet hovers in his window and then turns and leaves. Lights change but the music continues. The saxophonist then strolls onstage playing his instrument. He is actually Zeno. He is interrupted by musician 1*.)

MUSICIAN 1: Hey Zeno! What's your take on this race?

ZENO: Oh, I'll tell you in a minute.

(*Musicians play a fugue on a sopranino, guitar, bass guitar, and drum. When it ends, Zeno still loiters on stage, but is summoned to the music area by the musicians. He scuttles back quickly*.)

MUSICIAN 2: I say guys, how come Tortoise always wins races? He's not even a great runner.

MUSICIAN 1: (*Laughs*) Great runners don't always win races. Look at that one for instance. Do you see him?

MUSICIAN 2: Yes I do. Who is he?

MUSICIAN 1: Hamlet. His mind ran faster than any feet. But then he lost his nerve.

MUSICIAN 2: (*Muttering*) Lost his nerve? The other lost a thumb. What is happening here? (*Heavy music, ominous but fast, starts up. Blackout.*)

Act 2

(*Music from the last scene continues and the lights in the windows come on. We see Hamlet striding quickly through them. Then he enters. The same square of light comes on and he walks into it. He turns and hears a whisper.*)

GHOST: Mark me. Pity me not.

HAMLET: What's there?

GHOST: Lend thy serious hearing …

HAMLET: What's out there?

GHOST: … to what I shall unfold.

HAMLET: Are there answers outside knowledge?

GHOST: I am forbid to tell the secrets, that would freeze the blood of man.

(*Arjuna enters between the puppet screens. S/he says the following and disappears behind a screen to appear on it as a tortoise. And after that his/her words run simultaneously with those of the Ghost.*)

ARJUNA: (*Laughs*) It's a mystery why hares always ask this question!

HAMLET: Who's that?

GHOST: Remember me. I am thy father's spirit.

ARJUNA: Remember me?

HAMLET: Why are you here? You belong there.

GHOST: Doomed for a certain time to walk the night, walk the night, walk the night, walk the night …

HAMLET: What do you want?

GHOST: Revenge, revenge, revenge.

ARJUNA: To compare notes.

HAMLET: About what?

ARJUNA: His foul and most lamentable murder.

GHOST: Remember me.

HAMLET: Hallucination?

ARJUNA:
Wake up! Wake up!
Let's race!
Let's play!

(*Pause. Hamlet connects to Arjuna.*)

HAMLET: Play? (*Pause*) Do I know you?

ARJUNA: It doesn't matter. Let's play.

HAMLET: Yes. Let's play! The Play is the thing! (*The guitar strikes up, the stage brightens, a new energy seems to enter and Hamlet starts dancing and then singing.*) This could … this could have a major impact on my mood, my self-esteem and my relationships.

ARJUNA: Come here!

HAMLET: Wait! (*He runs towards the screen behind which Drona was seen and we see him there as a shadow, dancing to his song.*) It could affect the way I treat Ophelia and Polonius, in a way that could change their fate. It could affect the way I think about killing my uncle. (*He appears in the window, training Arjuna in the sights of the make-believe gun in his hand. Arjuna runs onstage and stands there, alert to danger. Hamlet walks towards her and puts his gun to her head and says*) And that could change the fate of Denmark. (*He gets out of performance mode, relaxes. Arjuna gives a silent laugh.*)

HAMLET: How was that?

ARJUNA: Good! Good! (*Pause*) Now I'll tell you my story.

(*But before Arjuna can do so, Hamlet starts telling it as though it is familiar—because it is very similar to his own. Arjuna is startled, but joins him and also in the jig that accompanies it. They dance upstage together.*)

HAMLET: Once upon a time … The times were rotten …

ARJUNA: My hand trembled …

HAMLET: I couldn't kill my enemy …

ARJUNA: I shrank from the burden of living …

HAMLET:
    This beautiful earth,

ARJUNA: this air,

HAMLET: this golden sky

ARJUNA: was a mask.

HAMLET: Was a mask.

ARJUNA: I was disillusioned!

(*Hamlet turns slowly to look at Arjuna. He asks seriously and earnestly, wanting to know the answer.*)

HAMLET: How did you recover?

ARJUNA: (*Equally quietly and earnestly*) With a soliloquy.

(*Hamlet annoyed at this appropriation of his speciality, jabs Arjuna with his finger, emphasising each word as he backs him/her to the left.*)

HAMLET: Those are mine!

(*Arjuna throws Hamlet's jabbing finger away, backs him to the right of stage, doing a jig while responding.*)

ARJUNA: Yes. But mine was a meta-meta-meta-meta soliloquy.

HAMLET: (*Pushes Arjuna off him to centre-stage*) What's that?

ARJUNA: (*Pause. Slowly, mysteriously, Arjuna starts practising a combat figure of movement, and, at the same time, explains the meta soliloquy. Hamlet watches her interestedly. It's different from what he is acquainted with.*) Well, a meta soliloquy is a soliloquy about a soliloquy. You simply step out of your soliloquy and soliloquize about it. I'm talking about a meta soliloquy, but you can take it to the power of infinity.

(*Pause. Hamlet finds the intricacies of the combat movement difficult. He dismisses it.*)

HAMLET: What rubbish!

ARJUNA: (*Shrugs her shoulders*) Try it. (*Continues to complete her figure.*)

HAMLET: (*Takes up the challenge*) Where do I start? (*Falling into the game and doing the figure of movement. In the middle of the movement they meet, and both stop.*) Have you read me on my depression?

ARJUNA: (*Goes into a dramatic posture as she quotes Hamlet from Hamlet*) 'I have of late lost all my mirth, forgone all custom of exercise.'

HAMLET: (*Warming to the subject*) Mine is the most famous description on the condition.

ARJUNA: (*Laughs and says mockingly*) Modern man in search of his soul. (*Runs off-stage laughing, to disappear behind the puppet screen.*)

HAMLET: (*Furious. Runs behind her*) You are laughing at me. I'm not going to play if ... don't go.

(*Hamlet re-enters and hovers near a window. Heavy metal music on the guitar during the following unspoken bit. Arjuna stands near the other window. Each eyes the other. Hamlet hesitantly walks onstage and silently pleads with Arjuna to join him. What follows is a communication only with eyes, gesture and stance. Arjuna requests a musician to bring a chair on to the stage. On seeing the chair [Psychiatrist's couch] Hamlet moves away in fright. Arjuna gestures to Hamlet to sit on the chair. Reluctantly he does so. Music stops. Arjuna paces behind the chair, waiting for Hamlet to open up.*)

HAMLET:
Is my depression due to a chemical imbalance? Or an emotional conflict?
Do I need medication or psychotherapy? Or both?

ARJUNA: What are your symptoms?

HAMLET: Weight loss, early morning awakening, diurnal variation of mood, disgust with sex, drink, food and physicality in general.

ARJUNA: What are the causes?

HAMLET: My struggle with the slings and arrows of outrageous fortune …

ARJUNA: Outrageous fortune?

HAMLET: My dysfunctional family and society …

ARJUNA: What else?

HAMLET: Doubts about the ethics of revenge, confusion about how to be in the world …

ARJUNA: That one? That one I know intimately!

HAMLET: You do? Tell me!

ARJUNA: Try a meta-meta soliloquy! (*Arjuna disappears behind the darkened screen.*)

HAMLET: (*Gets off his chair in a rush and turns to the screen where Arjuna has disappeared. Bitterly*) What a fool you make of me.

(*Turns and studies the chair, which becomes the throne of Denmark. He caresses it longingly*) I lack advancement.

(*Music starts up, sad brooding music. Hamlet seems to be making love to the chair. He walks towards it as though on a tightrope. A parody of 'to be or not to be'. Then he falls onto the chair, slithers over and around it and finally falls abruptly from it. The entire movement is a dance of sadness to music, which ends abruptly with his fall.*)

ARJUNA: (*Appears in a window, unseen by Hamlet*) You should heal yourself. (*Disappears.*)

HAMLET: (*Shakes with silent laughter. Slowly he picks himself up and sits astride the chair*)
Let me feel.
Let me think.
Why must I do?
My depression is a sign of health.
It gives me time: to reflect, heal …
… be self-aware (*Pause*)
That's powerful action.

(*Musicians sing a* vaitari *as though calling Hamlet to action. Hamlet gets off his chair and starts an intricate pattern of movements with his feet. He runs thus repeatedly between the chair and the screen behind which he had danced. He plots carefully with his feet. The musicians continue their percussive* vaitari. *Suddenly Hamlet stops his planning and makes an emotive rejecting gesture towards the chair. He turns instead towards the screen. The light transforms it into a mirror. He sees his image reflected in it. It traps and seduces him. He is content to be a reflection. He does not want to change that. And then he sees the Angel of History within his image, whose force pushes him forward, in the direction of the chair, in spite of himself. He halts midway.*)

HAMLET: I don't want to run anymore.

ANGEL OF HISTORY: I am ready for flight.

HAMLET: I would like to turn back.

ANGEL OF HISTORY: Don't try to stop timeless time, you will have little luck.

(*Pause.*)

HAMLET: (*Low and falling*)
I want to stand still …

ANGEL OF HISTORY: … and walk backward like a crab? (*Pause.*) Nothing and no one in the world can stand still. Listen to this story.

(*Hamlet unfreezes and goes to sit on the chair/throne.*)

HAMLET: Whose story is this, Zeno?

MUSICIAN 3: A girl who ran with a red queen.

HAMLET: You mean Alice who ran fast on the same spot?

MUSICIAN 3: The same girl.

(*Musicians enter and play Alice's race with the Red Queen. A steady slow drum-beat signifies the status quo, while the saxophone races progressively ahead to signify movement. As it plays, Hamlet retards into a young infant, worshipful of his father. After a while, he returns to normalcy and interrupts the musicians.*)

HAMLET: What's the point?

ZENO:
The importance of being contemporary …

MUSICIAN 2: … and being in the present. (*The musicians retire.*)

HAMLET: The present … (*Starts laughing, then goes quiet.*) The present is out of joint my friend. (*Pause.*) Will I ever stand still?

MUSICIAN 2: Yes, when you lose your shadow.

HAMLET: How do I lose my shadow?

MUSICIANS: (*Laugh. Blackout. When the lights come on again, Hamlet has disappeared. Ganapati enters and dances. At the end of his dance, there is a blackout, and only the Ganapati puppet is lit up during the following song.*)

GANAPATI:
A lid was smashed, a veil was torn:
I *was* the World-I was new-born.
The race began simultaneously.
But I reached my goal instantly.

(*Light comes on and Hamlet is seen walking back slowly to his chair. He sits.*)

HAMLET: (*Pause.*) Isn't this resolution outside knowledge?

TORTOISE: Checkmate!

HAMLET: What?

TORTOISE: Checkmate!

(*Pause. Light changes. Soft, slow music. Light on Arjuna in a window, dancing. Very slowly, Hamlet gets up and makes a gesture of giving in. He slowly overturns his chair and sits on it.*)

ARJUNA: It's a mystery Hamlet, how you made the transition from 'to be or not to be' to 'let be'.

HAMLET: It must have happened off-stage.

ARJUNA: Off-stage? Ah! on the boat to England.

HAMLET: Maybe … Perhaps … Maybe.

(*Light fades on Hamlet and comes on to the screen, where Hare is dancing. Music. Hare sings.*)

HARE:
There was a knowledge seeker,
Hedged in by human limits.
He sacrificed the main road,
To take a zig-zag by-lane.

And though he lost much time,
He grew a wiser man.

(*Light goes off on the screen and comes on to fall only on Hamlet.*)

HAMLET:
There is a Divinity that shapes our ends
Rough-hew them how we will.
If it be now, 'tis not to come,
If it be not to come, it will be now,
If it be not now, yet it will come.
The readiness is all.

(*Blackout.*)

PUPPETS: Ready! Get set! Go! (*Musicians start up music of the race. And end it abruptly.*)

The End

From Aesop to Hamlet

*An Interview**

ANMOL VELLANI

ANMOL VELLANI: My first question is, why did you call it *The Hare and the Tortoise?*

VEENAPANI CHAWLA: That is the cover story.

VELLANI: Which cover story?

CHAWLA: The race … the race.

VELLANI: The race. The reason I asked is because I was slightly confused by that title. And my confusion was that when

* This interview was conducted in Puducherry on 3 April 2011.

somebody says *The Hare and the Tortoise*, I think of Aesop's fable. And in Aesop's fable what happens is that the hare loses the race because of his own conceit because he is so sure of himself, so self-confident, so absolutely certain about his own superiority over the tortoise, that he can let the tortoise go ahead, and he can sleep and he can eat cabbages, etc., etc., and he loses because he's so sure he's going to win. He leaves it till too late—and then doesn't win. So at least in Aesop's version there seems to be very little—apart from the fact that it is a race with two animals challenging each other—of the concerns at the heart of your production. So when I viewed the production, I asked myself, now what is Veenapani taking from the fable which is relevant? So that's why I am wondering whether you might have just confused the audience by referring to a fable that has nothing in it, apart from a race, which relates to anything I can see in the production.

CHAWLA: Interpretation allows a metaphorical reading of the fable. When we talk about the confidence of the hare—and let's forget about the moral problems of conceit, etc.—we are thinking of the hare operating within a known system over which he has total control. And the production's concerns are with being *outside* a known system. In a known system, yes, we feel we have control over things. But in moments of crisis, we do not have control because there are questions to which the operating system does not have answers. Therefore you have to go outside that system to find answers to those questions. The parallel texts in the production, which involve Hamlet, Arjuna/Ekalavya, Ganapati, Zeno, and Alice, are there to reinforce these concerns from a variety of different perspectives.

Also, I did not take the fable as it is and map the other stories on to it. In fact the text which really concerned me was the Hamlet/Arjuna story and the other texts accumulated in my mind because of a connection I sensed between them. I took a latent response from within myself, sensing a connection with the other stories and used that to structure the production. When we look at certain connecting texts, there is of course the self-evident element, but there is also a kind of latent thought, which is not so clear to one. It is not articulated completely, all the ends are not tied up. It is latent and it is connecting; and that is what I used.

VELLANI: So you're interpreting the hare as someone who functions within a certain system?

CHAWLA: Yes, the hare …

VELLANI: The hare is functioning from within a system. Let's just stay with that thought …

CHAWLA: … *known* system.

VELLANI: Known system, yes. You equate Hamlet and the hare. Hamlet is the hare, right? And he's constantly challenged, therefore. And I love that little square of light you create, which in the most recent version [of the production] is at the beginning, if I'm not mistaken. Hamlet is within that light and yet, occasionally, part of him goes out of that light as if struggling to go outside the known frame, which is the lit frame, but he doesn't quite make it out. Though his movements suggest that there is something outside that visual frame, he cannot quite get all of himself out of it. He's constantly drawn back into that square of light. Was that what you were intending?

CHAWLA: Yes. And I juxtaposed it with the scene which follows, when Ekalavya plays badminton/shoots arrows. But he is in a circular light—there is a quality of infinity about a circle, unlike the square. The square gives the impression of limitation, of being boxed in. Anyway, Ekalavya puts his foot outside that circle of light, he goes completely out … And then one foot is outside and one inside. He's astride both worlds.

VELLANI: So are you therefore trying to say … See, one way you could read the production is to say, okay, this is about different states of consciousness; this is about a knowledge frame, the epistemological frame, the subject-predicate frame, the knower-and-known frame, and another a state of being, which is outside that frame. But what I'm hearing you now say is that what's important is to belong to two frames at the same time, or to be able to traverse ...

CHAWLA: Yes it is about all that you say. However, you *may* belong to two frames simultaneously. I assume that if you step into another system, you will also know the one that you have left.

VELLANI: Yes, certainly ... certainly.

CHAWLA: So some part of you, being familiar with it, is identified with it. Familiarity. Yet there is something ...

VELLANI: But do you see that frame differently then because you have been able to go outside it and look at it from some other place?

CHAWLA: I think it remains a plane you know; and you see it more clearly from outside ...

VELLANI: ... for what it is.

CHAWLA: Yes. You see it more clearly. Subjectively your experience of it changes—and that is the point—but it remains what it is, objectively.

VELLANI: So it's the difference between being in a frame entirely and seeing it therefore in a certain way, and then being able to see it from some other place ...

CHAWLA: Yes.

VELLANI: ... which sort of frames it for you.

CHAWLA: You can know it better. You can see what you can do with it. And you have more tools to deal with the problems within it. For instance, Arjuna's crisis and its solution are about being within a known frame and then stepping out of it into another frame—where you find the solution to the problems of the earlier frame. Then having found the solution, you go back to dealing with the problem of the earlier frame with more tools, more capacity. Of course in my interpretation, the colloquy at Kurukshetra is a soliloquy, which enables Arjuna to step out of the crisis within the frame he occupies and then to deal with it. In the production, Arjuna advises Hamlet to try a meta meta meta meta soliloquy for solutions to his problems. For one can step out of systems and more systems and more systems and more systems. I suppose there are endless [systems], I don't know, empirically, but, yes, I think that is what it is. I don't want to use the word 'hierarchy'—but it is something like that.

VELLANI: Like a universe within a universe within a universe within a universe, right? So you can step back to other universes ...

CHAWLA: Yes.

VELLANI: ... and keep stepping back, really.

CHAWLA: Keep stepping out because then you equip yourself with more tools with which to deal with everything around. I must say that this concept of stepping out of known systems was reinforced in my mind when I read about Gödel's Incompleteness Theorem in [Douglas R. Hofstadter's] *Gödel, Escher, Bach*. Gödel critiques [Alfred North Whitehead and Bertrand Russell's] *Principia Mathematica* on the grounds that no particular system can be complete in itself; you always have to step outside that system to find answers to some of the questions.

VELLANI: So what is the tortoise, then, in *The Hare and the Tortoise*? You've told me what the hare is. The hare is functioning from within a certain system. So does the tortoise have a particular ...?

CHAWLA: The tortoise is the one who can [step out of the system]. He can occupy all the systems simultaneously. Ekalavya is a tortoise. He is like the tortoise in Zeno's Paradox. Zeno's Paradox is actually also about the failure of a system. He is talking about the fact that there is no such thing as movement.

VELLANI: Wait. What Zeno is trying to say is not the impossibility of motion—because the Paradox is itself built on assuming that two people are moving—but the illusion of motion.

CHAWLA: The illusion of motion.

VELLANI: Right? The illusion of movement. Which brings me to the other images which the production works with, plays with. Alice is moving fast on the same spot, for instance, which also suggests the illusion of motion ...

CHAWLA: Exactly. And also, there again, it's another system; it's another way of looking at life and existence and knowledge.

VELLANI: I was just thinking that the idea that Alice is moving fast in the same place could relate to another idea in the production ... For example, in the Kartikeya–Ganapati race, one guy runs and the other guy is ...

CHAWLA: Yes. It is also about the different consciousness that these two have. With Ganapati, the consciousness is such that just being where he is, he is also everywhere—a consciousness, which comprehends, apprehends but also knows by identity, knows by becoming the totality.

VELLANI: So being yourself the target and the bow.

CHAWLA: Yes, absolutely! That is exactly it. Kartikeya represents a physical travelling in time and Ganapati the experience of the space–time continuum. The moment of 'now' dilated to include all three dimensions of time—past, present, and future—and of space. In Einstein's space–time continuum, as time dilates, space contracts. And as one physicist, Edward Harrison said, 'In one heartbeat one can traverse the universe.'

It seems as though space–time generates a universal consciousness. Mystics experience this universal consciousness, where a specific existence expands and exists everywhere—is the universe; is the universe through another kind of knowing, that of becoming it, of knowing by identity rather than through the senses or the rational mind. All the tortoise characters have this universal consciousness.

VELLANI: Yes. Now in the play, very cleverly, Zeno's Paradox is not expressed or articulated in words, it is interpreted through music. And there is that very beautiful musical passage where the rhythm is completely fixed and simple, around which Pascal is racing in different ways. And his relationship to that fixed rhythm keeps changing. So how was the music expressing the Paradox in your understanding?

CHAWLA: I think the music you describe is the one which communicates Alice running on the same spot. Zeno's Paradox, which was also communicated through music, was expressed through a fugue. The fugue repeats a theme through infinite variations and so gives at once the sense of movement and of non-movement. The illusion of movement as you put it. And this is true of the Alice music as well. The fugue also gives you a sense of infinity; a temporal or finite way of expressing infinity—which too is a paradox! In my mind the notion of infinity runs through all the tortoise characters: the Tortoise—in both the fable and Zeno's Paradox—Alice, Ganapati, Ekalavya.

VELLANI: We were talking about frames. A very important thing happened as this production evolved. Whereas in the early versions, if I recall correctly, Hamlet appeared in the middle, what you've done now is have Hamlet begin, come through—weave through the production—and also end it. So Hamlet has become the framing device. What do you think that brought to the production?

CHAWLA: Well actually, that was how I had first written the script. Then I passed it around. For I must say that I was not very confident in the beginning. And people said, 'Don't begin like this; it doesn't make sense.' I think when you write something and it is just a fraction of what is in your mind, it doesn't communicate to everyone in the way it communicates to you. So, not being confident, I shifted Hamlet to the middle. Then when I saw the piece, I realized that it wasn't working. Because

Hamlet really frames the problem, or shall we say, images the problem, right at the beginning. The production uses his problem as the means to clearly focus on its concerns.

And the second thing had to do with Vinay as an actor. As an actor, he came on stage in the middle of the production, after doing all kinds of stage management jobs off-stage. It just didn't work for him. He needed to feel Hamlet running in him from the beginning to give a strong performance. So, as I said, it was important to go back to the way I had initially written it, as that reflected the main concern—Hamlet's dilemma. It was from there that everything else came—as parallel texts.

I could have made the parallel texts and the production more organic but I didn't because that would have been too manufactured. I wanted it to reflect an unconnected, slightly sensed rather than really apprehended latency, which I had felt at the start when I was just beginning to reflect on the piece. Because what happens, at least to me, is that the moment I explain, I lose something of the depth that lies below the expressed thought. I feel that there is so much explaining that we do on the surface that the weight below has gone from our expression. And we need to have that—at least I need to have that—otherwise I feel the work is too superficial. So that sense of even not knowing myself completely, not having all the knots tied up—that was important. Just to give a sense of that latent possibility, that sense that the audience and I are …

VELLANI: … are discovering all the time.

CHAWLA: All the time. That there is a weight. One loses that by explaining and making everything self-evident. And profundity comes when everything is not completely explained. You hint at it and you show the way. You just say go there and maybe …

VELLANI: It's very interesting, what you said; because Homi Bhabha, the cultural theorist, is busy writing a book at the moment where he says all art—and I suppose by that he means art that is worthwhile, worth bothering about—is art that is always at the point of revealing itself. So this being at that point allows art to have this quality—of profundity, of latent depths ...

CHAWLA: ... [it is an] invitation to go into these dark channels, discover them for yourself. Not to have it spelt out.

VELLANI: And therefore the connections between the different races and the different characters—you can read them in different ways at different times, even though there is a frame, a reason why you bring them together.

CHAWLA: I wanted to leave these as parallels and not necessarily connect them in an overly explained manner.

VELLANI: We talked about different states of consciousness, different states of being, different realities, different universes. It's very interesting, therefore, that you use these multiple idioms of performance in the play. You have the puppets, you have the actors—the human form. The puppet forms interact with each other; the puppet forms interact with the human form. You have the human form interacting with a shadow of a human form, and then the actor in front of the screen interacting with the puppet behind the screen. What was the impulse behind combining those idioms and having them speak to each other?

CHAWLA: The form was also trying to become the content.

VELLANI: You were trying to express something through the form of the play itself.

CHAWLA: Yes.

VELLANI: Has it to do with what you said at the beginning, which is that you can be in multiple frames at the same time? And also what you are trying to do is to say the same thing in multiple ways.

CHAWLA: Yes, multiple ways to achieve multiple perspectives. And you are right that the play deals with different realities, different frames, etc., and that the puppets contribute to this. But let me add here that I thought of using puppets in the first place because a shadow puppeteer lived with us at Adishakti—very poor but a genius; the last in line of an old family of shadow puppeteers from the Thanjavur region. We adopted him and he would perform for our guests and other audiences. But I wanted to extend his practice and our knowledge of it, so I toyed with the idea of using puppets in a production. And *The Hare and the Tortoise* was in my mind for our next production!

The hare and the tortoise are archetypes. And so it seemed apt that the shadow puppets should manifest them. The shadow nature of these puppets led me to explore the shadow as a device to portray memory, the past, history, etc. When Arjuna is practising his bow and arrow, he recalls Drona—the shadow behind him. And Hamlet's obsession with the past, with memory, keeps him from moving forward.

The human form interacting with the puppet came out of a memory of a shadow puppet performance I had seen by the Kerala shadow puppeteers at Adishakti. The performers introduced their work with a musical introduction in front of the puppet screen and then in a single file disappeared behind the screen and became the puppets. I was floored by this morphing of the three-dimensional form into a two-dimensional form. And it came to me that the only way I could hint at the four dimensions of the tortoise against that of the hare was to have a moment such as this.

With regard to the use of multiple idioms—I must add here that I have been looking to reflect the contemporary mind in my work; the changeable nature of its perception of reality, its multiple-sightedness. And I find one way of doing this is through a kind of aesthetic pluralism, one which gives equal weight or importance to all the modes of expression—the word, the aural image, the visual image, etc. And as each of these expressions communicates uniquely, you get the sense of multiple perspectives and of mutability rather than repetition.

In *The Hare and the Tortoise*, I used more idioms than I usually do because the content demanded it.

VELLANI: This was the last thing I wanted to know—this business of playing with different realities, the puppet reality and the human reality, and between those realities.

Six
Workshops

As Hollow as a Drum

*Actor Training the Adishakti Way**

JOY BROOKE FAIRFIELD

The *mizhavu* is a large urn-shaped copper drum that accompanies performances of the Koodiyattam theatre. To play the difficult instrument requires both strength and grace: firm and fearless hands dance a fluid duet with the slick taut hide. When played well, the mizhavu rings like a bell at each strike and also resounds with a deep, heavy thud that you can feel in your bones.

* This report was written by the author while visiting Adishakti, particularly to observe their training methods.

Every afternoon of the Adishakti workshop, the participants sit onstage in a large circle, each engaged in the personal struggle to make their mizhavu sing. For over an hour they press their bodies against the challenge of drumming, attending closely to the ever-changing rhythms that can reach impossible speeds. Led by skilled teachers who inspire and occasionally terrify, the students must focus intently or risk losing the beat. There is no room in this circle for the individual ego.

At first it sneaks in here and there. Sour faces exchanged over the pain felt in hands. Laughter at the mistakes made by self or the neighbour. But eventually sweat rolls down and expressions clear. The rigid rhythms require the constant attention not of the brain but of the moving, sensing body. In the heart-shaking din of the circle of drums, the mind goes magnificently quiet.

'We're not trying to make you drummers,' says master drummer Suresh Kaliyath at the beginning of the first class. 'But every actor needs to learn to feel rhythm in his body.' Over the course of the workshop you realize that in order to let those rhythms resonate in you the way they move through the mizhavu, you'll have to make yourself as hollow as a drum.

All actor-training programmes involve the sharing of tools considered necessary for the job. Actors need graceful bodies, strong voices, emotional expressivity, and fearlessness in the face of the audience's gaze. Many training institutes approach these goals with a variety of techniques applied *on top* of an actor's pre-existing body, voice, emotional core, and psychological makeup. The body, if addressed at all, is taught posture and sometimes dance. To speak well, actors learn to project their voices and enunciate their words. To express emotion, they practise the application of their personal experiences to imaginary circumstances. Confidence, their teachers hope, should unfold from the successful mastery of these techniques, leaving the actors adequately prepared for the task of representing realistic characters—at least those similar to their own age, gender, and type—on the stage or screen.

At Adishakti, the training takes a different path. The priorities are the same—graceful bodies, clear voices, emotional openness, and a strong presence. However, instead of an additive process of acquiring new tricks, the path they suggest is one of subtraction. An actor, like any human being, has been acted upon over her lifetime by personal and cultural circumstances, resulting in accumulated layers of social conditioning that are 'performed', often unconsciously, in daily life. Women, for example, are taught relentlessly the importance of looking pretty, while men are often conditioned to hide sorrow and fear. Different class backgrounds can result in unique physical carriages or ways of speaking. Even being an actor comes with its own set of habits. We are often taught to speak too loudly and to retain painful memories from our past for use in our work. While these conditioned ways of being can serve us in life—and sometimes onstage or on camera—they are also limiting. To face the great task of performance, an actor must be able to mobilize all possible energies and resources. The unifying theme of the diverse classes taught at an Adishakti workshop is this attempt to unlock the actor's habitual usage of her body, voice, emotions, and psyche. Following in the footsteps of the resident artists themselves, actors are invited to become creative scientists performing experiments on their own ways of being.

Polish theatre-director and innovator Jerzy Grotowski called this kind of training the *via negativa*, contrasting it with the 'positive' path of traditional acting schools. A term borrowed from classical Christian theology, the 'via negativa' is a type of philosophical contemplation intended to move the devout closer to an understanding of God's ineffability. Rather than proclaiming what God is, theologians contemplating the via negativa consider instead what He is not. For example, God is not in this house because the house was constructed by men. God is not this tree because the tree will someday die. God is not the sky above because even the sky has limits. At the end of the process of elimination, God is not absent but rather revealed as outside of human comprehension completely. First frustrated, the analytical mind is eventually encouraged to sit peacefully beside its own inability to understand. Like Zen monks contemplating *koans*, theologians who tread the via negativa must confront the limits of their own knowledge.

Actors who embark on a training method that embraces the principles of the via negativa must be willing to cut away at their ideas of who they are. Am I my stoic facial expressions? No. Am I my graceful feminine body movements? No. Am I the actor with the deep rumbling voice? No. Like novices undergoing initiation to an order of warrior-priests, the group joins together in the transformational space of training to see what they could become when they give up who they are accustomed to being. Unlike the spiritual seeker, though, the actor undergoes this practice of ego-vanquishing not towards the goal of transcendence but rather so she can feel her body's intersection with the world more sensitively and use its innate openness to resonate meaning outwards, towards others.

The traditional Kerala martial art Kalaripayattu, practised every morning during the workshop, jumpstarts the process of breaking down ingrained patterns in the actors' bodies and minds. On the first day, students watch the swift, powerful movements of master teacher Nimmy Raphel and think, I could never do that. Yet all participants, regardless of age, gender, or prior experience, are expected to aim for mastery. Just as they do not intend to transform the actors into drummers, they don't expect to turn all their students into Kalaripayattu experts over just a handful of days. The rigorous training can certainly open up new physical possibilities—greater strength, speed, flexibility, alertness, and responsiveness—but the practice also has the potential to instigate shifts in the actor's consciousness.

The instructors use the intensity of the form to shove performers *past* the limitations erected by their minds. We become habituated to the sedentary bodies of students or businessmen, to bodies that move like women or men, like Indians or Americans, like intellectuals or comedians. In the practice of Kalaripayattu, there is simply not enough time or space to retain these physiological representations of identity. Each gesture must be clean and clear, every moment accounted for in either stillness or movement. Though there is no such thing as completely neutral body usage, the physicality produced by Kalaripayattu is different enough from quotidian forms of embodiment for it to become a kind of aesthetic neutral. The shared space of the martial art provides a meeting place for the participants where concentration and accuracy are all that matter. Everything else must fall away. This struggle for precision cultivates an intensity of focus and full-body presence that connects actors not only to the specific historical tradition of Kalaripayattu but also to the archetype of the warrior-priest, the actor's spiritual predecessor.

Kalaripayattu is complicated enough to challenge everyone, including athletes, dancers, and those with training in other martial arts. Struggling with your own limits results not only in the ecstatic process of overcoming them but also in greater humility. It is hard to be too proud when you're dripping with sweat and tripping over your own feet. Kalaripayattu welcomes all workshop participants to a kind of beginner's mind that is the ideal space from which to approach physical theatre training. Moving through the complicated physical exercises, the group enters a state of collective vulnerability.

The openness cultivated by the morning's Kalaripayattu practice is key preparation for the other forms of training presented over the course of a workshop day. Breaking into smaller groups, students work intimately with teachers on emotional expressivity and spoken text, relying on the breath as the base resource for both explorations.

At Adishakti it is said that 'Breath is emotion is breath'. Through in-depth research into physiology, they have developed specific breath patterns that have the power to trigger within the performer, the physical experiences of the main emotions described in the Natyashastra. Working with master teacher Vinay Kumar, workshop participants are introduced to these physical techniques and taught to use the breath to generate expression in the face and voice. Breaking down the emotions into technical aspects such as breath length, air placement, mouth shape, and facial muscles is at first extremely tedious, like dissecting a joke so completely that it loses all its humour. Yet, over the course of the week, you watch the efficacy of this process of stimulating rather than simulating emotions. Actors are startled to witness each other produce emotionally affective expressions using breath and muscle triggers rather than the personal emotional recall used in method acting.

Emotional expressivity is rarely taught in acting class. There is a widespread assumption that 'if you feel it, the audience will see it'. However, emotional transparency, like everything else in human nature, is conditioned. Our access to emotions as well as our ability to share them through expression is limited by our personal and cultural experiences. Actors are often innately expressive people but habits of the breath, body, and psyche still limit our range. Working from the premise that everyone can access the full range of emotional experiences if nothing gets in their way, the teachers at Adishakti urge actors to traverse the via negativa en route to emotional expressivity. Attempting to figure out why an actor has a particularly shallow inhale, Kumar asks, 'Cold? Allergies? Stuffy nose?' The actor shakes his head three times. 'Ah,' the teacher says, eyes lighting up. 'Habit!' And promptly begins pounding firmly on the man's chest, trying to loosen up whatever has gotten stuck.

The self-revelations that occur through this work result in the development of shared vulnerability and trust within the group of actors. Some have passed out completely while experiencing anger or even mirth. Tears frequently fall while working with emotions of sadness, fear, or wonder. Participants watch each other struggle with certain breath practices whilst others come easily. They learn from their colleagues' successes and see their own issues reflected in each others' blockages. Always, through repetition, focus, and encouragement, it becomes possible to break down the self-imposed but unconscious barriers that limit expressivity. After a series of pounds, pokes, verbal jokes, and demonstrations, the shallowly breathing actor is finally able to begin inhaling more deeply and consciously, opening up the doorway to emotional expression that had previously been inaccessible.

In this strange circle of panting bodies, actors push the boundaries of their emotional expressiveness through stretching and strengthening the muscles of their faces and diaphragms. In prac-tising each specific breath pattern and focusing on the sensations of air moving through their tensing and releasing muscles, they understand more deeply and immediately what emotions actually feel like in the flesh. Using sensation awareness as the base of per-formance helps the actor stay present in the moment rather than constantly reaching backwards for shreds of still-active personal memories. Reliance on these bodily techniques also allows the actor access to emotional states she might not feel, or even be able to feel, in her daily life.

In addition to making possible a greater range of expressive-ness, these techniques also give the actor greater facility in con-trolling the flows of emotional energy in her body. In life, at peak places of emotion, we begin to lose our self-awareness. The actor cannot afford to do this. She must be able to skilfully surf a physi-cal experience of emotion but stick to the rhythm of the play and remain present to the other actors onstage as well as to the eyes of the audience. By learning the somatic foundations of emotions in this rigorous way, the actor gains the ability to shape and sculpt physical expression in the same way she might learn the steps to a dance. She can be alive in the moment, yet remain in control of the potentially uncontrollable emotional energy.

It is said at Adishakti that the work is intended to cultivate the inner landscape of the actor. At first this might seem strange, as most of the training revolves around apprenticing one's body to external forms. But in fact what is being taught is a new way of connecting one's inner experiences to one's creative, embodied output. This is the case with Kumar's work with the emotions, and also very evident in the class led by Veenapani Chawla on voice and text.

Using linguistic diagrams and charts, actors learn the exact placement of vowels and consonants in the mouth. Chawla's sensitive ear guides them towards an understanding of precisely where the vibrations of each sound hit the body—the lips, the tongue, the roof of the mouth. While other speech training tech-niques focus on how each vowel and consonant should sound to the audience, this work focuses on how they feel to the actor.

Through increasing their sensitivity to the movement of air and vibrations that make up human speech, the actors learn to fully experience the sensuousness of each word.

The point of this work is not simply to develop clear articulation so that actors can be heard from the back row of the theatre; rather, Chawla makes clear, that learning to feel each word from the inside out changes one's relationship with language. In the work with the emotions, the actor is reminded that human expression is ultimately a series of subtle and intricate physical actions. Similarly, in the voice and text class, the actor is confronted with the beautifully simple vision, that speaking is an embodied dance between the breath and the body. We may think of language as something superior to the human form or placed on top of it as the evolution of human consciousness progressed but in fact it is a deeply sensuous process that requires the lips to touch themselves, the tongue to tap the teeth and palate, the uvula to vibrate in the warm cavern of the back of the throat.

Chawla's embodied philosophy of speech does not prioritize mechanical articulation but rather full investment in the physical experience of each moment of speaking. Over the course of the workshop, actors learn exercises that isolate the mouth movements of the vowels and consonants so that they can be more fully conscious of the action of the breath. They also practise putting speech into motion and linking language with intention using running, throwing a ball, and volleying a badminton shuttlecock. Through these techniques, a new relationship with language is cultivated that transcends the purely rational-critical mode. Actors are able to experience speaking not as a way of simply sharing thoughts but as a new form of conscious embodiment through which precise meaning can be exchanged. While this might sound esoteric, the results are quite practical. By the end of the training, almost every actor can be heard and understood more clearly, even from the back row, and it becomes evident that clarity in language arises not from mechanical articulation or pushing for volume but from the power of consciousness investing itself fully into the moment of speech.

In addition to resulting in greater clarity, this approach to voice work also imbues language with a freshness that is crucial for the actor who must recite the same text night after night. It is difficult to attend to the same words with a constant sense of discovery if one conceives of language as purely a technical means to a communicative end. In Chawla's philosophy, however, a word is not a random assortment of sounds but rather has clues to its meaning coded inside its structure. 'The word "length" actually has length to it,' she explains. 'Try it! You cannot say the word without allowing your mouth to experience lengthening.' Working with a powerful speech by Lady Macbeth from Shakespeare's play, actors learn how the movement of air and body combine into a sort of magical incantation. Wider mouth shapes seem to summon the void itself, and consonant-heavy passages hit the air aggressively as if each cut of the breath were the stroke of a knife. What is ironic about this work is that while it might seem complicated, the actual struggle for the actor is to get out of her own way. Chawla encourages actors to let the sensual physicality of the words do the work for them and to simply be present to the speaking of the spell-like syllables. Again, this technique is not additive but a process of subtraction. If the actor can let go of her plan and release her preconceived notions, then she is free to tumble head-first into the moment of speaking. In doing so, the freshness that is so difficult to attain on the 20th night of performance, arises naturally.

Over the course of a workshop day at Adishakti, the performer takes a journey from the micro to the macro. In the early morning, even before the Kalaripayattu session, actors engage in 15 minutes of eye exercises, in which the smallest but arguably most powerful organs of creative expression are trained towards greater strength, endurance, and reach. After traversing the internal regions of the body, breath, and voice, the interpersonal emotional and verbal realms, and the collective space of the drum circle, in the evening the actor is confronted with the big picture perspective of full stage action.

This evening class, taught by Kumar, continues the embodied education of rhythm explored earlier in the day through drumming but goes several steps further. Actors are introduced to the notion of rhythm as an organizing principle for stage action— the play itself has a pulse, the expectation of the audience constitutes another pulse, and the actor's job is to work rhythmically within those contexts. More of a sensibility than a tool, rhythmic awareness can be applied to movement, speech, emotional expression, or other aspects of performance. In this class, cultivation of rhythm begins with clapping and counting to the steady beat of a metronome. As the exercises grow more complicated, seemingly simple tasks like listening, counting, and responding on cue become almost impossible challenges. In the failures, the split between what you intend to do and what you are able to do becomes painfully obvious. The successes prove the power of focus, practice, and attitude. All scenarios reveal the ongoing challenge of aligning the clapping, moving, speaking body with the planning, thinking, intending mind.

As with the emotions, the process towards greater rhythmic sensitivity requires becoming aware of your own habits. Are you always rushing the beat? Are your natural body movements slower than those of others? Do you have a hard time staying focused all the way through a particularly long pattern? Do you always end up joining your neighbour's beat when your task was to hold your own? There is nothing wrong with 'walking to the beat of your own drummer' in daily life; but actors must be comfortable in various rhythms, depending on the play, character, and moment.

In addition to understanding that rhythmic sensibility is necessary for performance, participants leave this class with a deep appreciation for the beauty of multiple overlapping rhythms. Using examples from visual art, popular music, and animation, Kumar shows how numerous independently operating rhythms in a work of art can provide greater interpretive options for the viewer. When possibilities for interpretation are increased, meaning is amplified. In this way, this class serves to draw students towards a new aesthetic, one that challenges simple narrative and transparent signifiers and engages viewers as participants rather than passive observers.

Training at Adishakti encourages the actor to be radical with herself. Over the course of the workshop, you learn to enjoy the feeling of pushing your own boundaries and tearing down the false effigies of who you thought you were. Watching others do the same is inspiring, and the group energy of exploration and rigour can pull even the hesitant along in its wake. While we think of radical training methods as often linked to the new and innovative, these techniques draw power through their connection to traditional forms. The kind of performance knowledge that is generated in the intersection of old forms with contemporary research is both grounded and groundbreaking. One does not become radical by putting on newer and stranger costumes but by using reliable tools to peel off the layers of conditioning that impede the resonance of the emptiness within.

Over the course of the 90-minute drumming class, the actor experiences pain in different places of her body—hands, shoulders, back, hips. Through attending closely to the impeccable technique of Kaliyath and the fluid fire of company member Arvind Rane, it eventually dawns on her that the pain in her hands arises not from the impact of flesh against hide but because of an almost imperceptible reflex of tension immediately before she makes contact with the drum. It is not the action itself but the attempt to protect herself from it that causes pain. So with the shoulders—they hurt not from the constant swinging motion but because of the subtle and unconscious ways the muscles attempt to control the swing. So with the back—it anxiously stretches forward towards the drum rather than allowing the negative space between the body and the copper to be part of the dance. So with the hips—they tense slightly upwards away from the chair rather than relaxing down and forming the sturdy bowl that can hold the body in its open grasp. Each instance of tension is a habit that has solidified in the body, conditioned in countless ways over the course of a human lifetime. The difficult and noble task of the actor is to radically cut away at all of these calcifications of body, breath, and behaviour so that the interaction between self and world can be as unencumbered as possible. But, as the resident artists demonstrate, this journey towards freedom can only take place through rigorous, conscious, intentional daily action. At Adishakti it is said that the goal of the actor is to become 'both the potter and the pot'; or in other words, the skilful artist who consciously crafts an object of beauty and the unconscious, material clay that allows itself to be shaped. Perhaps, additionally, it could be said that the goal is to become 'both the drummer and the drum'.

Through this workshop, the actor summons her inner drummer, the sweating, pulsing body pounding with all her might in the gallant attempt to release all shadows of fear that manifest as physical tension and pain. At the same time she seeks the conscious embodiment of the perfectly crafted mizhavu, the spacious, hollow vessel desiring nothing more than to resound the ineffable beauty of its own emptiness.

Source of Performance Energy[*]

RAM GANESH KAMATHAM

I must admit that I was extremely nervous about attending the Source of Performance Energy workshop at the Adishakti Laboratory for Theatre Arts and Research in Pondicherry. The biggest worry on my mind was that I had tossed up acting a while ago in favour of sitting at a desk and writing plays. I was dreading the prospect of actually going back to saying lines, as opposed to cursing under my breath every time a line was miffed, paraphrased or twisted by a performer in a way it was not meant to be. I figured I was at least half-prepared, since I am always happy

* Originally published in *PTNotes* (Prithvi Theatre's monthly newsletter), November 2010.

to do cartwheels, forward rolls, backward rolls—anything other than speaking a role.

In addition, the Adishakti workshops have acquired a bit of lore, mostly involving the intensity and stamina required to last through them and also the agony of the sessions on rhythm and percussion. 'I came out with blisters and bruises! My hands were black and blue. All the small bones in my hands shattered and now I can't hold chopsticks. You have to get up at seven in the morning ... every day'!—were some of the horrific statements I had heard from a number of serious actors. What follows are my personal notes from the workshop, in no particular order, and organised with no particular logic.

The first thing I realise in the workshop is how much we take for granted the existence of some body parts—small muscles in the eyes, the diaphragm, the muscles of the back, quadriceps and of course the hamstrings and thighs. The performer's tool is the body and the amount of energy spent in fine-tuning the body, is directly visible in the calibre of the performer. The training at Adishakti extends far beyond doing weights and buffing up. It focuses on manipulating much subtler energies.

On the evening before the start of the workshop, we receive folders (which had disconcerting 3D orcas on them), that outlined the structure of the workshop. At seven in the morning we would start with 15 minutes of eye-exercises. Then it was Kalaripayattu till 8:45 a.m. Then some voice work before we adjourned for breakfast. The group would then split into two. One group would work with breath practices for psychological expression, and the other on text. After a tea break, the groups would switch. Then it was lunch at one, a snooze break from two to three, and then the Koodiyattam rhythm session, another break, then it was working with body centres and the last session before dinner was, use of rhythm in performance. Then if you had any energy left, you could flop into the pool or bed, depending on which you thought more relaxing.

Vinay Kumar is a rock star. I am transported to the first moment of wonder that Adishakti created in my mind. It is 2004 and the Ranga Shankara theatre has just been built in Bangalore. I have carefully budgeted and bought all my tickets well in advance for select shows of the opening festival. It is with some alarm that, at a show titled *Ganapati*, I am handed a flyer that has detailed notes to the play. If you need notes to see a play I think, there is something quite wrong with the play.

As the show begins, I stare at the performers, clueless. I am watching a code I have never seen, let alone understood. Rhythm has replaced text as a signifier of meaning. It is like having a carpet yanked out from under your feet. And then Vinay Kumar, whacking away at a *mizhavu*, pulls a rabbit out of a hat. One minute he is playing the *mizhavu*, the next he cartwheels out, magically displacing himself from one position to another on stage. My jaw drops. It is like (if you will forgive the hyperbole) a one-inch punch. You see it work but you simply don't understand the physics that goes into it.

The first few sessions of breath work leave me mystified. We are working on *shringara*, a positive energy that fills one with a sense of well-being, a vague definition to an even vaguer catch-all

Vinay Kumar leaps in the air during the Source of Performance Energy workshop. Photograph courtesy of Aparna Jayakumar.

category of emotion. I am huffing and puffing away like a choo-choo train, but all I am getting is giddy, and I feel like my lungs are going to explode. This is all bogus, I think to myself. How the heck am I going to fill the top of my head with air when my respiratory system ends much further south. My pupils are dilating, my eyes are doing funny things and everyone else looks like they have defective electrodes in various parts of their bodies, but no *shringara*. After the session I am so oxygenated, I feel like I'm going to vaporise. I suppose that counts as a feeling of well-being.

Kalaripayattu is a load of fun. Vinay and Nimmy move like fluid. My muscle memory is not co-operating. I'm able to learn smaller movements, but unable to string together long sequences. I realise how careless I am with my knees, and have to constantly correct my posture. The stances give you the option to really stretch; so I'm constantly trying to put the pressure on my thighs and hamstrings and not blow out my knees and lower back.

My dreaded session is voice work. I'm trying to produce some decent sound and am trying to figure out the right posture for it. I seem to be making a mess of it, since Veenapani walks up to me and prods me a little. My hips are too far back. She asks me to root my movement correctly, and casually tosses out a leg sideways to demonstrate. I'm trying to figure out how she's adjusted her centre of gravity without registering it in her upper body. I'm also trying to understand how she can toss off a leg and half her base, without affecting the structure sitting on top of it. We do an exercise where we run till we are out of breath and then speak a few lines. I suddenly realise all this breath/centre/*chakra* business may not be bogus after all.

It's now time to work on the breathing of *adbhuta*, wonder. My cynical circuits have gone back into over-drive. We are making various monkey-like sounds and breathing like choo-choo trains on acid. I sound like a monkey, and my diaphragm feels like a football, and I'm trying to be as awestruck as I can. I make a hash of my attempt at *adbhuta* and figure it's time to abandon this hair-brained idea.

It is only after the session that I have my 'aha' moment. I'm jumping about like a monkey going O-O-O when suddenly the air hits a portion of my upper palate and I feel the impulse to jump. What's this then, I wonder to myself. I say the sound again and try to isolate the spot in my mouth. Once again, I hit the spot and instantly I feel the urge to spring upward and bounce up and down. I resolve to just work in the breath sessions in an open-minded, methodical way, and not try to come at the exercise from a pre-conceived notion of what the emotion should be.

The *mizhavu* is the only musical instrument that is meant, specifically, for theatre. It's a big copper drum that inflicts incredible amounts of pain when played. It's pretty apt as a metaphor for the relationship one has with theatre, as I found out after talking to more than a few people. It is unforgiving, unyielding and snooty. You can whack away at it all you like, it will still find a way to thwart you next time round. The rhythm session after lunch is a nightmare. Arvind Rane, the loveable local subversive element, has this gem to offer: 'If it hurts, hit harder'. He is right.

People find different ways to adapt to this gut-wrenching session. A couple of us find each other in the session, as we are able to match rhythms and play together. For some of us it's easier. I switch off my pain circuits and manage to hop-skip-stagger past the hurt into numbness; and then I'm working. Perhaps it's the stubborn writer in me that makes me plough through this legendary pain. It also helps to pull your eyes, face and mouth into funny shapes, as well as move your body around while playing. One, it helps mask the pain. Two, it makes phrasing easier, you're actually talking with/through the drum. Three, anything to take your mind off the pain!

We are working on *karuna*, compassion. It's scary. It's the respiratory equivalent of strangulation. I'm doubly worried because I know I can hold my breath for quite a long while, so I'm sure I'm just going to be sitting around as my heartbeat quickens, my body screams for air and everyone gets bored watching me blow another exercise. Vinay outlines the steps involved. Expel air sharply with a 'huh', lock the chest and accelerate the de-oxygenation in the body, which is the absolute reverse of swimming underwater for a long time. It's sickening. Your face melts, as if all your facial features are hot liquid. It feels like stabbing yourself in the chest with a hot knife. I get a sickening sensation of hot sticky black liquid being poured into my insides. I'm in that horrible place, where your body is confronting death and is saying to you, listen buddy, keep messing around like this and you are a gonner.

I've promised myself I'm going to go for it. I manage to nudge myself over some sick psychological threshold and take in a huge gasp of air. I bawl my guts out. Yeah, I've got this one figured. Vinay tells us we should be careful with this one, as it is addictive, the same as auto-erotic asphyxiation. For some reason I think of David Caradine. I'm edgy all evening as I try to shake off the after-effects of the exercise.

Suresh reminds me of Ganapati. He's always in shringara, smiling benevolently at some cosmic joke that only a human metronome knows. His hand reminds me of Ganesha's trunk. He dunks his hand on the *mizhavu* from an inch away and makes it sing like a bell. I'm reminded of the one-inch punch again. You see it work, but you simply don't understand the physics that goes into it! I wish I had fatter hands!

Eye exercises with Nimmy are incredible. We work at actively changing the focal length of our eyes and giving energy to the eyes. Vinay says Koodiyattam performers do eye exercises with ghee in their eyes. We're slacking off one day and Vinay threatens to put ghee in our eyes. The group is suddenly motivated!

A typical percussion session involves the customary howling in pain as the hands warm up. More than a few people cry and weep. Others book massages, then oversleep, thus finding a creative way to bunk the session. I discover I like percussion! It takes time for me to get my head around the tha-tha-keta-thak-a-tha phrasing, but once it sticks, it sticks—a weird combination of cognitive and muscle memory.

Raudra, anger, is a cinch for me. You create and hold tension in the muscles at the back of your neck. I tense my muscles so hard I get a horrible neck ache after. I'm so angry I see red and my entire skull starts vibrating. As with *karuna*, it takes time for the after-effects of the exercise to wear off. The negative emotions seem easier than the positive ones!

Voice work for me is pure torture. Veenapani is patient, but I'm making a total hash of everything. My dirty habits take their time leaving, and, in a panic, my voice heads straight for my throat and vocal chords. I've been telling actors to speak from the stomach, but for the first time I'm figuring out the actual mechanics of making that happen. 'Learn to use different resonators,' Veenapani says. I'm baffled. On the last day of the workshop, I'm aspirating my 'ha' like a champ, and suddenly I feel the sound resonating in my chest. My voice hits a register I don't recognise. I'm over-joyed! I manage to move the sound around from my throat to my chest to my head.

For some reason, Adishakti facilitates accelerated learning. Maybe it's because we seem to learn faster in groups, or maybe it's just the great energy of the place. Everyone is always trying things, so you just pick up stuff a lot quicker. A whole bunch of people make huge progress with their swimming—learning to swim, learning different strokes, handstands, flips—all while we work on our breathing. The swimming exercises take a bit of getting used to, since the breathing is not geared towards speed, and you don't grab air to the chest. Instead, you direct it much deeper. I realise that everything, every single thing in the world, has rhythm.

What is with these *chakras*? It really takes a leap of faith to work with them. Initially I was able to concede that these points are directly linked to balance since they are rooted in the spine; but then I figured there's an entire world of exploration there beyond physical matter. While physiology tells us what consti-tutes our physical body, the inner map of the body is quite differ-ent. It's the difference between perceiving gross matter and subtle matter, the difference between the light bulb, the filament, and the light itself. There is a self-made gross matter and then there is the subtle self. And here is the big question: how do you become fully aware of that subtle self? I stop myself. Perhaps this line of thinking is out of scope at the moment.

We do small presentations at the end of the workshop. It's amazing to see the learning that everyone takes back. It's also a joy to work with yourself, without the pressure of qualitative scrutiny. More than a few pieces move me. There are no less than three rounds of crying. Mysteriously, three pieces involve pornography. One piece is deeply spiritual. It leaves me deeply pensive all evening.

I think we are too easy on ourselves, too satisfied with safety. I think we are too comfortable thinking we know the answers, instead of asking the difficult questions. I ask a theatre senior about his thoughts on Adishakti. 'Veenapani operates from a different planet. She sets the bar so high, she's in a different league altogether.' I totally agree.

Seven
The Ramayana Festival

The Ramayana from Multiple Perspectives[*]

DEVINA DUTT

For three years, Veenapani Chawla and her team of actors at Adishakti hosted the Ramayana Festival, a wide-ranging and long-term exploration of the plurality of performance arts traditions, forms, and belief systems linked to the epic. The festivals, which stretched for an unbroken 10 days each year, were

[*] The writer responds to the three Ramayana Festivals Veenapani Chawla conceived and hosted at Adishakti from 2009 to 2011. As with all other conferences held here, this series too was devoted to initiating a dialogue, this time between traditional performers of the Ramayana, contemporary interpreters of the epic through dance, drama, and music, and artists and scholars who have studied the many tellings and retellings of the epic across South Asia.

held at the Adishakti campus, a three-acre area on the outskirts of Puducherry town. With its low-key, unshowy, traditional Kerala architecture, the space is quite distinct from similar looking resorts with their manicured lawns and 'tasteful' retreats carefully touched up with Indian chic.

For those who made the decision to attend the alternately gruelling and restful festival, Adishakti's spare, natural, and unadorned environment and space provided an immediate fore-taste of the nature of the gathering and its quest for a deeper and more subtle artistic experience of the epic. Each year, as the festival unfolded, the space would prove to be a key ally, nurturing a collective desire to come closer to the epic and its myriad narratives through undiluted performances and the fullest of discussions in equal measure.

Conceived as intense and deep creative investigations of the diverse ways of approaching each other's forms and thought processes around a single idea, scholars and performers, along with their listeners, found themselves constantly returning to some uncharted mystery or remembered detail of the epic. In trying to understand the appeal of its clean storyline and prominent characters, which seemed to endorse the hermeneutic rights of artists and communities to refashion them from time to time, the Ramayana Festivals were also conceived as a greater quest into the nature of cultural plurality and issues linked to exchanges between traditional artists and their knowledge systems and arts practitioners in India today.

Given the nature of these goals, it was clear from the very beginning that the usual rules of cultural programming would not do. For if performers, scholars, organizers, and participants had to come together to learn and interact over a number of days, they would need a structure that helped them balance the interplay of performances with reflection while remaining open and alert to the tremendous churning of responses elicited by the wealth of regional art forms and talks that made up the festival schedule.

In the second year, for instance, a partial glimpse of the schedule reveals that the festival began with a Sanskrit play by

Bhavabhuti, *Uttara Rama Charita*, adapted by Kavalam Narayan Panicker in Hindi; a sensitively modulated talk by writer Arshiya Sattar on reading the Ramayana as principally a love story and the very human failings and tragedy of its hero Ram; a lecture by Professor Srisurang Poolthupya, an expert on the Thai Ramkien; a Nangyar Koothu performance titled *Sita Parityagam* by Kapila Nagavallikkunnel and a discussion on the art form along with the musicians from her group; a session by Russian scholar Vladimir Latsenko on the chanting of the Ramayana; historian A.R. Venkatachalapathy's brilliant account of the Dravidian critique of the Ramayana; and a three-hour concert, *Bhavayami Raghuramam*, by Carnatic vocalist Aruna Sairam, exploring the Ramayana through music, followed by a long conversation on her experiences with voice training the following day.

Designing a Festival

Imaginatively curated by Veenapani Chawla and independent critic and dramaturg Rustom Bharucha, who attended the first festival as an interlocutor and stayed on to curate the next two festivals as its director, the festival was paced and arranged with great skill. Working within an intimate and unhurried scale, the Adishakti Festivals encouraged performers to present their form in its fullness, unapologetically, and without worrying about the much-feared short attention spans of the audience. The focus was on the performance and not on any notion of an 'event'.

In the first two years of the festival, the evenings were set aside for performances while the morning sessions the following day were devoted to related discussions with the artists. By the third year, the festival organizers felt that the festival had matured and could take on new challenges. The two sessions were therefore delinked, and the presence of leading scholars from India and abroad was increased, so that the intellectual component went down deeper even as a more subtle juxtaposition of ideas and emotional registers between performers and thinkers was attempted.

Each year though, the afternoons were left free; but as audiences soon discovered, far from being a concession, this break was

absolutely essential. The festivals left no place for passive view-
ing, and by the end of the experience, this would prove to be
the critical factor that differentiated them from other festivals.
Participants soon discovered that their attention was claimed
not just by the formal and conventional aspects of presentations
of the performances and their discussions, pure and undiluted as
they were, but by the host of interactions and transmission of
knowledge taking place on the margins, at informal groupings
and impromptu sessions, or when you walked into a rehearsal
or a sound check, or overheard an interesting conversation
at lunch.

The lack of a formal dividing line between the audience and
performers empowered the former in numerous ways. Not only
did they view diverse forms performed by traditional artists
across genres of folk, classical, theatre, and dance but, through
them, came to a closer understanding of the world views, cultural
values, and needs of these groups and practitioners. This did not
happen as part of a lecture or special session on the sociology of
culture but simply by being in the company of artists who had
been given the opportunity to present their art in its fullness;
and by being able to converse with them before and after their
shows. The unusual courtesies extended to artists and the form
they represented, irrespective of their celebrity or the lack of it,
meant that a lot of the distressing brassiness and excessive self-
regard of cultural presenters and impresarios was very effectively
eliminated from every aspect of the festival, reducing clutter and
festival stress.

All of this had a strong calming influence on the participants,
helped them relax and settle into a slowed-down but more intense
rhythm, where picking up fine points, exchanging, discovering,
and dwelling on one's responses along with other people's in
an honest, searching, and open way, could take place naturally.
In the process, participants had an opportunity to reflect on,
compare, and correct their own responses or ways of seeing,
leading to untypical encounters, especially in the discussions
with the artists that sometimes took place immediately after
the performances.

After the formal sessions of the Ramayana seminar are over,
animated discussions continue informally under the trees.
Photograph courtesy of Vinay Kumar.

After Maya Rao's dance theatre production, the specially commissioned *Ravanama*, an exploration of the exquisite and tense
fragility between Ravana and Sita presented through a series of
improvisations, the audience was divided right down the middle.
One group comprised viewers with more conventional expectations, who struggled visibly to formulate a response, and another
group was made up of actors, theatre crew, and dancers, who loved
the malleable quality of Maya's improvisations and its implicit
defence of artistic prerogative in the shaping of her vision. The
audience, spilling out of the hall, continued excitedly discussing
the issues arising out of the performance late into the night. The
artist had specially requested that the audience stay with their
experience before reacting to it. The discussion with her therefore took place on the following morning.

When the actor took questions from both sets of people the
following day, she surprised them both by revealing the amount
of conscious thought, careful deliberation, and intellectual
meshing of ideas that had fed into the improvisation-driven

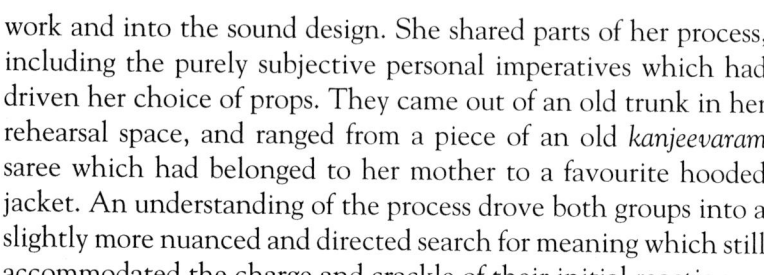

work and into the sound design. She shared parts of her process, including the purely subjective personal imperatives which had driven her choice of props. They came out of an old trunk in her rehearsal space, and ranged from a piece of an old *kanjeevaram* saree which had belonged to her mother to a favourite hooded jacket. An understanding of the process drove both groups into a slightly more nuanced and directed search for meaning which still accommodated the charge and crackle of their initial reactions.

A few evenings later when leading Thai dancer Pichet Klunchun performed *I Am the Demon*, based on the representation of the demon character in traditional Khon dance, assumptions on what constituted traditional, classical, or contemporary and the idea of purity of form and obedience to one's teacher, were once again questioned. This seemingly spare, clean, and modern-looking production had a pared-down serenity and was anchored in Pichet's deep bond with his teacher, to whom it was a tribute. It was also an enquiry into the meaning of his dance, the relationship between his master and himself and what constituted a perfect representation of the demon character within the traditions of an older, pre-tourism boom Thai culture, and the contemporary performance stage. The production travelled from its rigorous but exquisitely controlled opening moves, interspersed with video clippings of conversations on dance, before making way for a gradual softening, ending with a sense of inner realization achieved by the performer. Purged of the spectacularized pomp that much of Thai dance driven by the compulsions of cultural tourism finds itself in today, this was a thoughtful attempt by Pichet at having his say in an important contemporary debate on culture.

Imagining the Ramayana Festival

The idea of the Ramayana Festivals is closely linked to Adishakti's own journey as an arts initiative, which seeks to tap the knowledge systems of traditional artists as a way of discovering culturally rooted practices and a continuum in the group's attempt to create modern work informed by these roots.

When Veenapani Chawla began her search for traditional artists more than a decade ago, specifically in the context of her work on breath, she came face to face with practitioners of forms as diverse as Kalaripayattu and Koodiyattam. Till then, their encounters had happened in the course of festivals in which they participated, and interactions were confined to a few hurried back-room chats which did not lead to knowledge-sharing.

When she instituted a dialogue with these artists in the course of her own research, she found that they had begun to change through a process of historical attrition, like having to move out from their traditional performance space of temples to the stage in the auditorium.

The Adishakti workshops on breath underlined the importance of artists coming together across divides as members of the same community, who could share and contribute to each other's current practices. Chawla was intrigued by the different kinds of knowledge that she often encountered, of which the artists themselves were sometimes unaware in the absence of dialogue outside their tradition. They had failed to recognize the instrumentality of their knowledge in the practice of their performance art, or make wider connections beyond it. The process of talking closely to modern arts practitioners helped them seize upon these aspects, enabling them to discover new aspects of their art.

The Ramayana Festivals were an outcome of this line of thought which saw diverse performers coming together around a single idea with a desire to learn from and talk to each other at length, in the belief that these would prove to be rich and stimulating encounters.

Responding to the Adishakti Space

Although the sessions with scholars the morning after had been formally delinked from performances in the third year, and each was thus separated from the other, they had managed to inflect the other in interesting ways. So the sessions with scholars in the mornings were quite animated with the latter departing from their academic trappings to explain and be understood.

As some of India's leading intellectuals responded to the freshness of the forum, and the informality at Adishakti's eco-logically pure space, conversations conducted in the absence of formal timekeeping led them to shed their seminar habits. In the proximity of performers, their sessions took on a performative cast lending a more creative and speculative note to their talks. The participation of the participants, intelligent non-specialists for the most part, reflected the fact that there is a wider, keener interest in art and culture than is usually assumed, making for a higher than usual level of participation. In fact, a few popular performers, wedded to their perfunctory and slick habits on the urban performance circuit, failed to read the potential and nature of the Adishakti space. So Pt Channulal Mishra squandered a sizeable portion of his time on stage performing the standard set of *chaitis*, *horis*, and *kajris*, breaking off to recite some pedestrian poetry before getting down to the *Kevat Prasang* from Tulsidas's *Ramcharitmanas*. The performance was unfortunately marred by his propensity for excessive talk during the concert, denying the audience an opportunity to simply feel.

In contrast, Bharati Shivaji, who sought to expand the traditional universe of Mohiniattam with its admittedly limited traditional repertoire, in her specially commissioned work *Sita Parinamam*, gave us a work which affirmed the traditional purity of the dance form, enriched by a music design which used traditional Malayalam instruments like the *eddaka*. The dancer had selected some samples of progressive feminist writing on Sita by Malayalam poets including Vallathol, Ezhuthachan, and Kumaran Asan for her production. This was an intelligently conceived and executed work, which knew where to play by the rules, to placate the needs of tradition, and where to use artistic instinct for a well-judged adventure to break through with a sense of purpose. Her last piece, *Chintavishtayaya*, where Sita finds herself alone at the end of a life spent playing by the rules, was a fine example of how traditional *abhinaya* could be used to depict loss and the sense of being outplayed by destiny in an unusually extended but understated way.

In the conversation with the dancer after her two-hour long piece, there were some who felt that the abstraction of the dance form had been disturbed by the extended storytelling and abhinaya. This highlighted the plight of the sensitive classical dancers today, who make critical but visually less dramatic changes in their form. Not quite the definite departure of those who launch more experimental works with 'inventive' choreographies, the artistic intent of such efforts are usually not recognized. Not surprisingly, after playing safe for a while under the insistent questioning from the 'purist' perspective, the dancer replied that classical dancers were always under pressure in the modern urban environment for either being slow and difficult, and equally, for not rising above the traditional and limited dance repertoire. Sensitive viewers and supportive spaces were rare, said the artist, and that was why she had brought the new choreography, with its detailed storytelling, to Adishakti, conceding that she would probably not take it to the large performing venues in metros.

The emotional and intellectual arcs travelled in each festival, comprised argument, discussion, and the deepest felt responses, all of which made for a more direct and unmediated experience. And there lies its great value as a cultural conference; in the increasingly barren culturescape, where our views on aesthetics, ideas, and positions are rarely even stirred, the charged and often contentious festivals highlighted inner connections and internal contradictions, compelling spectators to subject themselves to the process of interpretation, review, and change from one session to the next. By the third year, a more subtle juxtaposition of energies had eventually emerged through the interplay of critical discourse and performance, just as the organizers had hoped; and in each case, plurality was visibly operating on more registers than they could have imagined.

The idea of plurality that revealed itself as the festival progressed, managed to shed light on its own inherent complexity too. In conjunction with the diverse performances, we were reminded of how difficult it was to form any kind of understanding of old texts and their meanings when approached with too orderly or pristine a world view. The wealth of open-ended material emerging from each session, performance, and discussion was proof enough of the fact that an understanding of plurality could only be possible if we left ourselves open to the necessary chaotic energies that seemed to lie at its heart.

Led by Performers and Thinkers

In its three years, the festivals brought together traditional performers and contemporary artists who showed new and often specially commissioned work from India and South East Asia, relating to some aspect of the Ramayana. They included scholars and writers like Paula Richman, Arshia Sattar, David Shulman, Anmol Vellani, Romila Thapar, Ashis Nandy, Sadanand Menon, C.S. Lakshmi, Leela Gandhi, A.R. Venkatachalapathy, Eddin Khoo (from Malaysia), Ghulam Mohammad Sheikh, and Kavalam Panicker. Apart from Yakshagana, Kattaikuttu, Koodiyattam, shadow puppetry, and Sattriya performers, there were musicians like Aruna Sairam and Channulal Mishra, and Mewati Jogis. Other performers included Mohiniattam dancer Bharati Shivaji, theatre person Maya Krishna Rao, Koodiyattam dancers Usha Nangyar and Kapila Venu, internationally known contemporary dancers Pichet Klunchun from Thailand and Sardono Kusumo from Indonesia, Javanese classical dancers Mugiyono Kasido, Sal Murgiyanto, and I Wayan Dibia, and Sufi singer and scholar Madan Gopal Singh.

Despite this diverse body of performers and scholars from the worlds of music, dance, literature, cinema, theatre, folk culture, the visual arts, across genres and styles, unfelicitous and modish words like cross-culture were never used to describe the exchanges. The festivals also escaped the blandness of officially approved ideas of plurality. They were, quite simply, a tracking of the prodigious plurality of the Ramayana, its many versions and forms and influences, its ability to slip into the life of a community and a culture by becoming a part of its most intimate knowledge and belief systems, and finding expression in its art forms.

One of the most distinctive features of the festivals was that they extended professional respect to all performers, unmindful of external hierarchies, so that performers—whether A-list classical musicians, internationally known stars, or unknown traditional artists from remote parts of rural India—were engaged with on a level of equality by their interlocutors and listeners. In the process, celebrity performers seemed to become more accessible, sharing more generously than they would have in the bland foyer and proscenium, time-bound stage show format. Similarly, the 'anonymous' traditional artists, like the 32 soft-spoken and unselfconsciously feminized Sattriya monks from Majuli, who sincerely believed they were Krishna's brides, and performed a full three hours of Shankardeva's *Ram Bijay* as well as the 50-strong troupe of Yakshagana artists, seemed to grow in confidence and stature. Groups like these put up shows which used the Adishakti outdoor space to the fullest.

The Yakshagana troupe of actors, for instance, wended their way on to the open air stage encircled by banana leaves, into the sacred square where the lead vocalist sang at the customary high pitch for nearly three hours of *Indrajit Vadhe*. After the performance, in an unplanned and magical gesture, the troupe led us back into the auditorium, which was their green room for the night, to introduce themselves. Here, in the presence of cast-off masks, open trunks, and costumes, the actors revealed themselves to be modest, shy young men, bank officers, medical representatives, computer students, hailing from the culturally vibrant villages across Karnataka, lured to Yakshagana by its mythological characters. It was a privilege to be so close to them so soon after a performance.

Madan Gopal Singh, the Sufi singer who performed next, had the deep yet unaffected erudition and empathetic sense of the cultural history of Punjab, which gave him a rare feel for his subject and made his listeners rethink the superficial and sharply reduced Sufi experience that one sees in market-based programming these days. As Singh explained, the folk and Sufi poets of the Punjab did not appear to take Ram as the central figure of the epic too seriously. From the twelfth to the eighteenth centuries, these poets had preferred to select fragments from the epic and work it into their songs. In a striking instance of how a culture can switch a received symbol or imagery with its own version, the golden deer of the Ramayana becomes the mysterious black deer in Punjabi Sufi songs, and it is on the latter that a besotted Sita expends her deep and obsessive passion in more than one song.

Taking a break from the traditional Indonesian dance of his early training, Sardono Kusumo, one of Indonesia's leading traditional dancers and modern choreographers, produced a charming improvisational piece on the three male characters of the Ramayana—Ram, Hanuman, and Ravan—in *Sita's Kitchen*. He was supported by Adishakti's actor Nimmy Raphel. Sardono's piece, sketchy as it was, aimed for a composite creative choreography. For the sensitive in the audience, the use of traditional Javanese dance skills, the transmutation of mythic characters through a dancer's own form, the contemporary approach, were all there to be seen and enjoyed as faintly perceived elements in the work.

Behind the artistic attempt was a less argued, more inward plurality. Unlike the notion of unity in diversity, which we in India often tend to disinterestedly flaunt, Sardono's little window to another culture hinted at the possibility of saying it differently. By seeking the underlying oneness in storytelling, text, art, and performance indicated in the pervasive animist traditions of an archipelago nation, which has found its own unique way of fashioning a unity out of its own kind of diversity, we experienced something new. It was befitting that a new notion of this central premise was hinted at in a festival dedicated to exploring the very idea of plurality inherent in the many versions of an ancient epic like the Ramayana.

New Pathways

The third year's festival, which saw a greater emphasis on scholars and performers from South East Asia, also allowed audiences in India the rare opportunity to look beyond the facts of their depositions to understand just how the Ramayana and its idealized characters sustained a people's idea of themselves and was an integral part of their relationships and life choices. It was in this context, soon after a talk on the concept of *taksu*, that complex combination of charisma and spiritual power that lies at the heart of a successful Balinese dance performance, that we heard dancer critic Sal Murgiyanto's talk titled 'Ramayana and I: A Javanese Dancer in Search of Self'. This was an intensely personal account which served as a socio-cultural reading of the Ramayana in his community of dancers in Java. Pointing out that his encounters with the Ramayana began as a child with the lullabies his mother sang, and as codes of good behaviour subsequently, Murgiyanto reflected on how his deep faith in the idealized characters from the epic, in particular the Sugreeva–Bali episode, had helped him put together an ethical code for his own life, which was unique to his circumstances, growing up as a young boy in a traditional village in Java and making his way in the world as an independent dancer.

Counterpointing the heartfelt Indonesian presentations, Eddin Khoo's talk titled 'Storm Clouds' was a brilliant account of the politics of culture in Malaysia in the last three decades of the 'Mahathir Project', an official policy which supported heavy industrialization in pursuit of its desire to be a model, economically advanced Muslim state but which was disquietingly silent on the hybrid foundations of Malay culture. Khoo traced the modern nation state's uncomfortable relationship with its diasporic past and its intensely racial political structures to a skewed desire for a puritan Islamic culture, purged of its myriad pasts. Disturbingly, this had led to the proscription of the shadow puppet traditions in the northeastern district of Kelantan.

The dismayed responses of the Indonesians, with their implacable faith in the epic and its heroes, came through especially in the aftermath of Romila Thapar's historically rigorous and unblinking enquiry into the variant versions of Valmiki's epic, in her examination of the Buddhist and Jaina versions, the *Jatakas* and *Paumachariyan*, and their implications for the hegemony of the former. This was an opportunity to measure the achievements and limitations of the intellectual approach as a counterpoint to those who simply elect to live by the epic. Soon after, Ashis Nandy's lecture, a passionately argued endorsement of a distinctive epic culture 'which is inherently pluralistic whether you like it or not', which went on to speak of its civilizational energy and strengths, was a critical moment in the festival. When he spoke of communities living by their versions of epics without wishing to hierarchize any particular version, we had already experienced a spectrum of stories and references from guests and performers at the festival with which to gauge his hypothesis.

As the festivals progressed, their influence could be judged by a certain quality of inwardness, and the idea began to grow that an aesthetic and philosophical quest of the Ramayana provided us, in the end, with a picture of ourselves. Its prodigious versatility, bare storyline, and clear characterization was used, time and again, as material to construct new and very personal stories.

Tamil author C.S. Lakshmi, in a talk entitled 'When Grandmother's Stories become Epic Texts: Experiences of Listening to the Ramayana, and Studying the Ramayana', was one such talk which also came closest to emulating the dynamics of a live performance. This was a decidedly personal account which blurred the lines between reality and fiction and was a tribute to the creative instinct mirrored in every retelling of the epic as well as the craft of writing. The participants responded with effortless empathy to Lakshmi's personal narrative and the pain of her veena-playing mother who had to set aside her beloved instrument for years, Lakshmi's own rudra veena lessons with a gracious guru who told her to regard it as not just an instrument but as her very life. These emotions were reflected in the exquisitely delicate story written by Lakshmi years later where Ravana approaches an ageing Sita with an offer of friendship and veena lessons, telling her, in this penultimate stage of her life, to approach the instrument as she would her life. Lakshmi's turning into fiction her earlier experiences and finding the Ramayana reflected as both truth and revelation, gave us a contemporary glimpse of what living by the epic could mean.

As the last festival came to a close, leading visual artist and scholar Ghulam Mohammad Sheikh shared 150 miniatures with us in a presentation titled 'Visualising the Ramayana'. In one of the most stimulating and unforgettable sessions of the festival, the artist-scholar combined a deep knowledge of his subject with a sense of wonder at how aspects and key moments of the Ramayana narrative could be uncovered only through subtle processes of visualization, which in turn, offer other ways of reading the epic.

The actors at Adishakti watched this session with particular interest, especially when Sheikh expertly but unobtrusively drew their attention to the element of performance, the use of space, and the stillness and control in the art-making. Referring to the device of continuous narration, where the repetition of the principal image in multiple actions is used to expand space and time within a single frame, we were shown a folio where Ram and Ravan's armies are ranged against each other but spill over their delineated borders. In another painting of the Guler school, as the young Ram and Lakshman cross the river with Vishwamitra, a diagonally devised river flows down the borders to 'inundate the viewer'. Each image came to the viewer, guiding them to the next, pointed out Sheikh. Responding to the notion of the movement in the visual, the Adishakti actors spoke later about this special session with great fervour, sensing that something about the way miniature artists approached their canvases might offer insights into ways of approaching the performance space. The tension between representation and performance in these folios also suggested that there was something they could intuitively apply to their own work as present-day actors.

Ending with a painting from the Shangri Ramayana, the participants were alerted to the manner in which the golden deer Maricha, in gold foil, is set against an identical mustard-yellow matt background. We had been told previously that a folio painting, designed to be held in the hand, was meant to be seen by one person at a time. In the representation of Maricha, therefore, as the hand holding the folio naturally shook, the impact of the colour of gold shifted from matt to shining, making the deer visible and invisible from time to time. 'You see from the eyes of Ram, don't you', said Sheikh, quietly bringing his lecture to a finish.

Over three memorable years, the Adishakti's Ramayana Festivals had achieved high standards of cultural programming and brought a world of experience to us; but this was one of its finest, most realized and illuminating moments.

The Last Word

SHANTA GOKHALE

It was said of Veenapani Chawla by some admirers of her work that her genius was too big to allow anybody from her team to grow and branch out on their own. Yet, all along she has been helping them to do just that—grow. She would never have been able to conceive and perform the kind of plays she wrote unless she had actors and musicians who were continuously growing. In private they were expected to work on themselves and during rehearsals, to contribute towards evolving the vocabulary they were working with.

The seminars and conferences Chawla organized at Adishakti were sources of intellectual growth for the team. The exercises they did in private to tune their minds for the work at Adishakti are a source of spiritual growth. Soon the time came when Chawla felt they needed to be given space to explore their creativity independently. First Vinay Kumar directed Ionesco's *Rhinoceros* and now, with the Ramayana Festivals as their source of inspiration, the team has been scripting solo works based on the epic for themselves. Two of the pieces are almost ready, and three are in the making. They are expected to be ready for presentation by the end of 2012.

Rhinoceros

In 2008, Vinay Kumar directed his first play, Ionesco's *Rhinoceros*. Speaking to this writer about why he chose it, he said it was because he had been familiar with Ionesco's work from his drama school days; but, more importantly, it was the relevance of the play to our times that drove the choice. 'In a fundamentally pluralistic, vibrant society,' he said, 'it is important to have so many different points of view. Alarmingly, the individual point of view is getting erased. Individual space and voice have shrunk. Debate, logic, and individuality are swept away by collective illogic and hysteria. Mass opinion washes over all discordant notes. In such conditions, the person who speaks out becomes a comical character.' In short, we are all in danger of turning into rhinoceros.

Vinay Kumar's radical editing of the play was aimed at highlighting this core idea. He cut out all characters and conversations that did not contribute to it, and then arrived at a physical language that would underline the argument. The thought that guided him was that in any exchange between two people, whether violent or friendly, one person attacks and the other retracts. Accordingly, his characters lean forward or back in rhythmic movements when they engage in debate.

His set is a set of boxes, around and on which all movement is centred. Sometimes the boxes serve an abstract purpose, and sometimes they represent objects, as when they become office tables at which the workers sit to do their monotonous, routine work. At times they are stacked up for characters to stand on, teetering dangerously, in moments of frenzied debate. In the final scene the stack of boxes on which Berenger sits underlines the isolation of the man who will not join the herd.

This ordinary man is made extraordinary by his stubborn preservation of his individuality. But his determination is lined with fear. What has seemed unavoidable for his friends and dear ones might turn out to be his fate too. For this reason he will not take off the bandage on his head. Who knows that he will not discover a horn growing there. The song he strums on his guitar is a nostalgic throwback to times when human beings were not under such extreme pressure to conform.

Works in Progress

After the Ramayana Festival which had fired up the imagination of the Adishakti team, Veenapani Chawla asked them to script plays, long or short, based on any theme of their choice from the epic and direct themselves in solo performances. The group has been working assiduously on the project since then, and are in the process of producing an extremely interesting collection of theatre pieces. Two of them were presented during the five-day seminar, 'Spaces of Theatre, Spaces for Theatre', held at Ninasam, Heggodu, in March 2012.

Nimmy Raphel's play titled *Nidravathwam* (In the State of Sleep), takes a look at the predicament of Kumbhakarna and Lakshman, brothers of the chief protagonists of the Ramayana, both of whom have contrasting problems with sleep. Kumbhakarna has mistakenly asked for sleep as a boon from Lord Brahma, and is gifted with six months of sleep every year. Lakshman, on the other hand, has asked sleep not to visit him for 14 years to enable him to guard Ram and Sita day and night during their exile in the forest. However, since somebody must take the sleep that he refuses to take, his wife Urmila does so.

The repercussions of the boon for Kumbhakarna are that his stories and actions can never be completed. Sleep always intervenes leaving him in a kind of suspended life. His confusion over his state is such that when he dies he is not sure whether he is actually dead or only dreaming of being dead.

Lakshman's loss of sleep causes him to lose concentration. He cannot think and act as an independent moral being. When Ram asks him to cut off Shurpanakha's nose, he is ridden with profound anxiety.

The two men meet on the battlefield. Kumbhakarna asks Lakshman to take his sleep from him for long enough to allow him to kill Lakshman. Meanwhile, Lakshman is caught up in an unsettling worry over whether his 14 years of wakefulness will be compensated at the end with 14 years of sleep or one day of sleep.

The play, about an hour long, is not a story but an exploration of the strange problem of sleep that links the two men. In finding a physical vocabulary for the play, Nimmy Raphel has introduced an element of what might be termed stylized *lokdharmi* into her narration, that enables her to move from abstraction to representation. The sequence in which Kumbhakarna brushes his teeth after waking from deep sleep is a case in point. Raphel's amazing body control is on full display throughout, alternately muscular and lissom. The sequences representing Kumbhakarna about to fall asleep or in a state of deep sleep are particularly well embodied.

At Ninasam, *Nidravathwam* was still a work in progress. Raphel received enough appreciative feedback from the audience there to give her courage to continue, and ideas to refine her work.

Suresh Kaliyath presented a delightfully mischievous *Hanuman Ramayana* at Ninasam, performed in an extended Ottan Thullal style of which he is a professional practitioner. Many of the key events from the Ramayana are present in his piece; but, seen from Hanuman's perspective, they take on a totally different tone and hue. His narrative is full of puckish humour which comes so unexpectedly that if you are not fully alert, you might miss it. At one point, he tells Valmiki, whom he ceremoniously welcomes, that the Hanuman Ramayana is better than the Valmiki Ramayana. Hunger, eating, and feeding occupy much of the time and space in the play, giving us some delightful passages of stylized representation.

In choreographing *Hanuman Ramayana*, Suresh's attempt has been to combine several seemingly disparate elements, while building on the strength of the basic form of Ottan Thullal. Like Raphel, he too switches from *natyadharmi* to lokdharmi, and from the role of the narrator to the roles of the characters. In an earlier version of the play there was more speech. He has cut that down to make for a tighter structure. He will continue to work on the piece with Chawla's inputs to refine it further.

Arvind Rane's piece, not completely scripted yet, turns around the idea of Luv's image in the mirror, his inability to tell his own story, and his encounter with his father.

Vinay Kumar is working on the idea of the 10th head of Ravana being unique amongst the others in temperament and thinking. This head unbalances symmetry which would have been achieved had he had nine heads—one in the centre and four on each side. Vinay Kumar has morphed his own head in different ways to represent the 10 heads and is planning to project them as a backdrop to his action.

Veenapani Chawla herself is working on Sita.

Postscript

When Veenapani Chawla directed her first play in Mumbai, Tom Stoppard's *Rosencrantz and Guildenstern Are Dead*, with a cast of students from the Arya Vidya Mandir, I did not know her personally. But I was impressed by the sophistication of the production.

This play came at a time when a wave of new plays was sweeping the city, from Pune and Nagpur, Delhi, Kolkata, and Bangalore. Young writers everywhere were wresting theatre away from the old guard, discarding old themes and old forms to experiment with the new. Gujarati theatre snapped ties with the old Bhangwadi style of musical theatre to venture into contemporary social issues and realism. The plays of Badal Sircar, Mohan Rakesh, Girish Karnad, and Vijay Tendulkar, and a little later of Mahesh Elkunchwar, Satish Alekar, and G.P Deshpande were being translated into Marathi, Hindi, and Bengali. English translations were being published in Rajinder Paul's theatre magazine *Enact*. It was a time of renewal. A strong new theatre movement was taking shape, with the Chhabildas School auditorium in Dadar, a Mumbai suburb, as its hub. This was a space you had to climb three rickety flights of stairs to reach. This was a space in which you sat on backless benches or dhurries. This was a space into which traffic sounds leaked. But what offset these problems was the spirit that fired the young play-makers who thronged to the space. The new theatre of the young hung on shoestring budgets, but who cared? Directors like Satyadev Dubey made do with basic lighting, improvised costumes, and symbolic sets to minimize losses. Actors subsidized their own travel costs.

As against this, *Rosencrantz and Guildenstern Are Dead*, staged at the newly opened, brilliantly designed, well-equipped Prithvi theatre in the northern suburb of Juhu, boasted a proper set complete with a boat and well-designed costumes and lighting. Most importantly, the play distinguished itself on two counts from the long-established English language theatre of south Bombay. It was not a copy of the play's successful Old Vic production, and the actors did not speak in borrowed accents, but in the Indian way.

Veenapani's *Oedipus* with Naseeruddin Shah in the lead followed in 1981, confirming that a strong new voice had appeared on the Mumbai stage. The press sat up and took notice. Veenapani's next two plays, *The Trojan Women* and *Savitri*, were widely covered by newspapers in Mumbai and in other cities to which it travelled. As a journalist writing on the performing arts, I too was called upon to cover her plays. Doing so proved to be a rich experience, one that gave me insights into a way of doing theatre that was very different from the Chhabildas plays whose rehearsals I had watched. At a dress rehearsal of *The Trojan Women* at an open air theatre in the northern suburbs, I marvelled at the rigour with which Veenapani was breaking the urban bodies of her actors into sinuous Chhau movements which formed the basis of the play's body language. In her next play, *Savitri*, she used Kalaripayattu and Tai Chi movements to evolve the body language.

I watched rehearsals of *Savitri* on the terrace of Veenapani's Mumbai home. This was the first time she had herself written the script for a play she was directing. It was a monumental task which involved carving a spare 40 lines from Sri Aurobindo's 24,000- line epic poem. Veenapani's engagement with economy of words had begun, as also with experiments in music. Meanwhile, it was evident that there was no money to support her theatre work. How are you managing, I asked with concern. She merely smiled in answer. But one of her actors said she is managing by selling her gold.

By now Veenapani and I were not just professional associates who met during rehearsals, but friends. So when she moved to Puducherry and Vinay Kumar, her actor from *Savitri*, enrolled at the local university to do his PhD in order to work with her, we continued to meet. I visited her in her tiny flat in Vazhakulam where I watched fascinated while Vinay Kumar worked on transforming his face into masks to signify the multiple characters he was going to play in *Impressions of Bhima*. His rehearsal space was the gap between a bed and a wall. Veenapani sat cross-legged on the bed, watching and commenting. That is how *Impressions of Bhima* was made.

Some time later, on another visit, Veenapani showed me a plot of land near Auroville that an admirer of her work had given her. There was nothing but scrub on it, but this was where she dreamt of building a theatre laboratory and research centre for Adishakti. Over the next few years, every visit I made threw up new surprises. First it was her beautiful house, built using an old and forgotten local technology. A short distance away was the rehearsal shed where every day her actors jammed with musicians from Auroville. Later a guest house came up, and finally the theatre. Meanwhile the land around grew thick with shrubs and trees, cutting the glare of the southern sun.

Three challenging plays followed, and Veenapani began passing on the techniques she had developed to young actors from all over the country through workshops. She was also organizing interesting seminars that would expose her actors to other arts and ideas. It was December 2007 when I thought it was time to document her work for the benefit of practitioners and students of theatre elsewhere. I knew at once that the book would not, should not, be written in a single voice, mine. It had to be a compilation of many voices, to reflect her own approach to theatre which was multicentred and consciously hybrid. Another decision I made was to undertake the project under my own steam, since there was nothing in it that would pull at funders' purse strings. My visits to Puducherry continued, but now with the book in view.

I participated in some of Adishakti's seminars and saw how they were contributing to expanding the minds and vision of the Adishakti actors. I also saw how the actors were being encouraged to develop new skills with every new play. It came as no surprise then, that while my work on the book progressed, Veenapani was making plans to push her actors into scripting and enacting a set of plays on their own, with her as guide.

During these visits I also came to understand the depth and completeness of Veenapani's belief in Sri Aurobindo's philosophy. I could see that every part of her life, every thought, and every action was informed by it. The Mother was not an external crutch. Her place was at the very centre of Veenapani's being. It was necessary for me, a diehard rationalist with no spiritual leanings, to understand this if I was to give my all to compiling and editing the book. If this was the force that had inspired her to create her unique theatre, if this was the force that gave her the strength to live the simple, joyous, all-inclusive life that she lived, then it was a good force.

Chugging along under my own steam, it has taken me five years to complete this book. It has been an exciting and stimulating journey. It is a matter of great joy to me that it is finally out there—*The Theatre of Veenapani Chawla*, my labour of love.

Appendix I

Reviews of the Mumbai Plays

A Triumph[†]

Aditi's production of Tom Stoppard's *Rosencrantz and Guildenstern Are Dead* at the Prithvi is a triumph. It doesn't signify that most of the already sparse audience on the second night never returned after the interval—the play is long and the spectators may have been afraid of missing the last train, or sleepy. And if they were uncomprehending—because certainly the play is complex—they are more to be pitied (for what they missed) than the players are to be censured.

Veenapani Chawla has rehearsed her performers admirably; they understand their roles and the concerns of the play very well and speak with all the lucidity and wealth of implication

[†] Smriti Nevatia's review of Veenapani Chawla's production of Tom Stoppard's *Rosencrantz and Guildenstern Are Dead* appeared in *The Sunday Observer* on 5 June 1983.

that Stoppard's double entendre requires. This is esecially true of Rosencrantz (Aditya Bhattacharya), Guildenstern (Shiv Kumar) and the Player, leader of the troupers (Kenneth Desai), the major characters who are given the most to say and who function at more levels than the rest. The other characters are all in white face, some because they are, within the play, professional actors; some because they—Claudius (Yusuf Mehta), Gertrude (Nandita Thakur), Polonius (Mihir Thaker), Ophelia (Leela Gandhi)—are in the play, which is, of course, *Hamlet*. Of this group only Hamlet (Naseeruddin Shah) himself transcends the Shakespearean barrier, notably to lounge in a deck chair in the shade of a beach umbrella and smoke a pipe on the way to London.

Stoppard's play itself derives from a most original inspiration: a feeling of compassion for those two poor fools in Shakespeare's tragedy, Rosencrantz and Guildenstern, and who knows which is which, friends of Hamlet's youth who are made pawns in the game of royal intrigue and consigned to their deaths. How about *Hamlet* from their point of view?

That idea, however, might have been simplistic, merely clever. What Stoppard does, working in the absurdist tradition (the play reverberates with echoes of Beckett), is to tune his fancy into a meditation of chance and destiny; freedom of action—here theatre itself becomes a brilliantly sustained metaphor for life; the problems of identity, ambiguity, uncertainty, death. Most remarkable is the way in which Stoppard raises puns and wordplay to the level of philosophy (or brings philosophy down to earth).

Rosencrantz ... is marvellously witty. Actual speeches from *Hamlet* are perfectly integrated with stretches of apparently inconsequential conversation. Suddenly someone cries out for some 'sustained action' and the wordplay dissolves instantly into horseplay. 'To be or not to be ...' is condensed into a piece of hilarious mime: Hamlet walks in lost in thought, teeters for a moment on the edge of a drop, shakes his head, walks on. Modern critical references are presented tongue-in-cheek, like the allusion to the 'provocative ambiguity' of Hamlet's relationship with his mother.

Every bit player is considerably better than competent, and they are, almost all of them, amateurs. Bhattacharya as Rosencrantz is excellent, his range of voice and mobility of expression are made good use of, although he tends to overdo the pop-eyed look. The casting of Shiv Kumar as Guildenstern is a little unconvincing to start with, but he grows into his role and subtly emerges as the more melancholy and cynical of the two. But the star of the show is Kenneth Desai as the mercurial, obscenely know-it-all yet detached Player; he really generates electricity, as when he explains, 'We're actors. We're the opposite of people'.

All the performers move with great agility; considering how wordy the play is, there is plenty of beautifully co-ordinated movement, none of which seems superfluous. That, in fact, is the kind of thing that reveals how well the production fulfills its task and justifies its existence—it makes you appreciate and want to read the text itself, but it gives the audience more than any mere reading could, because it is inspired, living theatre.

There are small patches where concentration flags, or where consistency suffers, but it is a difficult play and perfection is an extremely tall order. Indira Dayal's costumes are perfect, from Rosencrantz and Guildenstern's flowing capes down to the absurd yellow socks of Alfred (Vinesh Gandhi), the actor in drag who is called upon to play the queen (and who is responsible for the functional sets and effective lighting). As it stands—and moves and breathes—Aditi's production might conceivably have been better; on the other hand, it might much more conceivably have been very much worse and then, to indulge in a mixed metaphor, Stoppard style, the boot would have been on the other foot. Non-sequitur: love-one.

Intelligent Adaptation[†]

When *The Trojan Women* of Euripedes was performed in Athens in 415 BC, there was much topicality in the play. The theme of war's brutality and senselessness must have appealed to audiences caught between two phases of the Peloponnesian War, which would end a decade later with the capitulation of their city-state. Now that the

[†] Smriti Nevatia's review of Veenapani Chawla's production of Euripedes's *The Trojan Women* appeared in *The Sunday Observer*, undated.

glory of Greece was ebbing away, it must have been heartening to be reminded that chaos often paved the way for order, that the fall of Troy had led to the rise of Hellas. The memory of past greatness was doubtless comforting. And in the central figure of Queen Hecuba, enduring the unbearable loss of her kingly husband and heroic sons, many must have found release through identification and, moved by her nobility, in the end, hope.

But is it possible 24 centuries later to perform *The Trojan Women* in Bombay and make anything significant of it? Only raw amateurs are, usually, brash enough or unimaginative veterans rash enough to tackle something like classical Greek tragedy. And their productions differ only in slickness; both as a rule are equally dead. Happily Veenapani Chawla's version at the Prithvi belongs to a separate and rare category: a truly modern rendering of a classic in a form that restores it to life while routing it in a vital artistic context.

To conceive of the drama in the Mayurbhanj Chhau dance form of Orissa was inspired, and the result in a way is a theatrical event. Of the three schools of Chhau, Mayurbhanj is the least stylised in that it does not use masks: thus the performers are able to bring facial expression into play, although the emphasis remains on acting through movement and mime. The unbridled vigour of the form is made more balletic for the purpose of this production, which manages simultaneously to be culture-specific and universal.

Six months of rehearsals have ensured that the performers are more at ease in their chowk stances—the square, squat posture typical of Chhau—than their spectators are in their spill-over onto the aisle of the overcrowded theatre. Not that there is much rustling or fidgeting once the show begins. One is too mesmerised by the intimate circle of footlights, the huge stark background cut-outs of a ravaged Troy, the rising and falling beat of the lone *nagara*, the slitherings and whisperings of the black-clad chorus, the awful grief of Hecuba with her shorn head, the sudden martial twists and leaps, the long eerie lamentations collectively sung. The text is intelligently adapted—the conspiracy of the gods, for instance, is left out, reducing the sense of a mechanistic fate.

A major shortcoming because it reflects a flaw in the communication of the dramatic logic essential to tragedy, is the failure to convey Hecuba's temporary fall from greatness: her railings against Helen, *cause celebre* of the war and author of the Trojans' misery, are supposed to be vicious and baseless accusations; instead, Hecuba comes across as understandably bitter, at the most a shade too righteous.

Another problem is the unevenness of the accents and the missing cadences in certain speeches. Sohaila Kapur as Cassandra is a little weak; Neena Gupta as Andromache dances well but needs to work on her speech rhythms; Leela Gandhi lacks definition as Helen, but the very low tones of her voice carry to great effect. Aditya Bhattacharya with his set, twitching countenance, wins sympathy as King Menelaus of Saprta, Helen's husband, who must now decide her fate. Javed Jaffri as the Greek herald Talthybius establishes credibly the conflict between duty and his own increasing distaste for carrying out his superiors' orders. Sushmita Mukherjee succeeds in bringing depth and maturity to her moving, pivotal role as Hecuba. Her crouching stride slows down, her face is practically a mask of suffering, which appears to deepen as the sorrows mount.

Strangely, while supposedly revolutionary theatre is becoming decadent, this staging of a Greek tragedy is one of the most progressive endeavours in recent memory. Narrowly escaping the danger of turning into an audio-visual feast, teetering at times on the edge of the drop, it indicates one way out for the state of the art which seems to have reached a stalemate.

Missing the Rhetoric[†]

Spotlight kept its promise to provide quality theatre to Delhi by bringing Veenapani Chawla's *A Greater Dawn* over from Bombay recently. The play is an adaptation of Sri Aurobindo's epic poem

[†] Keval Arora's review of Veenapani Chawla's production *A Greater Dawn*, based on Sri Aurobindo's *Savitri*, appeared in *The Pioneer* on 5 November 1992.

Savitri and is inspired by an eclectic host of Indian performance traditions.

The story of Savitri and Satyavan is too well-known to need re-telling. In its common version, it affirms a patriarchal code of values through its celebration of a wifely devotion that transcends even death. In recent times its account of Death being outwitted by a woman has been seen as a proto-feminist exploration of female potential.

In Aurobindo's 24,000-line *Savitri*, the tale becomes an occasion for a larger meditation on spirit and evolution. The brochure note outlined the focus as: 'Satyavan is the soul of the world and Savitri's confrontation with Death is a journey of the avtar into the realms of unconsciousness so as to illumine and transform it'.

A Greater Dawn distils 24,000 lines of such a text into a 75-minute performance. Veenapani combined movement, chants, music, lights, rhythm, colours and images to provide Aurobindo's words with a dynamic spatial texture.

The stage was bare except for an oval silhouette upstage which pulsated with blue light. It turned to orange at the end when the conflict between Savitri and Death was resolved. The interplay between light and shade, as also between colours, focussed the polarised nature of the conflict perfectly. The contestants extended this principle of conflict by posing a fine study in contrasts. The gulf between Savitri (played by Mita Vasishth) and Death (played by K.C. Manavendranath) was emphasised through costumes, gestures, voices and even their respective body builds.

Some unity was provided by a six-member chorus that amplified the situation, articulated the antagonists' separate viewpoints and provided vital visual and aural depth. Greater cementing came from a dramatic musical score and a performance style with a defined sense of movement and speech. These were inspired by diverse sources: Kerala's Kudiattam, Kalaripayattu, Chhau, Kathakali, Buddhist chants, Manipuri death music, Tai Chi, and quite a bit else.

A Greater Dawn was a thoughtful combination of graceful ease and taut, disciplined energy. At times the sheer poetry of the movements deflected one's attention from the words. But otherwise the production did justice to Veenapani's talent for meticulousness and her ability to conceptualise performance in holistic terms.

And yet the play had a distinctively cool, as opposed to warm tone to it. It remained impressive without quite coming alive. In one sense, emotions were held at bay in *A Greater Dawn*. When they did surface, they were sublimated through a stylised utterance. However, stylised art is not necessarily a cold art, as any classical form can testify. Veenapani's decision to stylise in order to embody the philosophical text is intrinsically sound. The problem lies in the subject itself.

Savitri is a difficult text because it uses philosophical categories that require an audience of receptive, if not trained, minds. For those familiar with Aurobindo's work, the play can assume a sacral air as it did when the group performed at the Pondicherry Ashram. For Veenapani too, *Savitri* is very special. But for a general audience, the text proves impossibly elusive.

A Greater Dawn thus has all the makings of a cold, formal exercise, whose appeal lies not in what it says but in how it says it. It overawes by the wealth of its sources and the skilled use it makes of them. Nevertheless, its fractured quality is evident in the fact that its formal elements have a separate beauty of their own, independent of the detailed nuances of the spoken word.

Audiences may very well, in the manner of T.S. Eliot, react: 'We had the experience but missed the meaning'.

Appendix II

Scores for Ganapati

Percussion Score by Veenapani Chawla

Score 1

1	x	2	x	3 x	1	x	2	x	3	x

Ta   ki   ta   Di   ki   ta – 1st speed

Ta   k   ta   k   ta   k ta k   ta   k ta k – 2nd speed

Tak tak tak tak tak tak tak tak tak tak tak tak – 3rd speed

Taka taka taka taka taka taka Taka taka taka taka taka taka – 4th speed

Score 2

1	x	2	x	3 x	1	x	2	x	3	x

Ta   k   ta   k   ta   k ta k   ta   k ta k – 2nd speed – all 4
      percussionists [2 cycles]

Tak tak tak tak tak tak tak tak tak tak tak tak – 3rd speed – 1st & 3rd
      percussionists [2 cycles]

Ta k ta k ta k ta k ta k ta k – 2nd speed – 2nd &
4th percussionists [2 cycles]

Taka taka taka taka taka taka Taka taka taka taka taka taka – 4th
speed – 1st & 3rd percussionists [8 cycles]

Tak tak tak tak tak tak tak tak tak tak tak tak – 3rd speed – 2nd
percussionist [2 cycles]

Ta k ta k ta k ta k ta k ta k – 2nd speed – 4th
percussionist [2 cycles]

Taka taka taka taka taka taka Taka taka taka taka taka taka – 4th
speed – 2nd percussionist [4 cycles]

Tak tak tak tak tak tak tak tak tak tak tak tak – 3rd speed – 4th
percussionist [2cycles]

Taka taka taka taka taka taka Taka taka taka taka taka taka – 4th speed
– 4th percussionist [2 cycles]

All play together at this tempo for four rounds

Score 3

1   x   2   x   3   x   ½   1   x   2   x   3   -½
Ta ka ta ka ta ki ta   Tho m   tho m   tho m – 2nd, 3rd, & 4th
percussionists [5 cycles]

Score 4

1   x   2   x   3   x   ½   1   x   2   x   3   -½
Ta   ta   ta   ta   ta   ta   ta   ta   ta   ta ta ta   ta   –   1st
percussionist

Score 5

1   x   2   x 3 x 4 x 5 x 6 x 7 x 8
Taka taka Taka taka Taka taka Taka taka Taka taka Taka taka
ta ta ta –

1   2   3   4   1   2   3   4
Ta   ka   ta   ka   ta   ka   ta   ka

Tata tata tata tata tata tata tata tata – 3rd percussionist

All join the 3½ beat

Score 6

Improvisation between 3rd percussionist and Ganapati/1st percussionist

1   x   2   x   3   x   ½   1   x   2   x   3   -½

Ta ka ta ka ta ki ta   Tho m   tho m   tho m

Kit kita – 1st

A- thak a- thak a- thak taktaktak A- thak a- thak a-thak – 3

tatatatatatatatatata

A- thak a- thak a- thak taktaktak A- thak a- thak a-thak taktaktak

Ta ta kita Ta ta kita

A- thak a- thak a- thak taktaktak A- thak a- thak a-thak taktaktak

tatatatatatatatatata tatatatatatatatatata tatatatatatatatatata
    tatatatatatatatatata tatatatatatatatatata tatatatatatatatatata

A- thak a- thak a- thak taktaktak A- thak a- thak a-thak taktaktak

tatatatatatatatatata tatatatatatatatatata tatatatatatatatatata
    tatatatatatatatatata tatatatatatatatatata tatatatatatatatatata

Score 7

Improvisation between the 3rd and 2nd percussionists

1   x   2   x   3   x   ½   1   x   2   x   3   -½

Ta ka ta ka ta ki ta   Tho m   tho m   tho m

thakrithom   thakrithom   thakrithom   ta   thakrithom   thakrithom
    thakrithom ta – 1

din takita tatata dindin takita tatata takrtom takita takita takrtom
    takrtom kakita – 2

Takataka   takatakatakata   katakataka   Takataka   takatakatakata
    katakataka [2 cycles by both percussionists]

Takataka takatakatakata katakataka [4 cycles by both percussionists]

Takataka [4 cycles by both percussionists]

Takataka   takatakatakata   katakataka   Takataka   takatakatakata
    katakataka [2 cycles by both percussionists]

Score 8

Improvisation between the 3rd and 2nd percussionists

1   x   2   x   3   x   ½   1   x   2   x   3   -½

Ta ka ta ka   ta ki ta   Tho m   tho m   tho m

thakrthakr   thakrthakr   thakrthakr   taka   thakrthakr   thakrthakr
thakrthakr taka – 1

Takataka Takataka   Takataka taka   Takataka   Takataka   T a k a t a k a
taka – 4

Score 9

Improvisation between 1st and 3rd percussionists on the tabla bols with
hands and feet

1 2 3 4 5 6 7 8 9 10 11 12

Dha dha dhin dha ka tak dhin dha the-te ko-te ga-te ka-ne – 3rd
percussionist

Dhi-terekite dhin- na tun-na ka- tha dhi-dhi-na dhi-dhi-na – 1st
percussionist

Takrtom

Takrtom

Takrtom takrtom takrtom ta [4 cycles by both percussionists]

Score 10

1   2   3   4   5   6   7   8

Tata tata tata tata tata tata tata tata   –   2nd,   3rd,   &   4th
percussionists

Score 11

1   x 2   1   x 2

Ta dum tata Ta dum tata – Ganapati percussionist [6 cycles]

2nd, 3rd, 4th percussionists join with a single beat on mizhavu

Ta ta Ta ta – 2nd, 3rd, & 4th percussionists [8 cycles]

takrtaka takata takrtaka takata – Ganapati percussionist on the ghatam
[4 cycles]

takataka takrta takataka takrta – Ganapati percussionist on the ghatam
    [3 cycles]

tatatatatatata tatatatatatata – Ganapati percussionist on the ghatam
    [1 cycle]

Taka taka ta   Tak taka taka ta 2nd, 3rd, & 4th percussionists [8 cycles]

Ganapati percussionist moves to chenda

a taka a taka   a taka a taka – Ganapati percussionist [7 cycles]

tatatatatatata tatatatatatata – Ganapati percussionist [1 cycle]

Score 12

1   x   2   x   3   x   4   x   5   x 6
Tak tak   takatakata takatakata takatakata taktak   tata
Tak tak takatakata   takatakata taktak   tata-
Tak tak takatakata taktak tata -
tak tak   takatakata taktak   tata -
tak tak   tata -
tak tak tata
tak tak   tata

Score 13

All together

1 2   3 4 5 6 7 8 9 10 11 12
Ta ta ta ta ta ta ta ta ta ta ta ta
Ta ta ta ta ta ta
Ta ta ta ta
Ta ta
Ta ta

Score 14

1   2 3 - 1 2 3
Takataka takataka takataka Takataka takataka takataka – 4th speed –
    6 rounds

Score 15

1   2   3   4
Takataka takataka takata ka   takataka – 4 beat
1   x 2 x 3
Takataka takataka takataka
1st, 3rd, & 4th musicians on 4 beat, 2nd percussionist improvisation on 4 beat

1   x   2   x 3   x   4   x
Taka taka taka taka taka taka   taka taka – 1st, 3rd, & 4th percussionists
Tataka taka   taka taka taka – 2nd percussionist
taka ka taka taka ka taka – 2nd percussionist
ditaka ditaka ditaka ditaka ditaka ditaka ditaka ditaka – 2nd percussionist
ditaka ditaka ditaka ditaka ditaka ditaka ditaka ditaka – 2nd percussionist
Ta ta ta ta Ta ta ta ta Ta ta ta ta Ta ta ta ta – 2nd percussionist
taka taka   taka taka – 2nd percussionist
ta ta ta ta ta ta ta ta ta ta ta ta ta ta ta – 2nd percussionist [6 cycles]
A taka A taka A taka A taka – 1st percussionist [2 cycles]
Takataka   takatakatakata   katakataka   Takataka   takatakatakata katakataka – 1st percussionist [2 cycles]
Takataka takatakatakata katakataka – 1st percussionist [4 cycles]
Takataka – 1st percussionist [4 cycles]
ta ta ta ta ta ta ta ta ta ta ta ta ta ta ta – 2nd percussionist
Water pouring sound on mizhavu and kutty by all 4 musicians

Score 16

1   x   2   x 3   x   4   x
Taka taka taka taka taka taka   taka taka – 1st percussionist
Taka taka taka taka taka taka   taka taka – 1st, 3rd, & 4th percussionists [5 cycles]
Taka taka taka taka taka taka   taka taka – 1st, 2nd, 3rd, & 4th percussionists [1 cycle]

Ta taka taka ta tadi ta kida – 1st, 2nd, 3rd, & 4th percussionists

Taka taka taka taka taka taka   taka taka – 1st, 2nd, 3rd, & 4th percussionists [1 cycle]

Ta taka taka ta tadi ta kida – 1st, 2nd, 3rd, & 4th percussionists [1 cycle]

Taka taka **Taka** taka **Taka** taka **Taka** taka – 1st, 2nd, 3rd, & 4th percussionists [1 cycle/head]

Taka taka taka taka taka taka   taka taka – 1st, 3rd, & 4th percussionists [2 cycles/rotation head]

_ _   _ _   _ _   _ _   _ _   _ _   _ _ditrem – 1st, 3rd, & 4th percussionists [1 cycle/neck stretching]

Score 17

1   x 2   x   1   x 2

taka taka taka ta   Tak taka taka ta

Ta dum ta Ta dum ta

Ta dum ta Takr tata tatata – 1st percussionist on chenda later shifts to djembe

Ta taka takataka Ta taka takataka

di taka dikata di taka dikata – 2nd percussionist on mizhavu

Ta taka takataka Ta taka takataka

Takr tata Takr tata Ta taka takataka – 3rd percussionist on mizhavu later shifts to thappu

Dingtak din dingtak Dingtak din dingtak – 4th percussionist on djembe

Score 18

3rd percussionist plays a roll on the chenda and then the transition beat.

Ta taka taka ta ta di ta kidati threm – 3rd percussionist on chenda

Then all together play the transition beat. The interval between the sequence reduces as it is repeated and gets fainter:

Ta taka taka ta ta di ta kidati threm 123456

Ta taka taka ta ta di ta kidati threm 12345

Ta taka taka ta ta di ta kidati threm 1234

Ta taka taka ta ta di ta kidati threm123

Ta taka taka ta ta di ta kidati threm12
Ta taka taka ta ta di ta kidati threm1

Score 19

1   x   2   x 3   x   4   x

Taka taka taka taka taka taka   taka taka – 1st percussionist [1 cycle]

Taka taka taka taka taka taka   taka taka – 1st, 2nd, 3rd, & 4th
     percussionists [2 cycles]

Text

Vaitari

1   2   3   4   5   6   7   8

taje   nutadimi tahata   jam tari tamtat   anatam   tajonutam
   tadimi – 1st percussion

Text

Water sound on the mizhavu – 4th percussionist

Vaitari

1   2   3   4   5

tarikidimkutaka deemkutakitataka deem deem kukuta deem kukuta
   kukuta – 1st percussionist

Text

Vaitari

1   2   3   4

di tam tadhi tam takadimi takajonu taka tadim kinatom – 1st
   percussionist [2 cycles]

dim dim dim – 2nd & 4th percussionists on mizhavu and timpani

takataka – 3rd percussionist on chenda [2 cycles]

1   2   3   4

Takataka takataka takataka takataka takataka takataka takataka
   takataka – 2nd, 3rd, & 4th percussionists

Text

1   2   3   4

Takataka takataka takataka takataka takataka takataka takataka takataka – 2nd, 3rd, & 4th percussionists

Text

1   2   3   4

Tatata   ta tatata   ta tatata   tatata tatata tata

Dimtata   tatata ta   tatata   tatata tatata tata – 3rd percussionist – 2nd speed

Takataka takatata takataka takataka – 3rd percussionist – 3rd speed

Takatakatakataka   Takatakatakataka   Takatakatakataka Takatakatakataka – 3rd percussionist – 4th speed

Ta   ka   ta   ka – 3rd percussionist – slows down from the 1st speed

Text

Single beat on *elathalam* – 2nd percussionist

Score 20

1   x   2   x 3   x   4   x

Taka taka taka taka taka taka   taka taka – 3rd percussionist

Taka taka taka taka taka taka   taka taka –1st, 3rd, & 4th percussionists [12 cycles]

1   ½   1   ½   1   ½   1   ½

Ta   tata Ta tata Ta tata Ta   tata – 4th percussionist [the shuffle]

Improvisation by 2nd percussionist on the 4th percussionist's shuffle

Tata dum

Ta ta

Dum ta dum

Takata dikutadikuta

Tata tata dum

Ta   ta ta dumtaka takata ta

Ta ta

Takata dikutadikuta

dikutadikuta   dikutadikuta   ta

tata   tata tata tata

Takuk ta takadum takuk ta takadum

Takuku takuku tata Takuku takuku tata-

Takukutakuku Takukutakuku Takukutakuku-

Takukutakuku Takukutakuku Takukutakuku

Takukutakuku Takukutakuku Takukutakuku Takukutakuku

Takukutakuku Takukutakuku Takukutakuku Takukutakuku

1   ½   1   ½   1   ½   1   ½

Ta   tata Ta tata Ta tata Ta   tata – 4th percussionist

1   x   2   x 3   x   4   x

Taka taka taka taka taka taka   taka taka – 1st & 3rd percussionists on
     fast tempo

Takataka takataka takata ka   takataka – 2nd percussionist on chenda
     [2 cycles]

Takataka takataka takata ka   takataka – 2nd percussionist on djembe
     [2 cycles]

Takataka takataka – 2nd percussionist on chenda [4 cycles]

takata ka takataka – 2nd percussionist on djembe [4 cycles]

Takataka takataka takata ka   takataka – 2nd percussionist on chenda
     and djembe [3 cycles]

(*Fade out.*)

Score 21

The smaller numerals indicate the interval between each beat

In the 8-beat rhythm, 4-6-8 are played on the mizhavu by the elephants
     [1st and 2nd percussionists]. The other beats are not sounded till
     the numerals in the intervals disappear.

In the 7-beat rhythm, 3-5-7 are played on the mizhavu by the percussionists at the back [3rd and 4th]. The other beats are not sounded till the numerals in the intervals disappear.

11234 21234 31234 41234 51234 61234 71234 81234

11234 21234 31234 41234 51234 61234 71234 81234

1123 2123 3123 4123 5123 6123 7123 8123

112   212   312   413   512   612   712   812

11   21   31   41   51   61   71   81

1   2   3   4   5   6   7   8 [4 cycles]

1   2   3   4   5   6   7   8 [fast tempo–
4 cycles]

1 2   3 4   5 6 7 8 [continous from this point]

Takataka Takataka Takataka Takataka Takataka Takataka Takataka Takataka

In 6 cycles the tempo gradually increases and the next 6 cycle's tempo gradually decreases.

1   2

Ta-taka taka-ta – 3rd &4th percussionist – 2 beat [4 cycles]

Shift rhythm to the 10 beat

1	2	3	4	5
Takataka	Takataka	Takataka	Takataka	Tatatatatata
6	7	8	9	10
Tatatatatata	Tatatatatata	Tatatatatata	ta	khali – 3rd per-cussionist on chenda [5 cycle]

2nd musician dances to the 10 beat

1	2	3	4	5
Ta	ta	ta	ta	khali – 1st per-cussionist on mizhavu [3 cycles]

The 1st percussionist shifts to 10 beat

1	x	2	x	3	x	4	x	5	x
Takat aka		Taka taka		Taka taka		Taka taka		Tatata tatata	
6	x	7	x	8	x	9	x	10	

Tatata tatata Tatata tatata   Tatata tatata   ta   _   00 – 1st percussionist on mizhavu [2 cycles]

Then the 1st percussionist shifts to 3½ beat

1	x	2	x	3	x	½	1	x	2	x	3	-½

Ta ka ta ka   ta ki ta   Tho m   tho m   tho m   –   1st   percussionist [3 cycles]

1	x	2	x	3	x	4	x 5	x 6	x 7	x

Taka taka   Taka taka Taka taka Taka taka Taka taka Taka taka Taka
taka – 4th percussionist [7 cycles]

1	2	1	2

Ta-taka taka-ta   Ta-taka taka-ta – 4th percussionist [4 cycles]

Score 22

1	2	3	4	5

Takataka   tatatata   tatatata   tatatata   tatatata

6	7	8	9	10

tatata   ta   ta   _   tata   –   3rd   percussionist
[Siva] on djembe [2 cycles]

1	x	2	x	3	x	½	1	x	2	x	3	-½

Ta ka ta ka   ta ki ta   Tho m   tho m   tho m –
3rd percussionist on djembe [5 cycles]

1	x	2	x	3	x	4	x	5

Ta	ta	ta	ta	_

Ta   ta   ta   ta   _   –   2nd   percussionist
[Ganapati] on edakka

Ta	ta		ta	ta
Ta	taka	ta	taka	ta
Taka	taka	taka	taka	taka
Ta	ta	ta	ta	ta
Di	taki	di	taki	di
Tata	tata	tata	tata	tata
Taka	taka		taka	taka

Ta   ta   ta   ta   _

1   x   2   x   3   x   ½   1   x   2   x   3   -½

Ta ka ta ka   ta ki ta   Tho m   tho m   tho m   – 1st percussionist on mizhavu [10 cycles]

Shifts to thapattam 3½ beat

Ta kum ta kum dum - taka Ta kum ta kum dum taka – 1st percussionist
on mizhavu [8 cycles]

1   x 2 x 1   x 2

Ta-taka taka-ta Ta-taka taka-ta – 4th percussionist on mizhavu [15
cycles]

1   x 2 x   1   x 2 x

Dum taka takaka taka Dum taka takaka taka – 4th musician on mizhavu
[8 cycles]

Score 23

1   x   2   x   3   x   4

Takatakatakataka   Takatakatakataka   Takatakatakataka
Takatakatakataka – 3rd percussionist on djembe [4 cycles]

Takatakatakataka Takatakatakataka [4 cycles]

Takatakatakataka [4 cycles]

Taka taka taka taka taka taka taka taka [4 cycles]

Text

Fire sound on mizhavu and djembe

1   x   2   x   3   x   4

Takatakatakataka Takatakatakataka Takatakatakataka Takatakatakataka
– 3rd percussionist on djembe [1 cycle]

Takatakatakataka Takatakatakataka Takatakatakataka Takatakatakataka
– 1st & 4th percussionists on mizhavu [1 cycle]

Takatakatakataka Takatakatakataka – 3rd musician on djembe [2 cycles]

Takatakatakataka Takatakatakataka – 1st & 4th percussionists on the
mizhavu [2 cycles]

Takatakatakataka – 3rd percussionist on djembe [4 cycles]

Takatakatakataka – 1st & 4th percussionists on mizhavu [4 cycles]

Blackout – music

Takatakatakataka Takatakatakataka Takatakatakataka Takatakatakataka
   – 4th percussionist on chenda [3 cycles]

Takatakatakataka Takatakatakataka Takatakatakataka Takatakatakataka
   – 1st percussionist on mizhavu [2 cycles]

Takatakatakataka Takatakatakataka – 4th percussionist on chenda
   [2 cycles]

Takatakatakataka Takatakatakataka – 1st percussionist on mizhavu
   [2 cycles]

Takatakatakataka – 4th percussionist on chenda [4 cycles]

Takatakatakataka – 1st percussionist on mizhavu [4 cycles]

Score 24

The rhythm of Ganapati's head movements. The numerals indicate the
   intervals between the rhythm.

ta - 1234

ta 12 ta ta - 1234

takita dikita takita dikita ta - 123456

taka taka taka taka - 1 2

kidataki kidataki kidataki kidataki - 1234

kidataki kidataki kidataki kidataki kidataki

kidataki kidataki kidataki ta - 1234 5678

ta ta ta ta ta ta ta ta - 1234

ta ta ta ta ta ta ta ta ta ta ta ta ta ta ta ta

ta ka ta - 12345678

ta din din ta da din ta din din ta ta din - 1234

ta ta ta ta

ta taka ta ka ta

ta ta ta

taka taka takataka takataka takataka

ta ta - 1234

ta ta - 1234

ta ta - 123

ta ta - 12

ta - 12

ta - 1

1   ½

Tat a dum ta

1   2

Ta taka   taka ta

1   2   3

Ta   ta   ta

1   2   3   4

Takataka   takataka   takataka   takataka

ta ta ta – ta ta - 12345678

(Blackout.)

Score 25

The exploration

1   ½   1 2 1 2   3 1   2   3   4

Tat a dum ta Ta taka taka ta Ta   ta   ta   Takataka   takataka
takataka takataka

Tat a – 1st ta – 3rd   taka – 4th

      dum ta – 2nd ta – 1st   takataka – 3rd

      Ta taka – 4th Ta   ta – 2nd takataka – 1st takataka – 3rd

Tat a dum ta – 4th   Ta tata – 2nd Takataka – 1st takataka – 3rd

      Ta taka taka – 4th tata – 2nd takataka takataka – 3rd

Tat a dum ta Ta taka taka ta Ta   ta   ta – 2nd [*the theme*]

Variations on the theme:

The sequence starts in slow tempo with the 2nd percussionist being the first to pass on the rhythm sequence.

1   1 2 1

Tat a dum ta Tat a dum ta Ta taka taka ta Tat a dum ta – 2nd musician pass to

2 3 1

Ta taka taka ta Ta ta ta   Tat a dum ta – 3rd musician pass to

2 3 4

Ta taka taka ta Ta ta ta Takataka takataka takataka takataka – 4th musician pass to

1   2 3

Tat a dum ta Ta taka taka ta Ta ta ta – 1st musician on *pakhavaj* – pass to

4   1 2 3

Takataka takataka takataka takataka Tat a dum ta Ta taka taka ta Ta ta ta

1 2 1 1 1 2

Tat a dum ta Ta taka taka ta Tat a dum ta Tat a dum ta Tat a dum ta Ta taka taka ta

1 2

Tat a dum ta Ta taka taka ta – 3rd musician on djembe – pass to

3 1 2

Ta ta ta Tat a dum ta Ta taka taka ta – 1st percussionist pass to

3 4 1

Ta ta ta Takataka takataka takataka takataka Tat a dum ta – 4th percussionist on small djembe and mizhavu

The passing goes into the 4th tempo

2 3 1 2 1 1

Ta taka taka ta Ta ta ta Tat a dum ta Ta taka taka ta Tat a dum ta Tat a dum ta

1 2 1 2 3

Tat a dum ta Tataka taka ta Tat a dum ta Ta taka taka ta Ta ta ta – 2nd percussionist pass to

1   2   3

Tat a dum ta Ta taka taka ta Ta ta ta – 3rd percussionist pass to

4   1   2

Takataka takataka takataka takataka Tat a dum ta Ta taka taka ta – 4th
    musician pass to – 1st speed

3   4   1

Ta ta ta Takataka takataka takataka takataka Tat a dum ta – 1st musician
    – gradually speeding the rhythm

2   3   1

Ta taka taka ta Ta ta ta Tat a dum ta – 2nd percussionist pass to

2   1   1   1   2

Ta taka taka ta Tat a dum ta Tat a dum ta Tat a dum ta Ta taka taka ta

1   2   3

Tat a dum ta Ta taka taka ta Ta ta ta – 3rd percussionist pass to

1   2   3

Tat a dum ta Ta taka taka ta Ta ta ta – 1st percussionist pass to

4   1   2

Takataka takataka takataka takataka Tat a dum ta Ta taka taka ta – 2nd
    percussionist pass to

3   4 1

Ta ta ta Takataka takataka takataka takataka Tat a dum ta – 4th
    percussionist pass to

2   3   1

Ta taka taka ta Ta ta ta Tat a dum ta – 1st percussionist pass to

2   1   1   1   2

Ta taka taka ta Tat a dum ta Tat a dum ta Tat a dum ta Ta taka taka ta

1   2   3

Tat a dum ta Ta taka taka ta Ta ta ta – 3rd percussionist pass to

1   2   3

Tat a dum ta Ta taka taka ta Ta ta ta – 1st percussionist pass to

4   1   2   3

Takataka takataka takataka takataka Tat a dum ta Ta taka taka ta Ta ta
    ta-

1	2	1	1	1	2

Tat a dum ta Ta taka taka ta Tat a dum ta Tat a dum ta Tat a dum ta Ta taka taka ta

1	2	3	1	2	3

Tat a dum ta Ta taka taka ta Ta ta ta Tat a dum ta Ta taka taka ta Ta ta ta

4

Takataka takataka takataka takataka – 2nd percussionist

Score 26

Text

1	½	1 2 1	2	3 1	2	3	4

Tat a dum ta Ta taka taka ta Ta   ta   ta   Takataka   takataka takataka takataka

4th percussionist on small djembe

2nd percussionist dances to the rhythm

Text

1	2

Takataka du dum – 1st percussionist accompanies the 2nd percussionist in his fall downward

2nd percussionist rises to the following beat and a long note on the saxophone

1	2	3	4 5	6	7

Tata ta tata ta tata ta aaa   _

The speed gradually increases and when it reaches its peak, stops

Text

1	2	3	4

Takatakatakataka Takatakatakataka Takatakatakataka Takatakatakataka

5	6	7	8

Takatakatakataka Takatakatakataka Takatakatakataka Takatakatakataka

– 1st, 3rd, & 4th percussionists on mizhavu

Text

1   x   2   x 3   x   4   x

Taka taka taka taka taka taka taka taka – 1st, 3rd, & 4th percussionists
on mizhavu [4 cycles]

Tatakataka   taka taka taka

taka ka taka di taka di taka di taka di taka

Ta ta ta ta   ta ta ta ta   ta ta ta ta   ta ta ta ta

        taka taka taka taka taka taka

A taka A taka A taka A taka

ta ta ta ta ta ta ta ta ta ta ta ta ta ta ta – 2nd percussionist on kutti

Text

1   2   3   4   5   6

Ta ta ta takata takata takata – 2nd percussionist on kutti

While the 2nd percussionist plays this beat, the 1st percussionist jumps
and stands behind him

1   ½   1 2 1   2   3 1   2   3   4

Tat a dum ta Ta taka taka ta Ta   ta   ta   Takataka   takataka
takataka takataka

Tat a –   ta   taka-   Takataka takataka

        dum ta – taka ta taᵗ   takataka-

                Ta taka Ta   ta takataka- takataka

Tat a dum ta Ta taka taka ta Ta   ta   ta

Tat a dum ta   Ta tata Takataka takataka

        Ta taka taka ta ta takataka takataka

Tat a dum ta   taka ta   Ta tata Takataka takataka – 4th percussionist
plays on the djembe. The saxophone plays a long note.

Score 27

The saxophonist enters

1   ½

Tat a dum ta – the 1st percussionist

Saxophone

1   2

Ta taka   taka ta – 3rd & 4th percussionists

Saxophone

1   2   3

Ta   ta   ta – 1st, 3rd, & 4th percussionists

Saxophone

1   2   3   4

Takataka takataka   takataka   takataka – 3rd & 4th percussionists

Saxophonist's solo improvisation

The percussionists join the saxophone

1   2 3   4

Takatakatakataka Takatakatakataka Takatakatakataka Takatakatakataka [16 cycles]

1st percussionist on djembe

2nd percussionist on timpani

3rd and 4th percussionists on mizhavu

1   2 3   4

Takatakatakataka TakatakatakatakaTakatakatakataka Takatakatakataka – fast roll on djembe by 1st percussionist

1   2 3   4

Takatak Takatak Takatak Tata – [16 cycles] on the 4th tempo

1st percussionist on djembe

2nd percussionist on timpani

3rd and 4th percussionsits on mizhavu

Saxophone

1 ½

Tat a dum ta – saxophone

1 ½   1 2 1 2   3 1 2   3   4

Tat a dum ta Ta taka taka ta Ta ta ta Takataka takataka takataka takataka

[6 cycles]

Gradual reduction of sound without reducing the speed.

Score 28

1	½	1 2 1	2	3 1	2	3	4

Tat a dum ta Ta taka taka ta Ta   ta   ta   Takataka   takataka
takataka takataka

4th percussionist on mizhavu

The 3rd percussionist joins on the second beat of the 4th percussionist on the 2nd round

1	½	1 2 1	2	3 1	2	3	4

Tat a dum ta Ta taka taka ta Ta   ta   ta   Takataka   takataka
takataka takataka-

3rd percussionist on mizhavu

The 1st percussionist joins on the 3rd beat of the 3rd percussionist on the 3rd round

1	½	1 2 1	2	3 1	2	3	4

Tat a dum ta Ta taka taka ta Ta   ta   ta   Takataka   takataka
takataka takataka

1st percussionist on mizhavu

The 2nd percussionist joins on the 4th beat of the 1st percussionist on the 4th round

1	½	1 2 1	2	3 1	2	3	4

Tat a dum ta Ta taka taka ta Ta   ta   ta   Takataka   takataka
takataka takataka

2nd percussionist on chenda

On the 5th round the saxophone joins the four percussionists playing on mizhavu

Dialogue with the saxophone and the other percussionists – [improvisation]

1   2 3   4

Takatakatakataka Takatakatakataka Takatakatakataka Takatakatakataka – 3rd & 4th percussionists on mizhavu, 2nd percussionist on chenda [24 cycles]

The sequence is a fast improvisation where the saxophonist and the 1st percussionist have a dialogue. The percussionist plays the 8-beat in fast tempo.

1   2 3   4

Takatakatakataka Takatakatakataka Takatakatakataka Takatakatakataka – x 2 – 1st percussionist on mizhavu

A thak athak athak athak A thak athak athak athak A thak athak athak athak [4 cycles]

Takatakatakataka taktak Takatakatakataka taktak Takatakatakataka taktak [4 cycles]

Tarikida tarikida Tarikida tarikida Tarikida tarikida Tarikida tarikida [4 cycles]

Tarikida tarikida tatata Tarikida tarikida tatata [2 cycles]

Tatatatatatatatata Tatatatatatatatata [3 cycles]

1   2 3   4

Takatakatakataka Takatakatakataka Takatakatakataka Takatakatakataka – 3rd & 4th percussionists on mizhavu, 2nd percussionist on chenda [8 cycles]

The 1st percussionist shifts to the 4th tempo of the 4-beat

Tatatatatatatatata Tatatatatatatatata [2 cycles]

Dudududududududu Dudududududududu [2 cycles]

Tatatatatatatatata Dudududududududu [2 cycles]

Tatatata Dudududu [4 cycles]

Tatatatatatatatata Tatatatatatatatata [3 cycles]

All the percussionists together shift to the medium tempo of the theme –

the saxophone joins them

Score 29

1   ½   1 2 1   2   3 1   2   3   4

Tat a dum ta Ta taka taka ta Ta ta   ta Takataka   takataka   takataka
takataka

[6 cycles]

Gradual reduction of sound without reducing the speed

The End

Saxophone Score by Pascal Sieger

Act 2

Score P-1 (Entry)

Score P-2 (Duet)

Percussionist Two

1   x   2   x 3   x   4   x

Taka taka taka taka taka taka   taka taka

Tat- aka taka   Tat- aka taka Tat- aka taka Tat- aka taka [4 cycles]
2nd musician

ditaka ditaka ditaka ditaka ditaka ditaka ditaka ditaka [2 cycles]
  2nd musician

ditaka ditaka ditaka ditaka tataka takata tadita kitadi [1 cycle]
  2nd musician

Score P-3 (The elephant)

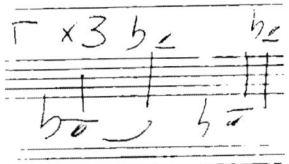

Score P-4 (Around the egg)

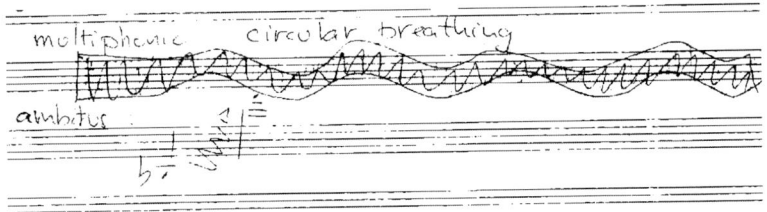

Score P-5 (The sloughs of despondence)

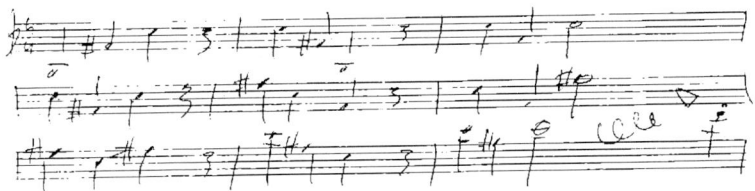

Score P-6 (Martanda)

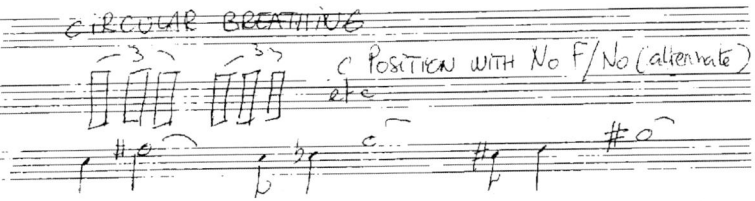

Score P-7 (More than you receive)

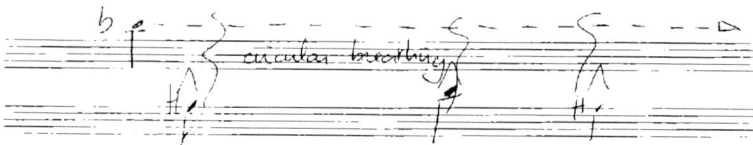

Score P-8 (Handclaps)

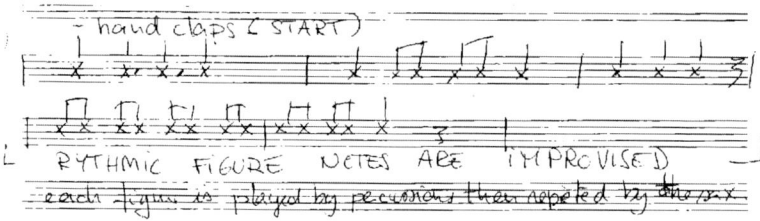

Score P-9 (Sax solo)

Score P-10 (Around the musicians)

Score P-11 (Playing for the kutti)

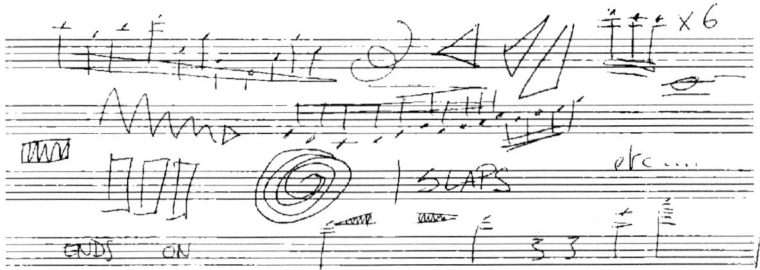

Score P-12 (Calling the drums)

Score P-13 (Finale)

Appendix III

Appointments and Awards

1997   Nominated an expert in the field of traditional, folk, and indigenous arts by the Department of Culture, Government of India.

1998   Appointed Trustee on the Board of Trustees of the National Folklore Support Center, Chennai.

2006   Received the Zee Astitva Award—Theatre Person of the Year 2006.

2008   Appointed on the Board of Editors for *Theatre, Dance and Performance Training*, a theatre journal to be published by Routledge.

2011   Awarded the Sangeet Natak Akademi Puraskar for contribution to contemporary theatre as a director for the year 2010.

Bibliography

Chatterjee, Shoma A. 1992. 'The Rise of a Greater Dawn', *Sunday Financial Express*, Madras, 5 April.

Devi, Hima. 1993. 'Vibrant Spleandour of the Greater Dawn', *The Afternoon Despatch and Courier*, 14 May.

Doctor, Geeta. 1998. 'Exploring the Many Levels of Theatre', *The Economic Times*.

Gangadhar, V. 1981. '"Oedipus", Unforgettalbe Experience', *The Times of India*, 24 August.

—————. 1999. 'Looking beyond the Ordinary', *The Hindu*, 16 April.

Gokhale, Shanta. 1992. 'Out of the Throes of Death', *The Sunday Times of India*, 10 February.

—————. 1995. 'In Search of a Body Language', *The Telegraph*, 11 August.

—————. 1998. 'In Search of the Enigmatic Arjuna', *The Sunday Times of India*, 20 December.

—————. 2000. 'A Moveable Feast', *The Sunday Times of India*, 3 December.

Gokhale, Veena. 1986. 'From Blackboards to Spotlights', *Suburbia*, 17–23 May.

Jacinto, Leela. 1992. 'Stage of the Art', *Society*, April.

Komalavalli, R. 1991. 'Tough Choices for a New Idiom', *The Sunday Times of India*, 18 August.

————. 1992. 'Many Hues of Dawn', *The Pioneer*, 16 March.

Kothari, Sunil. 1994. 'A Symbolic Journey', *Indian Express*, 30 October.

'Living Tradition: An Interview with Veenapani Chawla', *The Golden Chain*, May 2005.

Paul, G.S. 2001. 'Drumming in Tradition', *The Hindu Friday Review*, 2 November.

————. 2004. 'Myths through Metaphors', *The Hindu*, 23 April.

Ramakrishnan, Deepa H. 2005. 'The Stage Their World', *The Hindu Metroplus*, 1 October.

Ramchandani, Kamala. 1992. 'Savitri, A Parable of Dawn', *The Afternoon Despatch and Courier*, 25 March.

Ramnarayan, Gowri. 2003. 'Breath Holds the Key', *The Hindu*, 19 December.

Saran, Sathya. 1995. 'Exploring the Many Shades of Myth', *The Times of India*, 20 April.

————. 2003. 'Living the Dream', *Femina*, 15 November.

————. 2011. 'A Fighter for Creative Space', *The Hindu*, 21 August.

Tak, Tarun. 1989. 'From Oedipus Rex to Kalaripayyat', *The Sunday Observer*, 15 October.

Thakore, Dolly. 1981. 'Excellent Performances Highlight *Oedipus*', *Mid-Day*, 26 August.

Vanita, Ruth. 1996. 'Minimal Props and Maximal Acting', Sunday, 7 April (from Veenapani Chawla's files).

Vaze, Madhav. 2004. 'Adhyatma, Taking a Different Path, Veenapani Chawla', *Saptahik Sakal*, Diwali special.

————. 2008. 'Natakatli Urja: Veenapani Chawla Yancha "Adishakti" Prayog', *Saptahik Sakal*, 1 March.

About the Editor and Contributors

KEVAL ARORA is Associate Professor in English at his alma mater Kirori Mal College, University of Delhi. He has been staff advisor to the college theatre society, The Players, since 1981, and has turned it into the most vibrant campus theatre group in the country. He has also written widely on theatre in *The Pioneer*, *First City*, and *Theatre India*, among others, for many years.

HIMANSHU BURTE is an architect and theorist teaching at the School of Habitat Studies, Tata Institute of Social Sciences, Mumbai. He is the author of *Space for Engagement: The Indian Artplace and a Habitational Approach to Architecture* (Seagull Books, 2008). His current research interests include the politics of urban space, contemporary Indian architecture, sustainable urbanism, and theatre design.

VEENAPANI CHAWLA established Adishakti in 1981. She has scripted and directed most of its performances. Her work has toured India as well as international destinations. She has been recognized with grants from the Ford Foundation, the Charles

Wallace India Trust, the Department of Culture, the Det Lange Udvalga, Denmark, and the India Foundation for the Arts. In 2006 she received the Zee Astitva Award for excellence in Theatre and in 2011 was awarded the Sangeet Natak Akademi Puraskar for Theatre Director.

GEETA DOCTOR is a well-known Chennai-based critic and writer. She describes herself as a lifestyle journalist whose commentaries on life, literature, and society have always sought to be provocative and controversial.

DEVINA DUTT is a Mumbai-based writer and covers the arts. She has been a business and news journalist and now runs a corporate communications consultancy in Mumbai. She has translated poetry, short stories, and film scripts from Indian languages into English, and has also edited books. She is currently working on a documentary film on musicians from Dharwad.

JOY BROOKE FAIRFIELD is a PhD student in Theatre and Performance Studies at Stanford University with prior degrees from Harvard and New York universities. She is a director of new plays and original devised works based in San Francisco, California. She was honoured to study at Adishakti during the summer of 2011 and hopes to return soon.

LEELA GANDHI is Professor of English at the Department of English Language and Literature, University of Chicago. Her publications include *Affective Communities: Anticolonial Thought, Fin-de-Siecle Radicalism, and the Politics of Friendship (Politics, History, and Culture)* (Duke University Press, 2006), *Measures of Home: Poems* (distributed by Orient Longman, 2000), and *Postcolonial Theory: A Critical Introduction* (Columbia University Press, 1998), and with Ann Blake and Sue Thomas has co-authored *England through Colonial Eyes in Twentieth-century Fiction* (Palgrave Macmillan, 2002). She is a founding co-editor of the journal *Postcolonial Studies*.

SHANTA GOKHALE, a well-known bilingual writer, translator, journalist, and theatre critic, was formerly associated with *The Times of India* (Mumbai) as the Arts Editor. She has written screenplays for several films, such as the national award winning documentary film *Narayan Gangaram Surve* (2002; dir. Arun Khopkar) and has also appeared in the Hindi film *Ardh Satya* (1983; dir. Govind Nihlani) and a 13-part TV series directed by Amol Palekar. Her critical study of Marathi theatre, *Playwright at the Centre: Marathi Drama from 1843 to the Present*, was published in 2000. As a translator she has worked on veteran actress Durga Khote's noted autobiography, *I, Durga Khote: An Autobiography* (Oxford University Press, 2006) and has published translations of several plays by leading Marathi playwrights, including Mahesh Elkunchwar and Satish Alekar.

SARAH JOSEPH is a novelist and short story writer in Malayalam. Her novel *Aalahayude Penmakkal* (Daughters of God the Father) won the Kerala Sahitya Akademi award in 2001, the Kendra Sahitya Akademi Award in 2003, and the Vayalar Ramavarma Award in 2004. She has been at the forefront of the feminist movement in Kerala and is the founder of Manushi, an organization of thinking women.

RAM GANESH KAMATHAM is a writer-director who has created works for stage, film, radio, comics, and video games. A recipient of several awards and fellowships, including the 2011 Sultan Padamsee Award for playwriting, the Asif Currimbhoy Playwriting Fellowship, and the Sarai–CSDS Independent Research Fellowship, he was the Executive Editor of *PTNotes*, the Prithvi Theatre's monthly newsletter, from 2009 to 2011. Some of his work for the stage includes *Ultimate Kurukshetra* (2010), *Project S.T.R.I.P.* (2009), *Creeper* (2007), *Crab* (2006), *Snakes & Ladders* (2005), *Dancing on Glass* (2004), and *Square Root of Minus One* (2002). His plays have been staged at festivals in India and abroad.

M.D. MUTHUKUMARASWAMY is the Director of the National Folklore Support Centre, a non-governmental, non-profit organization in Chennai dedicated to the promotion of Indian folklore research, education, training, networking, and publications. The aim of the Centre is to integrate scholarship with activism, aesthetic appreciation with community development, comparative

folklore studies with cultural diversities and identities, dissemi-
nation of information with multidisciplinary dialogues, folklore
fieldwork with developmental issues. and folklore advocacy with
public programming events.

SMRITI NEVATIA has worked as a film and theatre critic, and as
researcher, writer, and co-director on many television shows
and independent documentaries. She was Co-Curator of 'Queer
Nazariya' (2010), an international film festival held in Mumbai,
and Curator of 'Our Lives … To Live' (2012), a nation-wide festival of films and discussions around themes of gender violence. She
is one of the authors of the study *Breaking the Binary* (LABIA—A
Queer Feminist LBT Collective, 2013). Smriti conducts script-
writing workshops and freelances as a text editor. Her essays,
poetry, and short fiction have appeared in various anthologies
and magazines.

ALAKNANDA SAMARTH is an actress and teacher. She began in
leading roles opposite the legendary Ebrahim Alkazi in his Theatre
Unit, Mumbai. She went to Brandeis University, USA, as a Wien
Scholar and The Royal Academy of Dramatic Art, London, in
1963. She was the first Indian actress acclaimed in a major classic
lead at the National Theatre, London for *Phaedra Britannica*, in
1975. Her solo work over the years has constantly explored the
cross-cultural voice, gaze, and self in landmarks such as *Kunti*
and *The Human Voice, Medeamaterial, Alma Mahler, Karima,
Medearevisited 2010*. As a teacher she has explored the actors'
cultural and sound memory and how you hear other traditions.

ANMOL VELLANI has led the India Foundation for the Arts, an
independent philanthropic organization, from 1995 to 2013.
During 1986–95 he was the programme officer at The Ford
Foundation, New Delhi, with responsibility for grant-making
in the performing arts, folklore, and classical learning in South
Asia. He has written on a range of subjects, including the arts and
religion, corporate patronage, arts entrepreneurship, the role of
foundations, intercultural dialogue, and the performing arts. He
has also directed theatre productions in different languages and
locations, both in India and abroad, over the last 35 years.

Leela Venkataraman is a Delhi-based dance critic who began reviewing dance first for the *National Herald* and then for *The Patriot*. She moved to *The Hindu* when the paper began its Delhi edition. Her column in this paper is considered to be the most incisive commentary on the dance scene in the capital. She has authored *Indian Classical Dance: Tradition in Transition* (Roli, 2004), a compendium of Indian classical dance. Among her other publications are *Bharatanatyam: Step by Step* and *The Dancing Phenomenon—Birju Maharaj*.